**Cambridge School
Shakespeare**

King Lear

Edited by Elspeth Bain, Jonathan Morris and Rob Smith

Series Editor: Rex Gibson
Director, Shakespeare and Schools Project

Series Editorial Group: Richard Andrews, Mike Clamp, Perry Mills, Rob Smith

CAMBRIDGE
UNIVERSITY PRESS

CAMBRIDGE UNIVERSITY PRESS
Cambridge, New York, Melbourne, Madrid, Cape Town,
Singapore, São Paulo, Delhi, Mexico City

Cambridge University Press
The Edinburgh Building, Cambridge CB2 8RU, UK

www.cambridge.org
Information on this title: www.cambridge.org/9780521735988

First published 1996
Second edition 2009
5th printing 2013

Printed and bound in the United Kingdom by the MPG Books Group

A catalogue record for this publication is available from the British Library

ISBN   978-0-521-73598-8 Paperback

ACKNOWLEDGEMENTS
Thanks are due to the following for permission to reproduce photographs:
Cover, v, vi, vii, vii, ix, x, xi, xii, 94, 97, 140, 170, 173, 196, 206, 208, 211, 221, 223, 225,
227, 228, Donald Cooper / Photostage; 4, Gordon Goode © Royal Shakespeare Company;
55, 120, Malcolm Davies © Royal Shakespeare Company; 16, 44, 188, Angus McBean
© Royal Shakespeare Company; 180, © RIA Novosti / Alamy; 72, 130, 194, Joe Cocks
Studio Collection © Shakespeare Birthplace Trust; 230, Maria Austria / MAI; 238*t*,
Ernest Daniels © Royal Shakespeare Company; 238*b*, MTI Photo; 239*t*, Filmways /
Athena / Lanterna / The Kobal Collection; 239*b*, Herald Ace / Nippon Herald /
Greenwich / The Kobal Collection.

Cover design by Smith

Contents

Cambridge School
Shakespeare

This edition of *King Lear* is part of the **Cambridge School Shakespeare** series. Like every other play in the series, it has been specially prepared to help all students in schools and colleges.

This version of *King Lear* aims to be different from other editions of the play. It invites you to bring the play to life in your classroom, hall or drama studio through enjoyable activities that will increase your understanding. Actors have created their different interpretations of the play over the centuries. Similarly, you are encouraged to make up your own mind about *King Lear*, rather than having someone else's interpretation handed down to you.

Cambridge School Shakespeare does not offer you a cut-down or simplified version of the play. This is Shakespeare's language, filled with imaginative possibilities. You will find on every left-hand page: a summary of the action, an explanation of unfamiliar words, a choice of activities on Shakespeare's language, characters and stories.

Between the acts and in the pages at the end of the play, you will find notes, illustrations and activities. This will help to increase your understanding of the whole play.

There are a large number of activities to give you the widest choice to suit your own particular needs. Please don't think you have to do every one. Choose the activities that will help you most.

This edition will be of value to you whether you are studying for an examination, reading for pleasure, or thinking of putting on the play to entertain others. You can work on the activities on your own or in groups. Many of the activities suggest a particular group size, but don't be afraid to make up larger or smaller groups to suit your own purposes.

Although you are invited to treat *King Lear* as a play, you don't need special dramatic or theatrical skills to do the activities. By choosing your activities, and by exploring and experimenting, you can make your own interpretations of Shakespeare's language, characters and stories. Whatever you do, remember that Shakespeare wrote his plays to be acted, watched and enjoyed.

Rex Gibson

This edition of *King Lear* uses the text of the play established by Jay L. Halio in **The New Cambridge Shakespeare**.

'Know, that we have divided / In three our kingdom'. *King Lear* dramatises the consequences of an elderly British king's decision to give up his power and land – while still retaining the title and status of king. Lear's three daughters, Gonerill, Regan and Cordelia, are asked to declare publicly how much they love him before learning how much of his kingdom they will have. Who might the strange character sitting at Lear's feet in this picture be?

Gonerill and Regan flatter their father extravagantly and are rewarded with shares of the kingdom.

'What can you say to draw / A third more opulent than your sisters?' Cordelia, the youngest sister and her father's favourite, is the last to speak. She loves her father deeply but refuses to play his flattery game, claiming only to love her father as a daughter should. Lear, hurt and enraged by her apparent defiance of his authority, publicly disowns and curses Cordelia.

'What wouldst thou do, old man?' The plain-speaking Duke of Kent intervenes on Cordelia's behalf and is rewarded with banishment. Although the Duke of Burgundy rejects the disgraced and dowerless Cordelia, the King of France – another of her suitors – willingly accepts her as his wife.

'Edgar I nothing am.' The Duke of Gloucester, a shocked witness of events, also has his family problems. His illegitimate son Edmond is secretly plotting to frame his elder brother Edgar and steal his inheritance. Edgar soon has to flee for his life, disguising himself as Poor Tom, a madman beggar.

The Earl of Kent (seen here seated right) has not gone into banishment but has also assumed a disguise, obtaining a position as the old king's servant. Lear's Fool (standing left) also remains with him.

'Not only, sir, this, your all-licensed fool, / But other of your insolent retinue / Do hourly carp and quarrel'. Lear plans to live alternately with Gonerill and Regan for six months at a time, but the arrangement soon breaks down. Gonerill is vexed by the king's insistence on retaining one hundred knights plus his Fool as his companions.

'O fool, I shall go mad.' Enraged by Gonerill's suggestion that he reduce the number of his knights, Lear sets off to go to Regan, meeting up with her at the Duke of Gloucester's castle. Gonerill arrives too, and both sisters insist the king has no real need of any followers. Lear is distraught and fears he will go mad. He leaves the castle accompanied only by his Fool. The night becomes stormy.

'This tempest in my mind'. As the storm rages, Kent searches for and finds
the king and his Fool wandering on the heath, where they also encounter
Edgar in his disguise as Poor Tom, a mad beggar. Lear's mind gives way
completely, but in his madness he develops a new concern and sympathy for
all the 'poor naked wretches' of this world.

'Go thrust him out at gates, and let him smell / His way to Dover.' Gloucester
helps get Lear to safety in Dover, where Cordelia has landed with a French
army. This loyalty to the king enrages Gonerill, Regan and her husband, the
Duke of Cornwall, who gouges out Gloucester's eyes in punishment and
throws him out into the storm (this is how the 2001 Shakespeare's Globe
production staged the blinding). However, Cornwall has been fatally wounded
by one of Gloucester's servants, who was trying to protect his master.

'Alack, I have no eyes.' Edgar, still acting the part of a madman beggar, meets his blind father and agrees to guide him to Dover, where Gloucester plans to throw himself off a cliff. Edgar, however, has a plan of his own that he hopes will make his father believe his life has been miraculously saved.

'How fares your majesty?' At Dover Cordelia and Lear are reunited. The king is calmer now, and when he recognises his youngest daughter he attempts to kneel before her to ask her to forgive him. Meanwhile, Gonerill and Regan are in competition for Edmond, each jealously eyeing the other.

'She's gone for ever'. Cordelia's French army is defeated in battle by Gonerill's and Regan's forces. Lear and Cordelia are captured and Edmond orders their deaths. Edgar, now disguised as a mysterious knight, accuses Edmond of treason and murder, challenges him to single combat and defeats him. The wounded and dying Edmond tries to revoke his death sentence on Lear and Cordelia, but the reprieve comes too late to save Cordelia. The king carries her dead body back on to the stage.

'The wonder is he hath endured so long'. Edgar and Kent both watch as Lear struggles to accept Cordelia's death before he dies himself. In this production Lear was played by a female actor, Kathryn Hunter.

Edgar speaks the closing lines of the play: 'We that are young / Shall never see so much, nor live so long.' Lear, Cordelia and Edmond lie dead. Gonerill and Regan have died off stage, Gonerill first poisoning her sister, and then committing suicide herself. Some productions, like this one, show their bodies on stage too.

List of characters

The Royal House of Britain

LEAR king of Britain
GONERILL his eldest daughter
REGAN his second daughter
CORDELIA his youngest daughter
THE DUKE OF ALBANY married to Gonerill
THE DUKE OF CORNWALL married to Regan

The Gloucester family

THE EARL OF GLOUCESTER
EDGAR his elder son and heir
EDMOND his illegitimate son

Other characters in the play

FOOL
THE EARL OF KENT (later disguised as CAIUS) } in the king's service

THE KING OF FRANCE
THE DUKE OF BURGUNDY } suitors to Cordelia

OSWALD Gonerill's steward
CURAN a courtier
A GENTLEMAN
AN OLD MAN Gloucester's tenant
A CAPTAIN
A HERALD
A SERVANT in Cornwall's household

Knights, gentlemen, soldiers, attendants, messengers, servants

The action of the play takes place in various parts of the kingdom of Britain.

Discussing King Lear's plan to abdicate and share out his kingdom, Kent and Gloucester are unsure about which of his two sons-in-law Lear favours. Gloucester introduces Edmond, his illegitimate son.

1 Introducing themes

Shakespeare often suggests in his opening scene the themes that his play will go on to explore. Make a list of the main topics of conversation in the script opposite (e.g. fathers and children), then use the list to make some predictions about how you think the play will develop. Write three sentences summarising your predicted story.

2 Gloucester gossips, Edmond listens (in groups of three)

Edmond hears himself described as the result of one of his father's sexual adventures, as a 'knave' and a 'whoreson'. He learns that he will soon be sent away again.

Take parts and speak lines 7–28. Read them once as though Gloucester is joking and showing real affection for his illegitimate son and then again as though he is being massively insensitive and cruel.

Afterwards, talk together about (a) your impressions of Gloucester; (b) what Edmond may be thinking about his father's conversation; and (c) how Kent might react at line 13 to cause Gloucester to ask 'Do you smell a fault?'

3 'The king is coming'

The way in which King Lear is treated by others is an important element in the play. How might a director ask Kent, Gloucester and Edmond to react to Lear's entrance in order to suggest how the rest of the court will behave in the king's presence?

---

affected favoured
qualities are so . . . either's moiety
  their merits are so evenly balanced, no
  one can predict what share of the
  kingdom they will receive
brazed to't hardened to it

issue result
by order of law born within marriage
knave rascal
whoreson bastard, son of a prostitute
out away for

The tragedy of King Lear

Act 1 Scene 1
King Lear's palace

Enter KENT, GLOUCESTER, and EDMOND

KENT I thought the king had more affected the Duke of Albany than
    Cornwall.
GLOUCESTER It did always seem so to us: but now in the division of
    the kingdom, it appears not which of the dukes he values most,
    for qualities are so weighed that curiosity in neither can make   5
    choice of either's moiety.
KENT Is not this your son, my lord?
GLOUCESTER His breeding, sir, hath been at my charge. I have so
    often blushed to acknowledge him, that now I am brazed to't.
KENT I cannot conceive you.   10
GLOUCESTER Sir, this young fellow's mother could; whereupon
    she grew round wombed, and had indeed, sir, a son for her
    cradle ere she had a husband for her bed. Do you smell a fault?
KENT I cannot wish the fault undone, the issue of it being so proper.
GLOUCESTER But I have a son, sir, by order of law, some year elder   15
    than this, who yet is no dearer in my account; though this knave
    came something saucily to the world before he was sent for, yet
    was his mother fair, there was good sport at his making, and the
    whoreson must be acknowledged. Do you know this noble
    gentleman, Edmond?   20
EDMOND No, my lord.
GLOUCESTER My lord of Kent; remember him hereafter as my
    honourable friend.
EDMOND My services to your lordship.
KENT I must love you and sue to know you better.   25
EDMOND Sir, I shall study deserving.
GLOUCESTER He hath been out nine years, and away he shall
    again. The king is coming.

Lear intends to divide Britain between his daughters. He sets them a test: whoever expresses the greatest love will be given the largest portion. Gonerill voices limitless love for him and wins a share.

From left to right: Cornwall, Regan, Gonerill, Lear, Cordelia and Albany. What do you think is the significance of the sword?

1 Enter King Lear (in large groups)

How might the entrance of Lear, his daughters and the members of the court be staged? See what kinds of effects you can create by staging it in different ways. For example, work out how a director could emphasise various aspects of Lear's character, his role as king or the different family relationships. The pictures of the opening scene on pages v and vi of the colour section and pages 16 and 206 will give you ideas about the different ways directors show this scene.

Sennet trumpet fanfare	**bounty** generosity
son son-in-law	**nature . . . challenge** natural affection
constant will firm intention	and good qualities are well matched
several dowers separate marriage	**bounds** limits, boundaries
gifts	**champains** plains
amorous sojourn visit as suitors	**meads** meadows
divest us both of part with	

Sennet. Enter KING LEAR, CORNWALL, ALBANY, GONERILL,
REGAN, CORDELIA, *and Attendants*

LEAR Attend the lords of France and Burgundy, Gloucester.
GLOUCESTER I shall, my lord.   *Exit*   30
LEAR Meantime we shall express our darker purpose.
       Give me the map there. Know, that we have divided
       In three our kingdom, and 'tis our fast intent
       To shake all cares and business from our age,
       Conferring them on younger strengths while we   35
       Unburdened crawl toward death. Our son of Cornwall,
       And you, our no less loving son of Albany,
       We have this hour a constant will to publish
       Our daughters' several dowers, that future strife
       May be prevented now. The princes, France and
          Burgundy,   40
       Great rivals in our youngest daughter's love,
       Long in our court have made their amorous sojourn,
       And here are to be answered. Tell me, my daughters
       (Since now we will divest us both of rule,
       Interest of territory, cares of state),   45
       Which of you shall we say doth love us most,
       That we our largest bounty may extend
       Where nature doth with merit challenge? Gonerill,
       Our eldest born, speak first.
GONERILL Sir, I love you more than word can wield the matter,   50
       Dearer than eyesight, space, and liberty;
       Beyond what can be valued, rich or rare,
       No less than life, with grace, health, beauty, honour;
       As much as child e'er loved, or father found;
       A love that makes breath poor, and speech unable;   55
       Beyond all manner of so much I love you.
CORDELIA [*Aside*] What shall Cordelia speak? Love, and be silent.
LEAR Of all these bounds even from this line, to this,
       With shadowy forests and with champains riched
       With plenteous rivers and wide-skirted meads,   60
       We make thee lady. To thine and Albany's issues
       Be this perpetual. What says our second daughter,
       Our dearest Regan, wife of Cornwall?

Regan claims that her greatest joy is her father's love. Lear gives her land equal to Gonerill's share. Cordelia refuses to join in the love test, saying that she simply loves her father as a daughter should.

1 Cordelia says 'Nothing' (in pairs)

Lear does not treat his daughters equally in the division of the kingdom. His words at line 81 suggest he has saved the best for Cordelia – his favourite, his 'joy'. But she refuses to join her sisters in flattering him, answering Lear's request for a declaration of love with 'Nothing', a word that will be used repeatedly in the rest of the play.

How should Cordelia speak the word 'Nothing'? Does Lear respond with instant rage or with embarrassed patience? In one production Lear and his courtiers thought Cordelia was joking and laughed indulgently at her words. (See pictures on page vi, top, of the colour section and p. 55.)

Take parts and speak lines 80–102 in various ways to discover which interpretation you prefer.

2 Three sisters (in groups of three)

While Gonerill and Regan emphasise their great 'love' for Lear (lines 50–71), Cordelia speaks only of her duty as his daughter, her 'bond' (lines 82–101). Take parts, and read aloud to each other what each sister says to Lear. Then try the following activities.

a Compare the language and imagery used by the different sisters. Consider also the length and complexity of the sentences they use and their specific choice of words.

b Talk together about what their different verbal styles suggest about the differing personalities of the sisters and how they really feel about their father. Sum up each sister in a sentence of your own.

c Look at the pictures on page v (bottom) of the colour section and on page 4, and suggest how the sisters' speeches could be staged to convey the character and unspoken feelings of each.

self-mettle same spirit	**opulent** rich
square of sense human body, perfect feeling	**bond** duty as a daughter
felicitate happy	**mar** damage
ponderous heavy, valuable	**begot** fathered
validity value	**bred** reared
interested admitted, married	**take my plight** accept my wedding vow

REGAN I am made of that self-mettle as my sister
        And prize me at her worth. In my true heart   65
        I find she names my very deed of love.
        Only she comes too short, that I profess
        Myself an enemy to all other joys
        Which the most precious square of sense possesses,
        And find I am alone felicitate   70
        In your dear highness' love.
CORDELIA [*Aside*]   Then poor Cordelia,
        And yet not so, since I am sure my love's
        More ponderous than my tongue.
LEAR To thee and thine hereditary ever
        Remain this ample third of our fair kingdom,   75
        No less in space, validity, and pleasure
        Than that conferred on Gonerill. Now our joy,
        Although our last and least, to whose young love
        The vines of France and milk of Burgundy
        Strive to be interested. What can you say to draw   80
        A third more opulent than your sisters? Speak.
CORDELIA Nothing, my lord.
LEAR Nothing?
CORDELIA Nothing.
LEAR Nothing will come of nothing, speak again.   85
CORDELIA Unhappy that I am, I cannot heave
        My heart into my mouth: I love your majesty
        According to my bond, no more nor less.
LEAR How, how, Cordelia? Mend your speech a little,
        Lest you may mar your fortunes.
CORDELIA   Good my lord,   90
        You have begot me, bred me, loved me. I
        Return those duties back as are right fit,
        Obey you, love you, and most honour you.
        Why have my sisters husbands, if they say
        They love you all? Happily, when I shall wed,   95
        That lord whose hand must take my plight shall carry
        Half my love with him, half my care and duty.
        Sure, I shall never marry like my sisters.
LEAR But goes thy heart with this?
CORDELIA   Ay, my good lord.

Enraged, Lear disowns Cordelia and divides her inheritance between Gonerill and Regan. He proposes that he and his one hundred knights live with Gonerill and Regan in turn. Kent protests.

---

1 A father's curse (in large groups)

In lines 102–14 Lear invokes ancient beliefs to curse and reject Cordelia. He is bitterly angry at her unwillingness to declare unqualified love for him. Here's one way to help you explore the force of Lear's angry words and their effect on Cordelia.

One person (volunteer only!) plays Cordelia. The others stand in a circle around her. Each one chooses a short section of Lear's words which they feel conveys his rejection of Cordelia. This extract can be five or six words, or as much as three lines. In turn, speak the words you have chosen. When you have spoken your words, turn your back on Cordelia.

Repeat the activity, adding suitable gestures to illustrate your words. Cordelia can try ways of gesturing and speaking lines from earlier in the script to respond to these attacks, but may not leave the circle.

After you have tried several versions of the activity, talk together about the way in which the language expresses Lear's feelings and the effect it has on Cordelia.

2 The language of authority (in small groups)

Lear asserts his authority in lines 115–33. He issues orders and proclaims his intentions. But to whom? Work through the lines, a sentence or small section at a time, identifying the person or persons addressed at each point.

3 Director's advice

Line 137 may mean 'stop blathering and get to the point' or 'I've made up my mind. Shut up or I'll make you suffer.' Suggest how an actor could experiment with saying this line and the gestures they could use to convey each of these different meanings.

Hecate   goddess of witchcraft
operation of the orbs   astrological influence of the stars
Propinquity . . . of blood   closeness and relationship
Scythian   cruel savage

makes his generation messes   eats his children (messes = meals)
Pre-eminence   high status
addition   titles, honours
sway   control
coronet   crown

LEAR So young, and so untender?   100
CORDELIA So young, my lord, and true.
LEAR Let it be so, thy truth then be thy dower.
       For by the sacred radiance of the sun,
       The mysteries of Hecate and the night,
       By all the operation of the orbs   105
       From whom we do exist and cease to be,
       Here I disclaim all my paternal care,
       Propinquity and property of blood,
       And as a stranger to my heart and me
       Hold thee from this forever. The barbarous Scythian,   110
       Or he that makes his generation messes
       To gorge his appetite, shall to my bosom
       Be as well neighboured, pitied, and relieved,
       As thou my sometime daughter.
KENT   Good my liege –
LEAR Peace, Kent,   115
       Come not between the dragon and his wrath.
       I loved her most, and thought to set my rest
       On her kind nursery. Hence and avoid my sight!
       So be my grave my peace, as here I give
       Her father's heart from her. Call France. Who stirs?   120
       Call Burgundy. – Cornwall and Albany,
       With my two daughters' dowers digest the third.
       Let pride, which she calls plainness, marry her.
       I do invest you jointly with my power,
       Pre-eminence, and all the large effects   125
       That troop with majesty. Ourself by monthly course,
       With reservation of an hundred knights
       By you to be sustained, shall our abode
       Make with you by due turn; only we shall retain
       The name and all th'addition to a king: the sway,   130
       Revenue, execution of the rest,
       Beloved sons, be yours; which to confirm,
       This coronet part between you.
KENT   Royal Lear,
       Whom I have ever honoured as my king,
       Loved as my father, as my master followed,   135
       As my great patron thought on in my prayers –
LEAR The bow is bent and drawn, make from the shaft.

[handwritten margin notes: "they can have Cordelia's dowry", "I do't wanna be king, but call + treat me like a king"]

Kent challenges Lear's decisions. Kent states his loyalty, but continues to criticise the king's actions. Lear warns Kent to stop his protest on pain of death. Lear is outraged, and begins to declare Kent's punishment.

1 Kent's plain speaking (in pairs)

In lines 138–48 Kent accuses Lear of madness, criticises Gonerill's and Regan's empty flattery, urges Lear to hold on to power and defends Cordelia's sincerity. He addresses Lear as 'thou', an inappropriately intimate term for a subject to use to his monarch (who would expect the courtesy of the plural 'you' in such a public conversation).

One student speaks Kent's lines. The other, as Lear, moves around the room, changing direction as often as they want. Kent must keep reading aloud, following Lear as closely as possible to make him listen. Lear must stop and turn round when Kent says something that bites deep into his feelings as a king and father. Afterwards talk together about which of Kent's remarks you think Lear would find the most hurtful.

2 Loyal Kent . . . the 'true blank'

Sight and blindness will become key themes. Kent implores Lear to 'See better', and offers to act as 'The true blank of thine eye' (lines 152–3). 'Blank' means centre of target or line of sight. Imagine that the actor playing Kent asks, 'Does it mean Lear should keep Kent in view, or that Kent is the model of an honest truth-teller, or what?' Make your reply.

3 Kent hears his 'reward'

Kent completes his protest (line 160) and Lear issues his verdict. On stage Kent could be shown to be overpowered by Albany and Cornwall or by Lear's soldiers. He could seem to be exhausted or he could appear to give up a hopeless attempt to alert the king. If you were the director, how would you stage the moment when Kent finishes his speech? For one production's version, see colour section, page vi (bottom).

---

fork   arrow-head
Reserve thy state   keep your powers
Reverb no hollowness   do not echo
 like an empty vessel
wage   stake, make war
Apollo   god of the sun

vassal   wretched slave
Miscreant   unbeliever, scoundrel
forbear   stop
Revoke   cancel, alter
vent clamour   make noise
recreant   traitor

KENT Let it fall rather, though the fork invade
       The region of my heart. Be Kent unmannerly
       When Lear is mad. What wouldst thou do, old man?   140
       Think'st thou that duty shall have dread to speak
       When power to flattery bows? To plainness honour's
         bound,
       When majesty falls to folly. Reserve thy state,
       And in thy best consideration check
       This hideous rashness. Answer my life, my judgement: 145
       Thy youngest daughter does not love thee least,
       Nor are those empty-hearted whose low sounds
       Reverb no hollowness.
LEAR   Kent, on thy life no more.
KENT My life I never held but as a pawn
       To wage against thine enemies, ne'er feared to lose it,   150
       Thy safety being motive.
LEAR   Out of my sight!
KENT See better, Lear, and let me still remain
       The true blank of thine eye.
LEAR Now by Apollo –
KENT   Now by Apollo, king,
       Thou swear'st thy gods in vain.
LEAR   O vassal! Miscreant!   155
ALBANY, CORNWALL Dear sir, forbear.
KENT Kill thy physician, and thy fee bestow
       Upon the foul disease. Revoke thy gift,
       Or whilst I can vent clamour from my throat,
       I'll tell thee thou dost evil.
LEAR   Hear me, recreant,   160
       On thine allegiance hear me.
       That thou hast sought to make us break our vows,
       Which we durst never yet; and with strained pride,
       To come betwixt our sentence and our power,
       Which nor our nature nor our place can bear,   165
       Our potency made good, take thy reward.
       Five days we do allot thee for provision
       To shield thee from disasters of the world,

[handwritten marginal note beside lines 149–151:] ? three-toning doesn't scare me

Lear banishes Kent from Britain, threatening execution if he remains. Kent praises Cordelia's honesty, and urges Gonerill and Regan to fulfil their words of love. Lear offers Cordelia in marriage to Burgundy, without a dowry.

1 Kent's parting words

Enraged by Kent's plain speaking, Lear banishes him. Kent has five days to prepare and must leave by the sixth day. If he is discovered in the kingdom after ten days, he will be executed.

In lines 174–81 Kent declares that he welcomes banishment if Lear insists on acting tyrannically. Before he says farewell, he addresses Lear, Cordelia and her sisters in turn, speaking each time in rhyming couplets. Write responses in the same style for Lear, Cordelia, Gonerill and Regan.

2 Who speaks line 182?

There are three possible candidates. The Quarto edition (see p. 240) gives the line to 'Glost' (i.e. Gloucester) while the Folio edition gives it to 'Cor', which could mean Cordelia or Cornwall. Which speaker would you choose to deliver the line? Give reasons for your choice.

3 The price of a princess (in pairs)

a Lear speaks about Cordelia as though she were a thing of little saleable value. Take turns to speak lines 190–5, emphasising Cordelia's lack of worth and treating your partner as Cordelia, the object of your scorn.

b 'Take her or leave her?' In lines 196–8 Lear states the five conditions on which he will give Cordelia to Burgundy. How do you think Cordelia feels about being discussed by Lear and Burgundy as if she were a commodity? Imagine that, at the end of each condition (after each of the first five commas), Cordelia speaks an Aside. What might she say? For ideas you could look back at Cordelia's Asides earlier in this scene (lines 57 and 71).

---

trunk body
Jupiter ruler of the gods
large speeches grand words
Flourish trumpet fanfare
rivalled competed
present dower marriage gift
tender offer, give

aught anything
little seeming substance small deceptive thing
pieced added
fitly like suitably please
owes possesses

And on the sixth to turn thy hated back
Upon our kingdom; if on the tenth day following   170
Thy banished trunk be found in our dominions,
The moment is thy death. Away! By Jupiter,
This shall not be revoked.
KENT Fare thee well, king, since thus thou wilt appear,
Freedom lives hence, and banishment is here.   175
[*To Cordelia*] The gods to their dear shelter take thee,
maid,
That justly think'st and hast most rightly said.
[*To Gonerill and Regan*] And your large speeches may your
deeds approve,
That good effects may spring from words of love.
Thus Kent, O princes, bids you all adieu,   180
He'll shape his old course in a country new.   *Exit*

Flourish. Enter GLOUCESTER *with* FRANCE *and* BURGUNDY [*and*]
Attendants

CORDELIA Here's France and Burgundy, my noble lord.
LEAR My lord of Burgundy,
We first address toward you, who with this king
Hath rivalled for our daughter. What in the least   185
Will you require in present dower with her,
Or cease your quest of love?
BURGUNDY   Most royal majesty,
I crave no more than hath your highness offered,
Nor will you tender less?
LEAR   Right noble Burgundy,
When she was dear to us, we did hold her so,   190
But now her price is fallen. Sir, there she stands.
If aught within that little seeming substance,
Or all of it, with our displeasure pieced
And nothing more, may fitly like your grace,
She's there, and she is yours.
BURGUNDY   I know no answer.   195
LEAR Will you with those infirmities she owes,
Unfriended, new adopted to our hate,
Dowered with our curse, and strangered with our oath,
Take her, or leave her?

13

Burgundy declines Lear's conditions. Lear advises France to reject Cordelia. France is amazed at Lear's sudden rejection of his favourite. Cordelia insists that she has been condemned for speaking honestly.

---

1 Characters under stress (in groups of three)

Take parts as France, Cordelia and Lear.

a France speaks lines 207–17 twice, first looking at Lear the whole time, and then gazing at Cordelia, ignoring the king. How might France's different attempts at eye contact alter the way Lear and Cordelia react to his words?

b Work through Cordelia's lines 218–28, suggesting which character she looks at as she speaks each line.

c France and Cordelia have been put in a difficult position here. What do the words they say suggest about their characters? If you were directing the play, what impression would you wish these two actors to make on the audience?

2 'Better thou hadst not been born' (in pairs)

Lear rejects his daughter in words (lines 228–9) that might seem excessively brutal and cruel. Experiment with various ways of delivering these lines. Lear could be:

- speaking quietly to Cordelia alone;
- making a great public announcement;
- saying the lines in some other way.

If you were directing the play, how would you wish the audience to react to Lear's words?

Election choice
stray departure
T'avert to redirect
argument subject, theme
balm comfort
dismantle strip away

fore-vouched previously promised
Fall into taint become rotten or decayed
reason without . . . in me only a miracle could make me believe
A still-soliciting eye always begging

BURGUNDY   Pardon me, royal sir,
        Election makes not up in such conditions.   200
LEAR   Then leave her, sir, for by the power that made me,
        I tell you all her wealth. [*To France*] For you, great king,
        I would not from your love make such a stray
        To match you where I hate; therefore beseech you
        T'avert your liking a more worthier way   205
        Than on a wretch whom nature is ashamed
        Almost t'acknowledge hers.
FRANCE   This is most strange,
        That she whom even but now was your best object,
        The argument of your praise, balm of your age,   *← Cordelia is his favorite*
        The best, the dearest, should in this trice of time   210
        Commit a thing so monstrous to dismantle   *proving his*
        So many folds of favour. Sure, her offence
        Must be of such unnatural degree   *previously promised*
        That monsters it, or your fore-vouched affection
        Fall into taint; which to believe of her   215
        Must be a faith that reason without miracle   *only a miracle could make me believe*
        Should never plant in me.
CORDELIA   I yet beseech your majesty –
        If for I want that glib and oily art,
        To speak and purpose not, since what I well intend,   220
        I'll do't before I speak – that you make known
        It is no vicious blot, murder, or foulness,
        No unchaste action or dishonoured step   *she did no foul things to have her father be angry*
        That hath deprived me of your grace and favour,
        But even for want of that for which I am richer –   225
        A still-soliciting eye, and such a tongue
        That I am glad I have not, though not to have it,
        Hath lost me in your liking.
LEAR   Better thou
        Hadst not been born than not t'have pleased me better.

Burgundy offers to marry Cordelia if Lear will guarantee the previously promised dowry. Lear refuses, and Burgundy rejects Cordelia. France takes her as his wife. Lear disowns Cordelia, and vows never to see her again.

---

1 Paradoxical truths (in groups of five to seven)

France describes the strange way Cordelia's fortunes are working out (lines 245–56). His words contain seven or eight antitheses (oppositions or paradoxes, such as 'rich'/'poor', 'losest'/'find'). Identify the antitheses and prepare a presentation of the lines with one person reading and the others miming. For example, the first mime represents 'rich' changing into 'poor'.

Cordelia's future is decided. Which line from the opposite page do you think is being spoken here and why?

---

tardiness in nature   natural reticence
history   inner thoughts, story
regards   other considerations
entire point   essential issue
respect and fortunes   status and wealth
kindle   warm, ignite

inflamed respect   passionate admiration
waterish   weak
unprized   unvalued
though unkind   even though they've been cruel and unsisterly
benison   blessing

FRANCE Is it but this? A tardiness in nature,   230
Which often leaves the history unspoke
That it intends to do? My lord of Burgundy,
What say you to the lady? Love's not love
When it is mingled with regards that stands
Aloof from th'entire point. Will you have her?   235
She is herself a dowry.
BURGUNDY   Royal king,
Give but that portion which yourself proposed,
And here I take Cordelia by the hand,
Duchess of Burgundy.
LEAR Nothing, I have sworn; I am firm.   240
BURGUNDY I am sorry then, you have so lost a father
That you must lose a husband.
CORDELIA   Peace be with Burgundy;
Since that respect and fortunes are his love,
I shall not be his wife.
FRANCE Fairest Cordelia, that art most rich being poor,   245
Most choice forsaken, and most loved despised,
Thee and thy virtues here I seize upon.
Be it lawful I take up what's cast away.
Gods, gods! 'Tis strange, that from their cold'st neglect
My love should kindle to inflamed respect.   250
Thy dowerless daughter, king, thrown to my chance,
Is queen of us, of ours, and our fair France.
Not all the dukes of waterish Burgundy
Can buy this unprized precious maid of me.
Bid them farewell, Cordelia, though unkind;   255
Thou losest here a better where to find.
LEAR Thou hast her, France, let her be thine; for we
Have no such daughter, nor shall ever see
That face of hers again. Therefore be gone,
Without our grace, our love, our benison.   260
Come, noble Burgundy.

Flourish. Exeunt [Lear, Burgundy, Cornwall, Albany, Gloucester,
Edmond, and Attendants]

FRANCE   Bid farewell to your sisters.

Cordelia asks her sisters to care for Lear. They reject her words and criticise her behaviour. Left together, Gonerill and Regan speak about Lear's erratic judgement and plan to work together to control him.

1 'So farewell to you both' (in groups of three)

How could the sisters speak their farewell conversation (lines 262–76)? One actress playing Cordelia said:

> You could so easily do it in a nasty, cynical way – in fact, that is how it is usually done. But in this production, it is just saying: 'I understand why you have behaved as you have, and I don't blame you. Here's a warning, but it is not a cynical warning.' Nevertheless, Regan and Gonerill resented my interference, and spoke their replies sarcastically. Gonerill's line 273, with its use of alliteration (repeated initial letter sound), especially lends itself to sarcasm.

Take parts and speak lines 262–76 to find your own interpretation of the mood in which you think the sisters say farewell.

2 Princesses in private (in groups of four)

The departure of the King of France and Cordelia leaves Gonerill and Regan alone to review the unexpected turn of events.

a Two of you read aloud Gonerill and Regan's private conversation (lines 277–98). Talk together about the advice a director might give to the actors playing the two sisters in order to make the differences between their characters as clear as possible.

b Select six different critical comments which Gonerill and Regan make about Lear in lines 277–98. When you have made your selection, two group members read aloud Gonerill's and Regan's earlier public statements (lines 50–6 and lines 64–71). The other two group members must then interject with their chosen critical comments, so that the sisters' truthful thoughts are heard as well as their insincere public voices.

---

professèd bosoms   publicly stated love
At fortune's alms   as a gift of charity
scanted   stinted, withheld
well are worth . . . wanted   deserve to be valued as nothing

plighted   hidden
engraffed   ingrained
choleric   ill-tempered
unconstant starts   unpredictable behaviour
i'th'heat   immediately

CORDELIA The jewels of our father, with washed eyes
　　　　Cordelia leaves you. I know you what you are,
　　　　And like a sister am most loath to call
　　　　Your faults as they are named. Love well our father: 265
　　　　To your professèd bosoms I commit him.
　　　　But yet, alas, stood I within his grace,
　　　　I would prefer him to a better place.
　　　　So farewell to you both.
REGAN Prescribe not us our duty.
GONERILL 　　　　　　　　Let your study 270
　　　　Be to content your lord, who hath received you
　　　　At fortune's alms. You have obedience scanted,
　　　　And well are worth the want that you have wanted.
CORDELIA Time shall unfold what plighted cunning hides;
　　　　Who covers faults, at last with shame derides. 275
　　　　Well may you prosper.
FRANCE 　　　　　　　　Come, my fair Cordelia.

Exeunt France and Cordelia

GONERILL Sister, it is not little I have to say of what most nearly
　　appertains to us both. I think our father will hence tonight.
REGAN That's most certain, and with you; next month with us.
GONERILL You see how full of changes his age is; the observation 280
　　we have made of it hath not been little. He always loved our
　　sister most, and with what poor judgement he hath now cast
　　her off appears too grossly.
REGAN 'Tis the infirmity of his age; yet he hath ever but slenderly
　　known himself. 285
GONERILL The best and soundest of his time hath been but rash;
　　then must we look from his age to receive not alone the
　　imperfections of long-engraffed condition, but therewithal the
　　unruly waywardness that infirm and choleric years bring with
　　them. 290
REGAN Such unconstant starts are we like to have from him as this
　　of Kent's banishment.
GONERILL There is further compliment of leave-taking between
　　France and him. Pray you, let us sit together. If our father carry
　　authority with such disposition as he bears, this last surrender 295
　　of his will but offend us.
REGAN We shall further think of it.
GONERILL We must do something, and i'th'heat. 　　　*Exeunt*

Edmond questions why he is regarded as inferior because his parents were not married. He is planning to replace his brother, Edgar, as his father's heir. Gloucester expresses concern about the events at court.

---

1 The truth about Edmond (in groups of four or five)

Lines 1–22 are a soliloquy, a speech either made by an actor alone on stage or unheard by anyone else present. The theatrical convention is that a soliloquy expresses what the character really thinks and feels. An actor can choose whether to address the audience directly, or to speak as if the audience overhears them thinking aloud.

Edmond complains about his treatment as a 'bastard' or illegitimate child. There was a considerable stigma attached to children born outside marriage in Shakespeare's day, especially amongst the nobility. Edmond, therefore, decides to take Nature as his deity or 'goddess', rejecting the social customs that condemn him as inferior. Explore Edmond's soliloquy through one or more of the following:

a Experiment on your own with different ways of speaking the lines.

b Share a group reading, taking turns to speak the words by changing readers at each punctuation mark or after each sentence.

c Make a list of Edmond's grievances. Compare the Edmond of these lines with the almost silent character you saw at the start of Act 1 Scene 1.

d Talk together about the impression of Edmond you gain from this soliloquy. Suggest four or five adjectives to describe his character.

e Make up three sixty-second dramas showing different incidents from Edmond's life which may have made him feel inferior to others because of his illegitimacy.

---

in the plague of custom condemned by the rules of society
curiosity of nations nit-picking laws
Lag of younger than
compact proportioned
issue child
composition bodily perfection

fops fools
speed succeed
Prescribed reduced
Confined to exhibition restricted to a small allowance
Upon the gad in haste

Act 1 Scene 2
The Earl of Gloucester's castle

Enter EDMOND

EDMOND Thou, Nature, art my goddess; to thy law
My services are bound. Wherefore should I
Stand in the plague of custom and permit
The curiosity of nations to deprive me?
For that I am some twelve or fourteen moonshines   5
Lag of a brother? Why 'bastard'? Wherefore 'base'?
When my dimensions are as well compact,
My mind as generous, and my shape as true
As honest madam's issue? Why brand they us
With 'base'? with 'baseness'? 'bastardy'? 'base, base'?   10
Who in the lusty stealth of nature take
More composition and fierce quality
Than doth within a dull, stale, tired bed
Go to th'creating a whole tribe of fops
Got 'tween a sleep and wake? Well then,   15
Legitimate Edgar, I must have your land.
Our father's love is to the bastard, Edmond,
As to th'legitimate. Fine word, 'legitimate'.
Well, my legitimate, [*Takes out a letter*] if this letter speed
And my invention thrive, Edmond the base   20
Shall to th'legitimate. I grow; I prosper;
Now gods, stand up for bastards!

Enter GLOUCESTER

GLOUCESTER Kent banished thus? and France in choler parted?
And the king gone tonight? Prescribed his power,
Confined to exhibition? All this done   25
Upon the gad? Edmond, how now? What news?

Edmond tricks Gloucester into reading a letter which he claims is from Edgar.
The letter suggests that Edgar is seeking his father's death in order to inherit
his wealth. Edmond lies about the origin of the letter.

1 'Nothing' – an echo

Once again, the word that will echo through much of the rest of the
play is heard: 'Nothing' (see p. 6). Here in lines 31–5, it is used by
a son and his father. You will find later in the play that Gloucester's
words, 'if it be nothing, I shall not need spectacles', are horrifically
ironic.

Think of three ways in which the situation developing in this family
is like that in Lear's family, and three ways in which it is different.

2 The language of uncertainty (in pairs)

Gloucester's language is full of questions, which suggest a troubled,
uncertain mind and possibly a mind vulnerable to Edmond's manip-
ulation. One person reads out all the questions Gloucester asks in lines
23–58, pausing after each question. In the pause, the other replies as
a member of the audience who has watched the play so far.

3 Father and son (in groups of four)

Edmond is working hard to manipulate and control his father in this
scene. Think about how the actors' movements and body language
can be used to indicate the characters' mood and feelings.

a One (or two) group members read out lines 23–44 while the other
  group members mime the actions of the two characters. Think
  about how it might be possible for Edmond to show the audience
  his true feelings whilst keeping them from his father.

b Use the letter as a prop. Begin with Gloucester's 'What news?'
  (line 26), and in pairs take turns to act out lines 26–44, with a
  piece of paper as the letter. Add gestures and movements to
  emphasise the sinister game of cat and mouse as Edmond dupes
  his father.

---

terrible dispatch sudden
  concealment
perused read
o'erlooking attention
essay . . . virtue test of my good
  nature
idle . . . bondage useless and foolish
  slavery

sways . . . suffered rules only
  because we tolerate it
casement window
closet private room
character handwriting
durst would, dare
fain rather

EDMOND So please your lordship, none. [*Putting up the letter*]

GLOUCESTER Why so earnestly seek you to put up that letter?

EDMOND I know no news, my lord.

GLOUCESTER What paper were you reading?   30

EDMOND Nothing, my lord.

Sudden hidig

GLOUCESTER No? What needed then that terrible dispatch of it
into your pocket? The quality of nothing hath not such need to
hide itself. Let's see. Come, if it be nothing, I shall not need
spectacles.   35

EDMOND I beseech you, sir, pardon me; it is a letter from my
brother that I have not all o'erread; and for so much as I have
perused, I find it not fit for your o'erlooking. *attention*

GLOUCESTER Give me the letter, sir.

EDMOND I shall offend either to detain or give it. The contents, as   40
in part I understand them, are too blame.

GLOUCESTER Let's see, let's see.

EDMOND I hope for my brother's justification he wrote this but as
an essay or taste of my virtue. *useless & foolish slaves*

[*Gives him the letter*]

GLOUCESTER *Reads* 'This policy and reverence of age makes the   45
world bitter to the best of our times, keeps our fortunes from us
till our oldness cannot relish them. I begin to find an idle and
fond bondage in the oppression of aged tyranny, who sways not
as it hath power but as it is suffered. Come to me, that of this I
may speak more. If our father would sleep till I waked him, you   50
should enjoy half his revenue forever and live the beloved of
your brother. Edgar.' Hum! Conspiracy! 'Sleep till I waked
him, you should enjoy half his revenue.' My son Edgar, had he
a hand to write this? a heart and brain to breed it in? When
came you to this? Who brought it?   55

EDMOND It was not brought me, my lord; there's the cunning of it.
I found it thrown in at the casement of my closet. *private room*

GLOUCESTER You know the character to be your brother's?

EDMOND If the matter were good, my lord, I durst swear it were
his: but in respect of that, I would fain think it were not.   60

rather

Gloucester curses Edgar, but Edmond develops the deception further by protesting that his brother cannot be a villain and by advising caution. Edmond proposes to talk to Edgar where their father can overhear them.

---

1 Deceiving words (in pairs)

Try one or more of the following activities to explore the way in which Edmond uses language cunningly in order to manipulate his father's feelings.

a Identify several lies that Edmond tells his father.

b Find three words or phrases of Edmond's that are probably intended to enrage his father. Find three or four other words and phrases that he uses to suggest his own honesty and loyalty.

c Compare Edmond's deceitful language in lines 62–90 with his soliloquy (lines 1–22), in which he states what he really thinks. Identify three or four examples to show the differences of style and content between his honest and dishonest language.

2 Can evil be comic? (in pairs)

Look back at this scene and decide whether it should be played for humour on stage. Edmond has some similarities to the Vice or Machiavel in medieval plays – a comic but evil figure who speaks confidentially to the audience, almost making them feel like fellow conspirators in his villainy.

- Talk about how the actor playing Edmond could try to engage the audience's sympathy and admiration, involving them in his wrongdoing.
- Suggest movements or gestures that Edmond could use to remind the audience of his real purposes.
- Talk about whether the actor playing Gloucester should play him as a dignified but deceived man, a gullible dupe or in some other way.

---

sounded you in asked your opinion about

sons at perfect age adult sons

testimony . . . intent information about his intentions

should . . . course won't go wrong

pawn down bet

meet appropriate

an auricular assurance the evidence of your own ears

wind me into him craftily discover his thoughts

unstate myself . . . resolution give everything to find out the truth

GLOUCESTER It is his.

EDMOND It is his hand, my lord, but I hope his heart is not in the
contents.

GLOUCESTER Has he never before sounded you in this business?

EDMOND Never, my lord. But I have heard him oft maintain it to   65
be fit that, sons at perfect age, and fathers declined, the father
should be as ward to the son, and the son manage his revenue.

GLOUCESTER O villain, villain – his very opinion in the letter!
Abhorred villain, unnatural, detested, brutish villain – worse
than brutish! Go, sirrah, seek him: I'll apprehend him.   70
Abominable villain, where is he?

EDMOND I do not well know, my lord. If it shall please you to
suspend your indignation against my brother till you can derive
from him better testimony of his intent, you should run a
certain course; where if you violently proceed against him,   75
mistaking his purpose, it would make a great gap in your own
honour and shake in pieces the heart of his obedience. I dare
pawn down my life for him that he hath writ this to feel my
affection to your honour and to no other pretence of danger.

GLOUCESTER Think you so?   80

EDMOND If your honour judge it meet, I will place you where you
shall hear us confer of this and by an auricular assurance have
your satisfaction, and that without any further delay than this
very evening.

GLOUCESTER He cannot be such a monster. Edmond, seek him   85
out: wind me into him, I pray you. Frame the business after
your own wisdom. I would unstate myself to be in a due
resolution.

EDMOND I will seek him, sir, presently, convey the business as I
shall find means, and acquaint you withal.   90

Gloucester sees Edgar's treachery as part of a breakdown in society foretold by the recent eclipses of the sun and moon. Edmond rejects such superstitious belief in astrology. He prepares to trick his brother, Edgar.

1 An old man fears for the future

Gloucester thinks that society is in decay and is disturbed by recent eclipses which he believes foretell the break-up of Lear's Britain. Human reason ('wisdom of nature') may understand the significance of eclipses, but the disasters that they bring are still devastating. He catalogues what he sees as unnatural disasters, from the decline of love to the rise of conspiracies ('Machinations') and insincerity ('hollowness').

Work through Gloucester's list of disasters in lines 94–100. How many can match with events so far in the play?

2 Edmond – realist and schemer (in pairs)

Edmond mocks people who choose to blame astrology and the stars ('heavenly compulsion' and 'spherical predominance') for their personalities. He says that he would have been wicked whichever star sign he was born under. He is what Nature made him.

Edgar's arrival is Edmond's cue to start the second part of his plot to inherit his father's wealth and status. His theatrical language emphasises that he is about to act out a role ('the catastrophe of the old comedy' refers to the abrupt ending of an old-fashioned play). He makes sure that Edgar overhears him speak fearfully of the recent eclipses in a mocking imitation of Gloucester's line 91, and he probably sings the words 'Fa, sol, la, me' (line 119) – they may refer to musical chords that the Elizabethans found disturbing and that some called 'the devil in music'.

Experiment with different ideas of what Edmond might be doing (or pretending to do) during Gloucester's lines 91–103 and when Edgar enters. What pieces of stage business could an actor incorporate to make Edmond seem even more two-faced?

---

sequent following
surfeits excesses
treachers traitors
whoremaster lecherous
lay . . . star blame his lechery on the stars

compounded had sex
Dragon's tail conjunction of the waning moon with the sun's orbit (thought to be an evil influence)
Ursa major star cluster (Great Bear)
Tom o'Bedlam a madman (see p. 74)

GLOUCESTER These late eclipses in the sun and moon portend no
good to us. Though the wisdom of nature can reason it thus
and thus, yet nature finds itself scourged by the sequent effects.
Love cools, friendship falls off, brothers divide. In cities,
mutinies; in countries, discord; in palaces, treason; and the   95
bond cracked 'twixt son and father. This villain of mine comes
under the prediction: there's son against father. The king falls
from bias of nature, there's father against child. We have seen
the best of our time. Machinations, hollowness, treachery, and
all ruinous disorders follow us disquietly to our graves. Find   100
out this villain, Edmond, it shall lose thee nothing. Do it
carefully. And the noble and true-hearted Kent banished; his
offence, honesty. 'Tis strange.   *Exit*
EDMOND This is the excellent foppery of the world, that when we
are sick in fortune, often the surfeits of our own behaviour, we   105
make guilty of our disasters the sun, the moon, and stars; as if
we were villains on necessity, fools by heavenly compulsion,
knaves, thieves, and treachers by spherical predominance,
drunkards, liars, and adulterers by an enforced obedience of
planetary influence; and all that we are evil in, by a divine   110
thrusting on. An admirable evasion of whoremaster man, to lay
his goatish disposition on the charge of a star! My father
compounded with my mother under the Dragon's tail, and my
nativity was under *Ursa major*, so that it follows, I am rough and
lecherous. I should have been that I am had the maidenliest   115
star in the firmament twinkled on my bastardising.

Enter EDGAR

Pat: he comes, like the catastrophe of the old comedy. My cue
is villainous melancholy, with a sigh like Tom o'Bedlam. – O
these eclipses do portend these divisions. Fa, sol, la, me.
EDGAR How now, brother Edmond, what serious contemplation   120
are you in?

Edmond warns Edgar that Gloucester has turned against him, and he is now in great danger. Edmond tells Edgar to hide, saying that he is on his side. Alone on stage, Edmond looks forward to succeeding by trickery.

1 Like father, like son (in pairs)

Edmond is as successful in deceiving his brother as he was with his father. Talk about why you think he finds it so easy to trick his family members. Look for examples of Edmond using misleading hints, delaying giving accurate information, asking worrying questions and apparently being very helpful and supportive.

2 Edmond – in his own words

Scene 2 begins and ends with soliloquies by Edmond. Identify similarities and differences in the two soliloquies. In particular, make clear the different use of the word 'nature' in each one.

3 Extra dialogue – extra insight?

The Quarto version of the play (see p. 240) includes six extra lines after 'unhappily' in lines 125–6. What could these additional lines, quoted below, suggest about the personalities of Edmond and Edgar?

> as of unnaturalness between the child and the parent, death, dearth,
> dissolutions of ancient amities, divisions in state, menaces and maledictions
> against king and nobles, needless diffidences, banishment of friends,
> dissipation of cohorts, nuptial breaches, and I know not what.
> EDGAR How long have you been a sectary astronomical?
> EDMOND Come, come,

To help you: 'diffidences' = doubts, 'dissipation of cohorts' = disbanding armies, 'sectary astronomical' = believer in astrology.

---

countenance looks
forbear avoid
with the mischief . . . allay hurting
  you would barely reduce his anger
have . . . forbearance keep a low
  profile, keep your head down

stir abroad go out
anon soon
credulous naive, unsuspecting
practices deceits
wit cunning
fashion fit use to my own purpose

EDMOND I am thinking, brother, of a prediction I read this other day, what should follow these eclipses.

EDGAR Do you busy yourself with that?

EDMOND I promise you, the effects he writes of succeed un- 125
happily. When saw you my father last?

EDGAR The night gone by.

EDMOND Spake you with him?

EDGAR Ay, two hours together.

EDMOND Parted you in good terms? Found you no displeasure in 130
him by word nor countenance?

EDGAR None at all.

EDMOND Bethink yourself wherein you may have offended him,
and at my entreaty forbear his presence until some little time
hath qualified the heat of his displeasure, which at this instant 135
so rageth in him that with the mischief of your person it would
scarcely allay.

EDGAR Some villain hath done me wrong.

EDMOND That's my fear. I pray you have a continent forbearance
till the speed of his rage goes slower; and as I say, retire with 140
me to my lodging, from whence I will fitly bring you to hear my
lord speak. Pray ye, go; there's my key. If you do stir abroad, go
armed.

EDGAR Armed, brother?

EDMOND Brother, I advise you to the best. I am no honest man, if 145
there be any good meaning toward you. I have told you what I
have seen and heard – but faintly, nothing like the image and
horror of it. Pray you, away.

EDGAR Shall I hear from you anon?

EDMOND I do serve you in this business. 150

Exit [*Edgar*]

A credulous father and a brother noble,
Whose nature is so far from doing harms
That he suspects none; on whose foolish honesty
My practices ride easy. I see the business.
Let me, if not by birth, have lands by wit. 155
All with me's meet that I can fashion fit. *Exit*

Gonerill complains about the unreasonable and unruly behaviour of her father and his knights. She instructs Oswald that he and the other servants should show Lear less courtesy and respect.

---

1 'I'll not endure it'

Some time has passed since Gonerill was last seen with her sister, Regan, in Scene 1. Lear has put his plan into effect, and has been staying with Gonerill, to her increasing annoyance and dismay. Gonerill is tired of her household being disturbed by the disorderly behaviour of Lear and his one hundred knights. But what exactly have Lear and his followers done?

Write a few lines for Oswald to speak following line 3, in which he gives actual examples of their riotous behaviour. Write them in blank verse if you can (see p. 235 for information on blank verse structure).

2 A short scene

Scene 3 is only twenty-two lines long. Imagine that a director decides to cut it from a production, and that you disagree with that decision. Make a list of reasons in favour of its inclusion, justifying its dramatic function in such matters as story, character and themes. Then decide whether you would also argue for the inclusion of the following additional lines which the Quarto version (see p. 240) gives to Gonerill after line 16:

> Not to be overruled. Idle old man,
> That still would manage those authorities
> That he hath given away! Now, by my life,
> Old fools are babes again, and must be used
> With checks as flatteries when they are seen abused.

---

chiding scolding, telling off
upbraids criticises
trifle trivial matter
come slack of former services
  become less courteous and helpful
  than before

Horns within sound of hunting horns
come to question made an issue
distaste dislike
hold my course follow my lead

Act 1 Scene 3
The castle of Albany and Gonerill

Enter GONERILL and her steward OSWALD

GONERILL Did my father strike my gentleman for chiding of his
    fool?
OSWALD Ay, madam.
GONERILL By day and night, he wrongs me; every hour
    He flashes into one gross crime or other   5
    That sets us all at odds. I'll not endure it.
    His knights grow riotous, and himself upbraids us
    On every trifle. When he returns from hunting,
    I will not speak with him. Say I am sick.
    If you come slack of former services,   10
    You shall do well; the fault of it I'll answer.
                [Horns within]
OSWALD He's coming, madam, I hear him.
GONERILL Put on what weary negligence you please,
    You and your fellows: I'd have it come to question.
    If he distaste it, let him to my sister,   15
    Whose mind and mine I know in that are one.
    Remember what I have said.
OSWALD Well, madam.
GONERILL And let his knights have colder looks among you:
    What grows of it no matter. Advise your fellows so.   20
    I'll write straight to my sister to hold my course.
    Prepare for dinner.
                           Exeunt

Kent hopes that his disguise as a poor man will enable him to re-enter Lear's service. In response to Lear's questions, Kent says he wants to serve the king.

1 Kent's disguise (in pairs)

Kent has not gone into exile but is risking his life to remain close to Lear. He plans to pose as a serving man who wishes to be employed by Lear. Kent hopes that he can disguise his voice as well as his appearance, and is often shown on stage using a rustic, West Country accent, but many other options are open to the actor.

a Decide on an accent for Kent, giving reasons for your choice.

b Kent has to convince Lear that he is worth employing as a servant. Act out lines 9–38 in turn, identifying the ways in which Kent succeeds in persuading Lear that he would be loyal and valuable.

c Discuss whether the actor should try to suggest any difficulties or struggle involved in a once-powerful nobleman maintaining his disguise as a humble servant.

2 Good and evil motives

Act 1 Scene 2 began with Edmond declaring his determination to get what he wanted at all costs. This scene begins with Kent's soliloquy planning a course of action motivated entirely by a 'good intent'. Choose one or two phrases from Kent's soliloquy (lines 1–17) and one or two from Edmond's soliloquy (Act 1 Scene 2, lines 1–17) which reflect their strongly contrasting beliefs.

3 'Authority'

Line 27 is often a dramatic moment in the theatre. Kent says that it is Lear's natural air of authority that makes him want to be his servant. At this point in the play the audience knows that Gonerill has ordered Oswald to encourage her servants to show open disrespect towards the king. How would you advise the actor playing Kent to say the word 'Authority' and how might the actor playing Lear react?

---

defuse disguise
intent intention
issue consequence
razed my likeness disguised my appearance
full of labours a hard worker

stay a jot wait a moment
What dost thou profess? what's your job?
countenance bearing, face
fain willingly

Act 1 Scene 4
The Great Hall of the castle of Albany and Gonerill

Enter KENT (*disguised*)

KENT If but as well I other accents borrow
　　　That can my speech defuse, my good intent
　　　May carry through itself to that full issue
　　　For which I razed my likeness. Now, banished Kent,
　　　If thou canst serve where thou dost stand condemned,　　5
　　　So may it come thy master, whom thou lov'st,
　　　Shall find thee full of labours.

Horns within. Enter LEAR, [*Knights*,] *and Attendants*

LEAR Let me not stay a jot for dinner. Go, get it ready.
　　　　　　　　　　　　　　　　[*Exit an Attendant*]
　　　How now, what art thou?

KENT A man, sir.　　10

LEAR What dost thou profess? What wouldst thou with us?

KENT I do profess to be no less than I seem, to serve him truly that
will put me in trust, to love him that is honest, to converse with
him that is wise and says little, to fear judgement, to fight when
I cannot choose, and to eat no fish.　　15

LEAR What art thou?

KENT A very honest-hearted fellow, and as poor as the king.

LEAR If thou be'st as poor for a subject as he's for a king, thou art
poor enough. What wouldst thou?

KENT Service.　　20

LEAR Who wouldst thou serve?

KENT You.

LEAR Dost thou know me, fellow?

KENT No, sir; but you have that in your countenance, which I
would fain call master.　　25

LEAR What's that?

KENT Authority.

LEAR What services canst thou do?

Lear decides to employ Kent. Oswald pointedly ignores a command from Lear. A knight comments on the growing disrespect being shown to the king. Lear says that he, too, has noticed the lack of courtesy.

1 Kent's self-portrait

Kent entertains Lear with a description of his own qualities and the services he can perform (lines 29–35). Invent a gesture for Kent to make to accompany each characteristic. For example, as he says 'I can keep honest counsel', he could tap the side of his nose to show that he can keep a secret. Afterwards, identify two of the qualities which, from your impression of Kent so far, most accurately reflect his personality.

2 'So please you –' (in pairs)

a Oswald has been told by Gonerill to adopt a 'weary negligence' towards Lear. Suggest ways in which Oswald could behave in this scene to really antagonise the king.

b Lear sends the knight after Oswald to bring him back to give an explanation for his rudeness. The knight returns, reporting that Oswald has flatly and insolently refused the king's command. Improvise the offstage conversation between the knight and Oswald.

3 Clues about the Fool

The Fool is not specifically named as appearing on stage until later in this scene, although he is sometimes shown playing a silent role in Scene 1 (see colour section, page v, top). In one production he was gagged for the opening scene, presumably to prevent him from interrupting the king's division of the kingdom. He is also mentioned by Gonerill when she complains to Oswald about the behaviour of the king's retinue (Act 1 Scene 3, lines 1–2).

What do lines 60–5 tell the audience about the Fool and Lear's relationship with him before he appears at line 81?

---

keep honest counsel keep a secret
diligence attention to the task
clotpoll idiot, blockhead
roundest most direct
wont used to
abatement reduction

the general dependants all the servants
conception perception, impression
very pretence and purpose deliberate act

KENT I can keep honest counsel, ride, run, mar a curious tale in
telling it, and deliver a plain message bluntly. That which   30
ordinary men are fit for, I am qualified in, and the best of me is
diligence.

LEAR How old art thou?

KENT Not so young, sir, to love a woman for singing, nor so old to
dote on her for anything. I have years on my back forty-eight.   35

LEAR Follow me; thou shalt serve me, if I like thee no worse after
dinner. I will not part from thee yet. Dinner, ho, dinner!
Where's my knave? my fool? Go you and call my fool hither.

[*Exit an Attendant*]

Enter OSWALD

You, you sirrah, where's my daughter?

OSWALD So please you –   *Exit*   40

LEAR What says the fellow there? Call the clotpoll back.

[*Exit a Knight*]

Where's my fool? Ho, I think the world's asleep.

[*Enter* KNIGHT]

How now? Where's that mongrel?

KNIGHT He says, my lord, your daughter is not well.

LEAR Why came not the slave back to me when I called him?   45

KNIGHT Sir, he answered me in the roundest manner, he would
not.

LEAR He would not?

KNIGHT My lord, I know not what the matter is, but to my
judgement your highness is not entertained with that cer-   50
emonious affection as you were wont. There's a great abatement of kindness appears as well in the general dependants as
in the duke himself also, and your daughter.

LEAR Ha? Sayest thou so?

KNIGHT I beseech you pardon me, my lord, if I be mistaken, for   55
my duty cannot be silent when I think your highness wronged.

LEAR Thou but rememberest me of mine own conception. I have
perceived a most faint neglect of late, which I have rather
blamed as mine own jealous curiosity than as a very pretence
and purpose of unkindness. I will look further into't. But   60
where's my fool? I have not seen him these two days.

KNIGHT Since my young lady's going into France, sir, the fool
hath much pined away.

Lear strikes Oswald for his rudeness. Kent joins in the assault. The Fool warns Kent about the dangers of following a king who shows such lack of wisdom in dealing with his daughters.

---

1 'who am I, sir?' (in small groups)

Ironically, Lear's question raises doubts about his own identity. He is no longer the all-powerful king that he was at the start of the play, and he is beginning to be aware of his changed status.

a Suggest three or four replies that Lear might expect in response to his question, 'who am I, sir?' (line 67)

b One student reads aloud Lear's lines 57–61. Talk together about whether you think that Lear is showing signs of softening and self-doubt.

c Why do you think Oswald's plain-spoken reply (line 68) angers Lear so much?

d Invent three or four alternative insults that Oswald could use in response to Lear instead of his deliberately disrespectful 'My lady's father.'

2 Oswald (in groups of four or five)

Oswald answers Lear (line 68) in a way that implies disrespect whilst not being openly rude. His words, however, may well make Lear aware of some uncomfortable truths. The last person to attempt this was Kent in Scene 1, and he was banished.

What seems certain is that Oswald causes such offence that he is physically humiliated and punished for it. Three people take the parts of Lear, Kent and Oswald and read out lines 67–79. The remaining group members should direct the physical movements and reactions of those reading to create suitably offensive gestures and expressions for Oswald and angry or outraged responses for Kent and Lear.

---

cur worthless dog
bandy hit to and fro, exchange
base lower-class, inferior
lubber clumsy oaf
tarry stay
earnest payment
Sirrah a contemptuous term of address to an inferior

coxcomb fool's cap
thou canst not . . . shortly if you cannot flatter, you'll be out of a job
nuncle my uncle
(a typical jester's address to his master)

LEAR No more of that, I have noted it well. Go you and tell my
daughter I would speak with her.   65

[Exit an Attendant]

Go you, call hither my fool.

[Exit an Attendant]

Enter OSWALD

Oh, you, sir, you, come you hither, sir, who am I, sir?

OSWALD My lady's father.

LEAR 'My lady's father'? My lord's knave, you whoreson dog, you
slave, you cur!   70

OSWALD I am none of these, my lord, I beseech your pardon.

LEAR Do you bandy looks with me, you rascal?

[Strikes him]

OSWALD I'll not be strucken, my lord.

KENT *[Tripping him]* Nor tripped neither, you base football player.

LEAR I thank thee, fellow. Thou serv'st me, and I'll love thee.   75

KENT Come, sir, arise, away, I'll teach you differences. Away,
away. If you will measure your lubber's length again, tarry; but
away, go to! Have you wisdom?

[Pushes Oswald out]

So.

LEAR Now, my friendly knave, I thank thee; there's earnest of thy   80
service.

[Gives Kent money]

Enter FOOL

FOOL Let me hire him, too; here's my coxcomb.

[Offers Kent his cap]

LEAR How now, my pretty knave, how dost thou?

FOOL *[To Kent]* Sirrah, you were best take my coxcomb.

LEAR Why, my boy?   85

FOOL Why? For taking one's part that's out of favour. *[To Kent]*
Nay, and thou canst not smile as the wind sits, thou'lt catch
cold shortly. There, take my coxcomb; why, this fellow has
banished two on's daughters and did the third a blessing
against his will; if thou follow him, thou must needs wear my   90
coxcomb. How now, nuncle? Would I had two coxcombs and
two daughters.

In spite of Lear's threat of a whipping, the Fool continues to be critical of him. In a series of jokes and rhymes the Fool chides Lear for disowning Cordelia and giving away his kingdom.

1 Painful truths in the Fool's jokes (in pairs)

a One person speaks lines 82–98. The other interrupts, saying 'Kent', 'Cordelia' or 'Gonerill and Regan' each time the Fool seems to refer to them.

b Decide how you would advise the actor playing Lear to react to the Fool's taunting use of the word 'nothing' in lines 114–16. Give your reasons.

c The Quarto version (see p. 240) includes an extra piece of dialogue after line 119 which is quoted below. If you were putting on a production of the play, why might you choose to include these lines?

FOOL Dost thou know the difference, my boy, between a bitter fool and a sweet one?

LEAR No, lad; teach me.

FOOL
        That lord that counselled thee
          To give away thy land,
       Come place him here by me,
          Do thou for him stand;
      The sweet and bitter fool
          Will presently appear,
      The one in motley here,
          The other found out there.

LEAR Dost thou call me fool, boy?

FOOL All thy other titles thou hast given away; that thou wast born with.

KENT This is not altogether fool, my lord.

FOOL No, faith; lords and great men will not let me. If I had a monopoly out, they would have part on't; and ladies too – they will not let me have all the fool to myself; they'll be snatching.

Lady Brach hunting hound, bitch
owest own
goest walk
Learn . . . trowest don't believe all you hear
Set . . . throwest don't gamble all you possess

unfeed unpaid
meat yolk
clovest divided
thou bor'st . . . dirt you were like the old man in the fable who foolishly carried his donkey on his back, trying to be kind

LEAR Why, my boy?

FOOL If I gave them all my living, I'd keep my coxcombs myself. There's mine; beg another of thy daughters. 95

LEAR Take heed, sirrah, the whip.

FOOL Truth's a dog must to kennel. He must be whipped out, when the Lady Brach may stand by th'fire and stink.

LEAR A pestilent gall to me.

FOOL Sirrah, I'll teach thee a speech. 100

LEAR Do.

FOOL Mark it, nuncle:

Have more than thou showest,
Speak less than thou knowest,
Lend less than thou owest, 105
Ride more than thou goest,
Learn more than thou trowest,
Set less than thou throwest,
Leave thy drink and thy whore,
And keep in-a-door, 110
And thou shalt have more,
Than two tens to a score.

KENT This is nothing, fool.

FOOL Then 'tis like the breath of an unfeed lawyer; you gave me nothing for't. Can you make no use of nothing, nuncle? 115

LEAR Why, no, boy; nothing can be made out of nothing.

FOOL [To Kent] Prithee, tell him so much the rent of his land comes to; he will not believe a fool.

LEAR A bitter fool.

FOOL Nuncle, give me an egg, and I'll give thee two crowns. 120

LEAR What two crowns shall they be?

FOOL Why, after I have cut the egg i'th'middle and eat up the meat, the two crowns of the egg. When thou clovest thy crown i'th'middle and gav'st away both parts, thou bor'st thine ass on thy back o'er the dirt. Thou hadst little wit in thy bald crown 125 when thou gav'st thy golden one away. If I speak like myself in this, let him be whipped that first finds it so.

[Sings]   Fools had ne'er less grace in a year,
For wise men are grown foppish,
And know not how their wits to wear, 130
Their manners are so apish.

LEAR When were you wont to be so full of songs, sirrah?

The Fool marvels at the contrasting treatment he receives from Lear and from Lear's daughters. Lear reproaches Gonerill for her sour expression. Gonerill criticises Lear's attendants for their loutish behaviour.

1 The Fool's-eye view (in pairs)

The Fool jokes about a topsy-turvy world where wise men become foolish and describes Lear as a child being punished by his daughters. Court Fools were often allowed great freedom to mock and criticise (Gonerill calls Lear's Fool 'all-licensed'). However, they had to judge carefully just how far to take their gibes to avoid being punished.

List the criticisms the Fool makes in lines 82–155 about Lear and his behaviour as if stating them directly rather than through the upside-down jesting with which he feels safe. Then write a brief speech for the Fool, criticising Lear by using these direct, frank comments.

2 Gonerill makes her case (in groups of four)

In lines 160–73 Gonerill, speaking in formal blank verse, mounts a powerful attack on the conduct of Lear's followers, accusing the king of encouraging their riotous behaviour ('put it on / By your allowance') and threatening, for the good of the state, to take drastic measures ('redresses') in the situation, even if this causes offence and brings shame to her father. (See also colour section, p. vii, top.)

- Take parts as Gonerill, Lear, the Fool and Kent. As Gonerill speaks lines 160–73, give her a respectful and quiet hearing.
- Gonerill reads the lines a second time, and the listeners respond more actively – perhaps giggling, busying themselves with eating or drinking or whispering words from the Fool's songs.
- On a third reading the listeners use phrases selected from the lines spoken by their characters earlier in the scene to heckle and interrupt. Gonerill should try to complete her speech despite the interruptions.

---

play bo-peep act like a child
pared sliced, shaved
O without a figure nothing
Mum, mum hush
He that keeps . . . some he who gives everything away will eventually want some of it back

shelled peascod empty pea-pod
all-licensed unchecked
carp criticise
rank unpleasant, offensive
safe redress sure remedy
put it on encourage it
censure criticism

FOOL I have used it, nuncle, e'er since thou mad'st thy daughters
thy mothers; for when thou gav'st them the rod and put'st down
thine own breeches,   135

[*Sings*]   Then they for sudden joy did weep,
              And I for sorrow sung,
              That such a king should play bo-peep,
              And go the fools among.

Prithee, nuncle, keep a schoolmaster that can teach thy fool to   140
lie. I would fain learn to lie.

LEAR And you lie, sirrah, we'll have you whipped.

FOOL I marvel what kin thou and thy daughters are: they'll have
me whipped for speaking true, thou'lt have me whipped for
lying, and sometimes I am whipped for holding my peace. I had   145
rather be any kind o'thing than a fool, and yet I would not be
thee, nuncle; thou hast pared thy wit o'both sides and left
nothing i'th'middle. Here comes one o'the parings.

Enter GONERILL

LEAR How now, daughter! What makes that frontlet on? You are
too much of late i'th'frown.   150

FOOL Thou wast a pretty fellow when thou hadst no need to care
for her frowning; now thou art an O without a figure. I am
better than thou art now; I am a fool, thou art nothing. [*To
Gonerill*] Yes, forsooth, I will hold my tongue, so your face bids
me, though you say nothing.   155

[*Sings*]   Mum, mum:
              He that keeps nor crust, nor crumb,
              Weary of all, shall want some.

That's a shelled peascod.

GONERILL Not only, sir, this, your all-licensed fool,   160
          But other of your insolent retinue
          Do hourly carp and quarrel, breaking forth
          In rank and not-to-be-endurèd riots. Sir,
          I had thought by making this well known unto you
          To have found a safe redress, but now grow fearful,   165
          By what yourself too late have spoke and done,
          That you protect this course, and put it on
          By your allowance; which if you should, the fault
          Would not 'scape censure, nor the redresses sleep;

Gonerill wishes that Lear would behave wisely. Lear questions both his own identity and Gonerill's. She criticises the debauchery of Lear's followers, and demands that he reduce their number.

---

1 'Does any here know me?' (in pairs)

Gonerill's criticism of Lear's moody and irrational behaviour (lines 179–82), the Fool's barbed comments and the king's own awareness of a general lack of respect all seem to make him unsure of his identity.

a Write advice for actors on how to perform Lear's lines at 178, 185–9 and 191, and the Fool's answer to Lear's question 'Who is it that can tell me who I am?' at line 189.

b Talk together about how much a sense of identity and self-worth depends on how we are treated by others.

2 The Fool falls silent

The Fool's 'Whoop, Jug, I love thee!' may just be nonsense, or may echo a popular song of the time. After his words at line 190 the Fool says nothing until line 270, later in this scene. Why do you think he falls silent and what could he be doing during all this time?

3 Gonerill makes demands (in groups of three or four)

In lines 192–207 Gonerill describes in detail the unacceptable behaviour of Lear's hundred knights. Directors staging the play must decide if she is deliberately exaggerating their 'disordered' behaviour and whether Lear's defence of them in lines 218–21 is, therefore, more accurate.

Read Gonerill's words (lines 192–207) in your group, changing speakers at the end of each sentence. Then each silently reread the lines and select from each line a key word. Your choice could emphasise her comments on Lear's age, her anger or her threats. Finally, read your pared-down speech to the group.

---

tender of . . . weal care for a healthy state
discreet proceeding sensible action
fraught furnished
dispositions moods
transport you change you
notion understanding

discernings / Are lethargied perceptions are dulled
admiration play-acting
deboshed debauched
epicurism gluttony
disquantity your train reduce your followers

Which in the tender of a wholesome weal   170
Might in their working do you that offence
Which else were shame, that then necessity
Will call discreet proceeding.
FOOL For you know, nuncle,
    The hedge-sparrow fed the cuckoo so long,   175
    That it's had it head bit off by it young.
So out went the candle, and we were left darkling.
LEAR Are you our daughter?
GONERILL I would you would make use of your good wisdom,
Whereof I know you are fraught, and put away   180
These dispositions, which of late transport you
From what you rightly are.
FOOL May not an ass know when the cart draws the horse? Whoop,
Jug, I love thee!
LEAR Does any here know me? This is not Lear: 185
Does Lear walk thus? speak thus? Where are his eyes?
Either his notion weakens, his discernings
Are lethargied – Ha! Waking? 'Tis not so!
Who is it that can tell me who I am?
FOOL Lear's shadow.   190
LEAR Your name, fair gentlewoman?
GONERILL This admiration, sir, is much o'th'savour
Of other your new pranks. I do beseech you
To understand my purposes aright:
As you are old and reverend, should be wise.   195
Here do you keep a hundred knights and squires,
Men so disordered, so deboshed and bold,
That this our court, infected with their manners,
Shows like a riotous inn; epicurism and lust
Makes it more like a tavern or a brothel   200
Than a graced palace. The shame itself doth speak
For instant remedy. Be then desired
By her, that else will take the thing she begs,
A little to disquantity your train,
And the remainders that shall still depend   205
To be such men as may besort your age,
Which know themselves and you.

Lear furiously declares that he will go to Regan. He attacks Gonerill's
ingratitude, and defends his followers' honour. He expresses anguish at his
treatment of Cordelia. Puzzled, Albany tries to soothe Lear.

In this Stratford production, the stage erupted at Lear's 'Darkness and devils!'
He kicked over a table, and his knights brawled with Gonerill's servants,
breaking up the furniture.

train followers	**The worships . . . name** their honour
kite scavenging bird of prey	**engine** destructive machine
parts accomplishments	**gall** bitterness, irritation
exact regard strict attention to detail	

LEAR   Darkness and devils!
    Saddle my horses; call my train together. –
    Degenerate bastard, I'll not trouble thee;
    Yet have I left a daughter.   210
GONERILL You strike my people, and your disordered rabble
    Make servants of their betters.

                    Enter ALBANY

LEAR   Woe that too late repents!
    Is it your will? Speak, sir. Prepare my horses.
    Ingratitude! Thou marble-hearted fiend,
    More hideous when thou show'st thee in a child   215
    Than the sea-monster.
ALBANY Pray, sir, be patient.
LEAR [*To Gonerill*]   Detested kite, thou liest!
    My train are men of choice and rarest parts,
    That all particulars of duty know,
    And in the most exact regard support   220
    The worships of their name. O most small fault,
    How ugly didst thou in Cordelia show!
    Which, like an engine, wrenched my frame of nature
    From the fixed place, drew from my heart all love,
    And added to the gall. O Lear, Lear, Lear!   225
    Beat at this gate that let thy folly in
    And thy dear judgement out. Go, go, my people.
ALBANY My lord, I am guiltless as I am ignorant
    Of what hath moved you.

Lear curses Gonerill with childlessness or unloving children. He leaves, but returns having discovered Gonerill's dismissal of fifty of his followers. Lear weeps and resumes cursing Gonerill, claiming that Regan will welcome him.

1 A father's curse (in pairs)

Lear has already called Gonerill 'Degenerate bastard' (line 209), and now he brings down a curse of childlessness upon her.

- One person speaks Lear's lines 230–44, while the other plays Gonerill and experiments with different ways to react to what Lear says.
- Afterwards, talk together about Lear's language. What makes it so powerful and disturbing? If you were directing the play, would you want the audience to feel any sympathy for Gonerill? Give your reasons.

2 Kent's version (in pairs)

Kent is only one of many silent or near-silent witnesses to the events of this scene. At line 244 Kent leaves with the king, but he has not spoken since Gonerill came on stage. Imagine that, immediately after he leaves, Kent speaks two lines of blank verse to Lear which he hopes will help the enraged king. Write Kent's two lines.

3 Lear weeps (in groups of three or four)

In lines 251–65 Lear is reduced to weeping. He is enraged by his own vulnerability, as well as outraged by Gonerill's attitude. Share out these lines and rehearse three group readings which emphasise in turn each of the following elements: Lear's sense of helplessness, his childishness, and his sensitivity about his manhood.

After your three readings, prepare a dramatic presentation of lines 251–65. All group members will represent Lear – divide the words between you as you choose. Add mime, gesture and movement.

---

increase reproduction
derogate degraded
teem bear children
spleen malice
thwart disnatured perverse unnatural
cadent falling

fret wear away
a clap one stroke
perforce against my will
untented woundings untreated injuries
temper soften

LEAR   It may be so, my lord.
    Hear, Nature, hear, dear goddess, hear: 230
    Suspend thy purpose, if thou didst intend
    To make this creature fruitful.
    Into her womb convey sterility,
    Dry up in her the organs of increase,
    And from her derogate body never spring   235
    A babe to honour her. If she must teem,
    Create her child of spleen, that it may live
    And be a thwart disnatured torment to her.
    Let it stamp wrinkles in her brow of youth,
    With cadent tears fret channels in her cheeks,   240
    Turn all her mother's pains and benefits
    To laughter and contempt, that she may feel
    How sharper than a serpent's tooth it is
    To have a thankless child. Away, away!
             Exeunt [Lear, Kent, Knights, and Attendants]

ALBANY Now, gods that we adore, whereof comes this?   245
GONERILL Never afflict yourself to know more of it,
    But let his disposition have that scope
    As dotage gives it.

Enter LEAR

LEAR What, fifty of my followers at a clap?
    Within a fortnight?
ALBANY   What's the matter, sir?   250
LEAR I'll tell thee. [*To Gonerill*] Life and death! I am ashamed
    That thou hast power to shake my manhood thus,
    That these hot tears, which break from me perforce,
    Should make thee worth them. Blasts and fogs upon thee!
    Th'untented woundings of a father's curse   255
    Pierce every sense about thee. Old fond eyes,
    Beweep this cause again, I'll pluck ye out
    And cast you with the waters that you loose
    To temper clay. Ha! Let it be so.
    I have another daughter,   260
    Who I am sure is kind and comfortable.
    When she shall hear this of thee, with her nails
    She'll flay thy wolvish visage. Thou shalt find
    That I'll resume the shape which thou dost think
    I have cast off forever.   *Exit*

Gonerill fears the dangers posed by Lear and his knights. She believes that such suspicion is safer than trust, and sends Oswald to warn Regan. Gonerill hints that Albany's gentle nature is a weakness in a ruler.

1 'the Fool follows after'

The Fool's words are often a mixture of sense and nonsense and it is frequently impossible to derive an exact meaning. If you can gain only a general sense of what he means in lines 271–5, don't worry. But the actor playing the Fool must somehow make the language significant to the audience. Suggest how he could 'convincingly' deliver lines 270–5 just before he leaves the stage to follow Lear.

2 Husband and wife (in pairs)

Gonerill interrupts Albany as he talks of his love for her. She speaks to him sarcastically about allowing Lear to keep a hundred knights, then challenges his judgement and strength of character.

a Take parts and speak everything Gonerill and Albany say to one another in lines 265–302. Afterwards, talk together about how you think they really feel about each other.

b How far do you agree with the student who said: 'The total difference between them, and between their outlooks, is summed up in what they both say in line 282'?

c At this point in the play how might the actors suggest to the audience what Albany would regard as a satisfactory outcome to the 'Lear problem' and what Gonerill would regard as satisfactory?

d Talk about Gonerill's possible movements and behaviour in this part of the scene. Should she ignore the Fool or react in some way? How might movement, gesture and placing on stage be used to suggest her relationship with Albany? Looking ahead to line 299, consider whether, or in what way, Gonerill should look at Albany as they talk.

---

partial biased
halter hangman's noose
politic sensible
At point armed and ready
buzz rumour
enguard protect

compact strengthen
This milky gentleness and course
these mild and gentle ways
ataxed blamed
harmful mildness gentleness that is
harmful to the state

GONERILL   Do you mark that?   265
ALBANY I cannot be so partial, Gonerill,
            To the great love I bear you –
GONERILL   Pray you, content.
            What, Oswald, ho!
            You, sir, more knave than fool, after your master.
FOOL Nuncle Lear, nuncle Lear, tarry, take the fool with thee.   270
            A fox, when one has caught her,
            And such a daughter,
            Should sure to the slaughter,
            If my cap would buy a halter;
            So the fool follows after.   *Exit*   275
GONERILL This man hath had good counsel. A hundred knights?
            'Tis politic and safe to let him keep
            At point a hundred knights? Yes, that on every dream,
            Each buzz, each fancy, each complaint, dislike,
            He may enguard his dotage with their powers   280
            And hold our lives in mercy. Oswald, I say!
ALBANY Well, you may fear too far.
GONERILL   Safer than trust too far.
            Let me still take away the harms I fear,
            Not fear still to be taken. I know his heart.
            What he hath uttered I have writ my sister: 285
            If she sustain him and his hundred knights
            When I have showed th'unfitness –

                    Enter OSWALD

                            How now, Oswald?
            What, have you writ that letter to my sister?
OSWALD Ay, madam.
GONERILL Take you some company and away to horse.   290
            Inform her full of my particular fear,
            And thereto add such reasons of your own
            As may compact it more. Get you gone,
            And hasten your return.
                                    [*Exit Oswald*]
                    No, no, my lord,
            This milky gentleness and course of yours,   295
            Though I condemn not, yet under pardon
            You are much more ataxed for want of wisdom,
            Than praised for harmful mildness.

Albany decides to wait for whatever happens. Lear sends Kent with letters to Regan. The Fool predicts that Regan's treatment of Lear will be the same as Gonerill's. Lear recalls his mistreatment of Cordelia.

1 Letters to Regan

Two messengers and two letters are on their way to Regan. Look back at Gonerill's instructions to Oswald in Act 1 Scene 4, lines 290–4, and contrast them with the ones her father issues to Kent in Act 1 Scene 5, lines 1–4.

- Sum up, using only a couple of sentences for each one, what the content of the letters might be.
- What reasons can you think of for the differences between the instructions?

2 The king and his Fool (in pairs)

The Fool directs a series of barbed jokes at Lear in Act 1 Scene 5, lines 6–38. Sometimes Lear appears to respond, but at other times he seems to be lost in his own thoughts about Cordelia or about revenge against Gonerill. In one production of the play the lines were played as though the two characters were a comedy double act. Each 'punchline' was accompanied by appropriate gestures and stamping of feet. In another production, the Fool was barely able to attract Lear's attention.

a Take parts and experiment with different styles of performing all the exchanges between Lear and the Fool in Act 1 Scene 5. Make clear by Lear's tone of voice or body language whether or not he is really listening to the Fool.

b Discuss whether or not you want to emphasise the humour or the pathos of this scene, and how you might demonstrate both.

---

mar make worse
th'event we'll see what happens
kibes chilblains
thy wit . . . slipshod your brain won't

need slippers because you don't have a brain
kindly in the same way as her sister
crab a small, sour fruit (crab apple)

ALBANY How far your eyes may pierce I cannot tell;
     Striving to better, oft we mar what's well.   300
GONERILL Nay then –
ALBANY Well, well, th'event.

Exeunt

Act 1   Scene 5
Outside the castle of Albany and Gonerill

Enter LEAR, KENT *(disguised), and* FOOL

LEAR Go you before to Gloucester with these letters. Acquaint my
daughter no further with anything you know than comes from
her demand out of the letter. If your diligence be not speedy, I
shall be there afore you.

KENT I will not sleep, my lord, till I have delivered your letter.   5

Exit

FOOL If a man's brains were in's heels, were't not in danger of
kibes?

LEAR Ay, boy.

FOOL Then, I prithee, be merry; thy wit shall not go slipshod.

LEAR Ha, ha, ha.   10

FOOL Shalt see thy other daughter will use thee kindly, for though
she's as like this as a crab's like an apple, yet I can tell what I
can tell.

LEAR What canst tell, boy?

FOOL She will taste as like this as a crab does to a crab. Thou   15
canst tell why one's nose stands i'th'middle on's face?

LEAR No.

FOOL Why, to keep one's eyes of either side 's nose, that what a
man cannot smell out, he may spy into.

LEAR I did her wrong.   20

The Fool continues his barbed jokes, but Lear's mind seems elsewhere as he thinks of seizing back the kingdom and of Gonerill's ingratitude. Lear fears insanity. As he leaves, the Fool makes a sexual joke.

1 Foolish jokes? (in pairs)

The Fool is playing the traditional role of the king's 'all-licensed fool' (see p. 226). He may be trying to cheer up the king, but he is also being very critical of Lear's behaviour, reminding him of the mistakes he has made.

- Work through lines 6–38 and remind each other of the cutting criticism in each of the Fool's jokes or riddles. (Don't spend too much time on this because the quickest way to kill a joke is to analyse it.)
- Invent and rehearse further jokes at Lear's expense which combine humour with reminders of his unwise behaviour.

2 What's in Lear's mind?

Try to identify who or what Lear is thinking of at lines 20, 27, 32 and 37–8.

3 'O let me not be mad'

Lear clearly feels he is no longer in control of events and seems very anxious. Some productions show his behaviour to be erratic and dangerous from the start, but in other productions this point in the play is where the first hint of mental breakdown may be seen.

If you were directing the play, would this moment of self-doubt be the first sign of madness, or would you choose to emphasise the king's dangerous misjudgements in Act 1 Scene 1 or his strong reactions to Gonerill's behaviour in Act 1 Scene 4?

4 Last words

Some critics claim that the Fool's final words are meant to be taken seriously. However, these lines clearly contain a sexual innuendo. Actors often emphasise the phallic joke with graphic gestures. Decide on possible reasons why Shakespeare chose to end the first Act on this sexual note.

case covering	**perforce** violently
asses fools, servants	**in temper** sane
mo more	**maid** virgin

FOOL Canst tell how an oyster makes his shell?

LEAR No.

FOOL Nor I neither; but I can tell why a snail has a house.

LEAR Why?

FOOL Why, to put 's head in, not to give it away to his daughters,   25
and leave his horns without a case.

LEAR I will forget my nature. So kind a father! Be my horses ready?

FOOL Thy asses are gone about 'em. The reason why the seven
stars are no mo than seven is a pretty reason.

LEAR Because they are not eight.   30

FOOL Yes, indeed, thou wouldst make a good fool.

LEAR To take't again perforce. Monster ingratitude!

FOOL If thou wert my fool, nuncle, I'd have thee beaten for being
old before thy time.

LEAR How's that?   35

FOOL Thou shouldst not have been old till thou hadst been wise.

LEAR O let me not be mad, not mad, sweet heaven!
Keep me in temper, I would not be mad.

[*Enter* GENTLEMAN]

How now, are the horses ready?

GENTLEMAN Ready, my lord.   40

LEAR Come, boy.

FOOL She that's a maid now, and laughs at my departure,
Shall not be a maid long, unless things be cut shorter.

Exeunt

Looking back at Act 1
Activities for groups or individuals

1 An interrupted ceremony

The play opens on a royal court awaiting the start of the ceremony to finalise the division of the kingdom. Directors have staged this in various ways, including as a tense political meeting, a series of public declarations recorded for broadcasting and a spectacular royal event of great pomp and grandeur. Yet, despite all expectation, the ceremony is never completed. The play's tragic events all stem from this interruption.

Plan how the division of the kingdom could be staged; where characters should stand, how they should behave and whether any props are to be used – in addition to the map which is mentioned in the script. Also consider how to stage the second part of the scene when the court has to deal with unexpected, unrehearsed events. See colour section, page vi (bottom) and page 16 for how two productions did this.

2 The map of the kingdom

In many productions the map mentioned in the opening scene plays a conspicuous role in the ceremony of division. You will see a design for a map in the colour section (p. v, top), and the picture opposite is of a production where the map covered the entire stage floor. Decide on an appropriate style of map to fit with your ideas for staging this episode.

3 The silent Fool speaks

The script first mentions the Fool appearing in Act 1 Scene 4, but productions often show him in attendance, uncharacteristically silent, during the opening scene. In one production this was explained by the fact that he was gagged. Look at the way he speaks in Scenes 4 and 5, and then write some Asides in a similar style for him to deliver at suitable moments in the opening scene, in which he comments on events – for example, after Gonerill and Regan have spoken, when Kent is banished, when Cordelia is disowned and when she leaves for France. Decide whether the Fool speaks in prose, blank verse, rhyme or a mixture of all three.

4 The bond

Some critics have said that Cordelia is smug and self-righteous in her refusal to participate in the love test. Cordelia loves her father according to her 'bond'. One of the meanings of 'bond' is a legal document or contract. Draw up a 'family bond' which states the duties and obligations of a modern father and teenage daughter towards each other.

5 Lear's folly

During Act 1 Kent, Gonerill and the Fool all accuse Lear of grave failures of judgement. Write three short statements in which each character lists specific misjudgements and comments on them. Try to make the style of each statement appropriate to the character concerned.

6 Different perspectives

Retell the events of Act 1 from each of the following viewpoints, as a:

- family saga dramatising problems between the generations
- political drama showing a struggle to take or hold on to power in a state
- feminist story – retold from a woman's point of view
- fairy story for very young children.

What does this moment from Scene 1 suggest about the relationship between Lear and Cordelia?

Curan informs Edmond of Cornwall and Regan's imminent arrival, and of the growing tension between Cornwall and Albany. Edmond tries to persuade the innocent Edgar to flee his father's castle.

1 Gloucester's castle: night (in pairs)

Britain is now awash with rumours and gossip about the strange and perplexing events of Act 1. Lear has divided his power and his kingdom between his daughters Regan and Gonerill, and disinherited his youngest and favourite daughter, Cordelia. Kent, one of Lear's trusted and loyal noblemen, has been banished on pain of death.

Act 2 opens with Curan, a courtier, adding to the tense atmosphere of concern and anxiety by telling of the growing rift and 'likely wars' between Cornwall and Albany. Rumours abound of the foolish behaviour of the king, of the bitter struggle for power between his beneficiaries, and of the volatile nature of domestic politics.

Take parts and read lines 1–13, exploring ways of creating a tense and unsettled atmosphere. Afterwards discuss your ideas for staging a dramatic opening to Act 2 and then write them up into a 'director's notebook'. Concentrate on action, gesture and movement. You could also sketch a possible set design.

2 Edmond sets to work (in pairs)

In lines 14–27 Edmond begins his plan to discredit Edgar. He appeals to the personified qualities of Briefness and Fortune to help him quickly seize and use the opportunity. As a result, his lines to Edgar are full of short, sharp statements, commands and questions.

Take parts and read aloud lines 19–32, changing over at each punctuation mark. Bring out the urgency of the way in which Edmond works on, and manipulates, Edgar, persuading him to run away. Afterwards talk together about the dramatic power of Edmond's speech and write a few notes of advice that you would give to an actor about how the lines might be delivered to best effect.

---

severally   separately
Save thee   God save you
pray you   please tell me
'twixt   between
perforce   by chance

queasy question   difficult nature
hither   here
Upon his party   on Cornwall's side
Advise yourself   think carefully

Act 2 Scene 1
The Great Hall of Gloucester's castle, at night

Enter EDMOND *and* CURAN, *severally*

EDMOND Save thee, Curan.

CURAN And you, sir. I have been with your father and given him
  notice that the Duke of Cornwall and Regan his duchess will
  be here with him this night.

EDMOND How comes that?   5

CURAN Nay, I know not. You have heard of the news abroad? I
  mean the whispered ones, for they are yet but ear-kissing
  arguments.

EDMOND Not I; pray you, what are they?

CURAN Have you heard of no likely wars toward 'twixt the Dukes   10
  of Cornwall and Albany?

EDMOND Not a word.

CURAN You may do then in time. Fare you well, sir.   *Exit*

EDMOND The duke be here tonight! The better, best.
      This weaves itself perforce into my business.   15
      My father hath set guard to take my brother,
      And I have one thing of a queasy question
      Which I must act. Briefness and Fortune, work!
      Brother, a word, descend; brother, I say!

Enter EDGAR

      My father watches: O sir, fly this place.   20
      Intelligence is given where you are hid;
      You have now the good advantage of the night.
      Have you not spoken 'gainst the Duke of Cornwall?
      He's coming hither, now i'th'night, i'th'haste,
      And Regan with him. Have you nothing said   25
      Upon his party 'gainst the Duke of Albany?
      Advise yourself.

EDGAR   I am sure on't, not a word.

Edmond stages a mock skirmish with Edgar, and deliberately wounds himself. Edgar flees, and Gloucester sends servants to pursue him. Edmond lies about Edgar's wicked intentions towards him and his father.

1 Shouts and whispers

Edmond hears his father coming and quickly devises a plan to stage a fight with Edgar. Edmond wants to disorient his brother, and heighten his father's fear and sense of imminent danger.

In lines 28–36 Edmond intends some words to be heard by Edgar alone, and some by the guards and Gloucester. An actor may even choose to make Edmond's 'I hear my father coming' (line 28) a statement aimed at Gloucester. Other words Edmond speaks to himself, or perhaps to the audience.

Explore different ways of speaking lines 28–36, then present your favourite version to others in your group.

2 Edmond persuades his father (in pairs)

Edmond sets out to convince his father of Edgar's guilt. He prepares by shouting for effect, by wounding himself, and by talking of things which he knows will have an impact on Gloucester. Edmond cunningly exploits Gloucester's superstitions and his hatred of the wickedness of offences committed against fathers. Earlier Edmond played on Gloucester's gullibility with the forged letter (Act 1 Scene 2, lines 27–103). Now Edmond continues to stress how 'unnatural' Edgar's intentions are, going against the natural duties and bonds of family.

Pick out the words or phrases in lines 37–55 which you think will have a strong effect on Gloucester. As one person reads the lines, the other speaks aloud what Edmond is really thinking. Afterwards identify which of Edmond's words are true and which are lies, then write a paragraph on your response to Edmond's behaviour.

---

quit you well   fight well
beget . . . endeavour   give the
  impression of my violent struggle
conjuring the moon   calling on the
  moon goddess
stand auspicious mistress   be his
  guiding goddess

parricides   father-killers
bend   aim
in fine   in conclusion
loathly opposite   bitterly opposed
in fell motion   with deadly thrust
unprovided   unarmed
latched   caught

EDMOND I hear my father coming. Pardon me,
    In cunning, I must draw my sword upon you.
    Draw, seem to defend yourself. Now, quit you well.   30
    [*Shouting*] Yield! Come before my father! – Light ho,
      here! –
    Fly, brother! – Torches, torches! – so, farewell.

                                   Exit Edgar

    Some blood drawn on me would beget opinion
    Of my more fierce endeavour.
                 [*Wounds his arm*]
                I have seen drunkards
    Do more than this in sport. Father, father!   35
    Stop, stop! No help?

     Enter GLOUCESTER, *and Servants with torches*

GLOUCESTER   Now, Edmond, where's the villain?
EDMOND Here stood he in the dark, his sharp sword out,
    Mumbling of wicked charms, conjuring the moon
    To stand auspicious mistress.
GLOUCESTER   But where is he?
EDMOND Look, sir, I bleed.
GLOUCESTER   Where is the villain, Edmond?   40
EDMOND Fled this way, sir, when by no means he could –
GLOUCESTER Pursue him, ho! Go after.
                          [*Exeunt Servants*]
                'By no means' what?
EDMOND Persuade me to the murder of your lordship,
    But that I told him the revenging gods
    'Gainst parricides did all the thunder bend,   45
    Spoke with how manifold and strong a bond
    The child was bound to'th'father; sir, in fine,
    Seeing how loathly opposite I stood
    To his unnatural purpose, in fell motion
    With his preparèd sword he charges home   50
    My unprovided body, latched mine arm;
    And when he saw my best alarumed spirits
    Bold in the quarrel's right, roused to th'encounter,
    Or whether ghasted by the noise I made,
    Full suddenly he fled.

Gloucester declares that Edgar must be caught and executed. Edmond continues to lie about Edgar. Convinced of Edgar's villainy, Gloucester plans to reward Edmond with his brother's inheritance.

---

1 Edmond forces his advantage (in pairs)

Edmond continues to persuade Gloucester of Edgar's villainy by reporting an alleged conversation with his brother. Edmond plays on contemporary prejudice against bastard children, and uses it to his own advantage.

Take turns to read aloud lines 66–76, in which Edmond imitates his brother. Try a variety of styles: mocking, sincere, deliberately exaggerated, and so on. Which do you think will work best to persuade Gloucester? Why do you think Gloucester is willing to let Edmond's words go unquestioned?

Together, look back at Act 1 Scene 1. How many similarities can you find between the behaviour of Lear then and Gloucester now? Share your findings with other pairs.

2 Two brothers (in groups of three or four)

Gloucester describes Edgar as a 'strange and fastened villain' (unnatural and confirmed villain), and Edmond as 'Loyal and natural'. Suggest other pairs of words to describe Edgar and Edmond: for example, Edgar as 'trusting and naive' and Edmond as 'plausible and confident'. As you read on, make your own list of descriptions. Amend or add to the list as you discover other aspects of their personalities.

---

dispatch be executed
arch lord
stake place of execution
pight determined
unpossessing landless
reposal placing
faithed believed

thou . . . world you must think people stupid
pregnant and potential spirits deep and powerful motives
Tucket trumpet call
fastened confirmed
capable able to inherit

GLOUCESTER   Let him fly far,   55
    Not in this land shall he remain uncaught;
    And found, dispatch. The noble duke my master,
    My worthy arch and patron, comes tonight.
    By his authority I will proclaim it,
    That he which finds him shall deserve our thanks,   60
    Bringing the murderous coward to the stake;
    He that conceals him, death.
EDMOND When I dissuaded him from his intent
    And found him pight to do it, with cursed speech
    I threatened to discover him. He replied,   65
    'Thou unpossessing bastard, dost thou think,
    If I would stand against thee, would the reposal
    Of any trust, virtue, or worth in thee
    Make thy words faithed? No; what I should deny
    (As this I would, ay, though thou didst produce   70
    My very character) I'd turn it all
    To thy suggestion, plot, and damnèd practice;
    And thou must make a dullard of the world,
    If they not thought the profits of my death
    Were very pregnant and potential spirits   75
    To make thee seek it.'
                Tucket within
GLOUCESTER   O strange and fastened villain!
    Would he deny his letter, said he?
    Hark, the duke's trumpets. I know not why he comes.
    All ports I'll bar, the villain shall not 'scape;
    The duke must grant me that. Besides, his picture   80
    I will send far and near, that all the kingdom
    May have due note of him; and of my land,
    Loyal and natural boy, I'll work the means
    To make thee capable.

Regan blames Lear's ill-disciplined knights for encouraging Edgar to murder Gloucester. Cornwall praises Edmond's efforts in thwarting Edgar's plans, and takes Edmond into his service.

---

1 Different people, different language (in pairs)

What characters say and how they say it often depend upon the status of the person they are addressing. When the Duke of Cornwall arrives, the language of Gloucester and Edmond undergoes a significant change.

Take parts as Edmond and Gloucester and speak lines 63–84, followed by Edmond's lines 96, 105 and 116–17 and Gloucester's lines 89, 92 and 95. Identify the contrasts between the way in which they speak before and after Cornwall and Regan enter. Suggest reasons why Edmond and Gloucester change their manner of speaking.

2 'I have heard strange news' (in groups of three)

Before Cornwall and Regan enter, someone has clearly told them about the sudden rift between Gloucester and Edgar. Remind yourselves of developments at the start of this scene, then improvise the conversation between this unnamed informant and Cornwall and his wife.

3 Accurate descriptions? (in groups of three or four)

Cornwall gives a glowing commendation of Edmond. In particular he praises Edmond's devoted, dutiful service of his father ('childlike office'). He also acknowledges Edmond's 'virtue and obedience' and his possession of a nature of 'deep trust'. Cornwall is unaware that his description is heavily ironic. All three of his assessments are inaccurate.

Consider each of Cornwall's judgements in turn, and rewrite it to express what Edmond is really like.

4 'You we first seize on'

Line 116 marks Edmond's first 'promotion' in the play as he is taken into Cornwall's service. Keep note of the steps of his continuing ascent to power as you read on.

How dost   how are you?
tended upon   waited upon, served
consort   company, gang
ill affected   disloyal
put him on   encouraged him to bring about

revenues   income
sojourn   stay
bewray   expose, reveal
strength   authority, power, resources

Enter CORNWALL, REGAN, *and Attendants*

CORNWALL How now, my noble friend, since I came hither,   85
    Which I can call but now, I have heard strange news.
REGAN If it be true, all vengeance comes too short
    Which can pursue th'offender. How dost, my lord?
GLOUCESTER O madam, my old heart is cracked, it's cracked.
REGAN What, did my father's godson seek your life?   90
    He whom my father named, your Edgar?
GLOUCESTER O lady, lady, shame would have it hid.
REGAN Was he not companion with the riotous knights
    That tended upon my father?
GLOUCESTER I know not, madam; 'tis too bad, too bad.   95
EDMOND Yes, madam, he was of that consort.
REGAN No marvel, then, though he were ill affected.
    'Tis they have put him on the old man's death,
    To have th'expense and waste of his revenues.
    I have this present evening from my sister   100
    Been well informed of them, and with such cautions,
    That if they come to sojourn at my house,
    I'll not be there.
CORNWALL   Nor I, assure thee, Regan.
    Edmond, I hear that you have shown your father
    A child-like office.
EDMOND   It was my duty, sir.   105
GLOUCESTER He did bewray his practice, and received
    This hurt you see, striving to apprehend him.
CORNWALL Is he pursued?
GLOUCESTER Ay, my good lord.
CORNWALL If he be taken, he shall never more   110
    Be feared of doing harm. Make your own purpose
    How in my strength you please. For you, Edmond,
    Whose virtue and obedience doth this instant
    So much commend itself, you shall be ours;
    Natures of such deep trust we shall much need;   115
    You we first seize on.
EDMOND   I shall serve you, sir,
    Truly, however else.
GLOUCESTER   For him I thank your grace.
CORNWALL You know not why we came to visit you?

Regan speaks of her hazardous night journey. She tells Gloucester that she urgently needs his advice. In Scene 2, Kent, in disguise, picks a quarrel with Oswald by insulting him.

1 Two letters, two points of view

Regan tells of receiving letters from Lear and Gonerill which express the growing rift ('differences') between father and daughter. Write Lear's and Gonerill's letters to Regan in which they offer their respective versions of events. Afterwards, as Regan, you could write replies. How might her responses to her father and sister differ?

2 Insulting Oswald (in large groups)

In lines 13–21 Kent mounts a passionate attack on Oswald. His language bristles with energetic and extravagant insults:

> 'broken meats' – leftovers from a meal
> 'worsted' – wool worn by servants
> 'lily-livered' – cowardly
> 'action-taking' – always going to law
> 'glass-gazing' – self-admiring, conceited
> 'superserviceable' – willing to serve in any way
> 'finical' – fussy
> 'bawd', 'pander' – pimp

One person plays Oswald (volunteers only!). The other group members stand in a circle around Oswald, and take turns to speak as Kent. Change the speaker at each punctuation mark. Repeat the activity with each Kent adding movement and gesture to their insult. Afterwards Oswald should talk about what it felt like to be on the receiving end of Kent's barrage. What do you think provokes this violent outburst of abusive language?

---

threading travelling with difficulty through
prize significance
from our home away from home
attend dispatch are waiting to be sent back

craves . . . use demands immediate action
I'th'mire in the bog
Lipsbury pinfold in my grip (pinfold = sheep pen)

REGAN Thus out of season, threading dark-eyed night?
　　　　Occasions, noble Gloucester, of some prize,　　　　120
　　　　Wherein we must have use of your advice.
　　　　Our father he hath writ, so hath our sister,
　　　　Of differences, which I best thought it fit
　　　　To answer from our home. The several messengers
　　　　From hence attend dispatch. Our good old friend,　　125
　　　　Lay comforts to your bosom and bestow
　　　　Your needful counsel to our businesses,
　　　　Which craves the instant use.
GLOUCESTER　　　　　　　　　　　　I serve you, madam;
　　　　Your graces are right welcome.　　　　*Exeunt. Flourish*

Act 2 Scene 2
The entrance to Gloucester's castle

Enter KENT *(disguised) and* OSWALD, *severally*

OSWALD Good dawning to thee, friend. Art of this house?
KENT Ay.
OSWALD Where may we set our horses?
KENT I'th'mire.
OSWALD Prithee, if thou lov'st me, tell me.　　　　5
KENT I love thee not.
OSWALD Why, then I care not for thee.
KENT If I had thee in Lipsbury pinfold, I would make thee care for
　　me.
OSWALD Why dost thou use me thus? I know thee not.　　　　10
KENT Fellow, I know thee.
OSWALD What dost thou know me for?
KENT A knave, a rascal, an eater of broken meats, a base, proud,
　　shallow, beggarly, three-suited, hundred-pound, filthy worsted-
　　stocking knave; a lily-livered, action-taking, whoreson glass-　　15
　　gazing, superserviceable, finical rogue; one-trunk-inheriting
　　slave; one that wouldst be a bawd in way of good service, and
　　art nothing but the composition of a knave, beggar, coward,
　　pander, and the son and heir of a mongrel bitch, one whom
　　I will beat into clamorous whining if thou deniest the least　　20
　　syllable of thy addition.

Kent insults Oswald again, and draws his sword. Oswald calls for help. Kent threatens Edmond, and Cornwall demands an explanation. Kent further insults Oswald, who seizes the chance to get his own back.

1 Kent versus Oswald (in pairs)

The exchanges between Kent and Oswald are often presented on stage in such a way that their comic aspects are highlighted. But stage-fighting needs a great deal of planning to make it appear spontaneous in performance.

Work out what advice you would give about lines 22–37 to the actors playing Oswald and Kent. In particular, think about:

- how Oswald responds to Kent drawing his sword (line 28)
- how Oswald responds to Kent's threats (lines 30, 35 and 37) whether or not Oswald feels in real danger
- when Oswald recognises Kent as the man who previously assaulted him
- why Kent is so keen to fight
- the effect on the combatants of the entrance of Cornwall.

2 'Help, ho, murder, murder!' (in small groups)

- First, two of you take parts as Oswald and Kent and work out a freeze-frame to capture Oswald's line 37.
- Then the rest stage the entrance of the other characters, freezing the action again to show the various reactions of each character to the argument that they witness. Each person should concentrate on displaying their particular character's facial expression and attitude towards what they see.

---

rail on insult
brazen-faced varlet determined rogue
make . . . moonshine of you puncture you full of holes to let in the moonlight
cullionly despicable, servile
barber-monger vain person
(spending time at the barber's)
carbonado your shanks slash your legs
goodman boy arrogant young man
disclaims renounces having any part
at suit in pity

OSWALD Why, what a monstrous fellow art thou, thus to rail on one that is neither known of thee nor knows thee!

KENT What a brazen-faced varlet art thou to deny thou knowest me! Is it two days since I tripped up thy heels and beat thee 25
before the king? Draw, you rogue! For though it be night, yet the moon shines. I'll make a sop o'th'moonshine of you, [*Drawing his sword*] you whoreson cullionly barber-monger, draw!

OSWALD Away, I have nothing to do with thee. 30

KENT Draw, you rascal. You come with letters against the king, and take Vanity the puppet's part against the royalty of her father. Draw, you rogue, or I'll so carbonado your shanks – draw, you rascal, come your ways!

OSWALD Help, ho, murder, help! 35

KENT Strike, you slave! Stand, rogue! Stand, you neat slave, strike!

OSWALD Help, ho, murder, murder!

Enter EDMOND, CORNWALL, REGAN, GLOUCESTER, *Servants*

EDMOND How now, what's the matter? Part!

KENT With you, goodman boy, if you please; come, I'll flesh ye; come on, young master. 40

GLOUCESTER Weapons? Arms? What's the matter here?

CORNWALL Keep peace, upon your lives; he dies that strikes again. What is the matter?

REGAN The messengers from our sister and the king?

CORNWALL What is your difference – speak! 45

OSWALD I am scarce in breath, my lord.

KENT No marvel, you have so bestirred your valour, you cowardly rascal. Nature disclaims in thee: a tailor made thee.

CORNWALL Thou art a strange fellow – a tailor make a man?

KENT A tailor, sir, a stone-cutter, or a painter could not have made 50
him so ill, though they had been but two years o'th'trade.

CORNWALL Speak yet, how grew your quarrel?

OSWALD This ancient ruffian, sir, whose life I have spared at suit of his grey beard –

Kent is enraged by Oswald's lie, and attacks the sycophantic, dishonest nature of great men's servants. Kent says that he dislikes Oswald's face, then insults Cornwall, Regan and the others.

1 No time for flatterers (in pairs)

Kent's tirade against Oswald is determined and direct. He threatens to crush Oswald into mortar ('unbolted' means refined or effeminate), and to daub him on the walls of a toilet ('jakes'). Kent attacks the dishonesty of 'smiling rogues', saying that they are villains who undermine marriages and family bonds ('holy cords'). Oswald is a flatterer who follows the moods of his master, inflaming his passions ('Being oil to fire') or feeding his melancholy ('colder moods') with further depression. A flatterer is like a kingfisher ('halcyon') whose beak follows the direction of the wind. Kent ends with an assault on Oswald's inane smiling ('epileptic visage') and threatens to drive him back to Camelot like a cackling goose.

In line 78 Kent explains that no one could be more unlike Oswald than he is ('No contraries hold more antipathy'). Using this idea of different personalities, talk together about why you think Kent detests Oswald so vehemently.

2 Plain-speaking

Kent says that he despises Oswald for his looks ('His countenance likes me not'). In lines 82–5 Kent extends this criticism and plain-speaking to include everyone present. On stage the moment can be both electric and amusing as the 'noble' characters take in the meaning of Kent's blunt insult. Consider in turn Kent, Cornwall, Regan, Edmond and Gloucester. Suggest how each would react as Kent speaks lines 82–5.

3 Appearance versus reality

A key theme of this play, as in all Shakespeare's plays, is that things are not what they seem. Here Kent is disguised as a servant although he's still a character of noble birth. No one recognises him (impenetrable disguises were a common stage convention). Collect other examples of things not being what they seem. Add to your list as you read on.

---

intrince tightly bound
smooth flatter
Renege deny
vary mood-shift

Sarum Salisbury
Camelot legendary city of King Arthur, and possibly home of cackling geese

KENT Thou whoreson zed, thou unnecessary letter! My lord, if you   55
will give me leave, I will tread this unbolted villain into mortar
and daub the wall of a jakes with him. Spare my grey beard,
you wagtail?

CORNWALL Peace, sirrah.
          You beastly knave, know you no reverence?   60

KENT Yes, sir, but anger hath a privilege.

CORNWALL Why art thou angry?

KENT That such a slave as this should wear a sword,
       Who wears no honesty. Such smiling rogues as these,
       Like rats, oft bite the holy cords a-twain,   65
       Which are too intrince t'unloose; smooth every passion
       That in the natures of their lords rebel,
       Being oil to fire, snow to the colder moods,
       Renege, affirm, and turn their halcyon beaks
       With every gall and vary of their masters,   70
       Knowing naught, like dogs, but following.
       A plague upon your epileptic visage!
       Smile you my speeches, as I were a fool?
       Goose, if I had you upon Sarum Plain,
       I'd drive ye cackling home to Camelot.   75

CORNWALL What, art thou mad, old fellow?

GLOUCESTER How fell you out? Say that.

KENT No contraries hold more antipathy
       Than I and such a knave.

CORNWALL   Why dost thou call him knave?
       What is his fault?

KENT   His countenance likes me not.   80

CORNWALL No more perchance does mine, nor his, nor hers.

KENT Sir, 'tis my occupation to be plain.
       I have seen better faces in my time
       Than stands on any shoulder that I see
       Before me at this instant.

Cornwall criticises Kent's blunt speaking. Kent uses exaggerated, courteous language, then claims truth in bluntness. Oswald lists Kent's actions against him. Cornwall decides to punish Kent in the stocks.

1 Blunt language, false language

Cornwall says that Kent pretends to be rough and rude well in excess of his true character ('Quite from his nature'). Cornwall mocks such plain-speaking and suspects that Kent's bluntness is a mask, concealing more evil intentions than any number of flattering, anxious-to-please attendants ('silly-ducking observants').

In lines 95–8 Kent deliberately mocks the insincere, deceitful language of false flatterers. He uses pompous terms that parody polite speech. In lines 99–102 Kent reverts to his customary plain blunt manner of speaking and uses prose instead of verse. Speak both sets of Kent's lines to make the contrast between them as pronounced as you can, and then suggest possible reasons for the switch from poetry to prose.

2 Point it out! (in groups of three)

Take parts as Oswald, Kent and Lear. As Oswald reads aloud lines 104–13 everyone points at whoever is mentioned; for example, 'I [point to Oswald] never gave him [point to Kent] any', and so on.

3 Ajax – the final insult?

Kent's reference to Ajax may be the last straw in triggering Cornwall's anger. Ajax was a foolish Greek warrior renowned for his gullibility. The reference is also a pun on a 'jakes', meaning toilet.

Try speaking Cornwall's lines 114–17 in different ways to express his displeasure towards Kent, then trace the steps that have led to Cornwall's decision to put him in the stocks. Does Kent deserve this treatment?

---

constrains . . . nature uses apparent bluntness for crafty purposes
stretch . . . nicely bow and scrape too much in all they do
Phoebus' front the sun's forehead
dialect manner of speaking
very late most recently

misconstruction misunderstanding
compact in league with the king
deal of man macho attitude
For . . . subdued for attacking a man who did not fight back
fleshment excitement

CORNWALL   This is some fellow   85
    Who, having been praised for bluntness, doth affect
    A saucy roughness, and constrains the garb
    Quite from his nature. He cannot flatter, he;
    An honest mind and plain, he must speak truth.
    And they will take it, so; if not, he's plain.   90
    These kind of knaves I know, which in this plainness
    Harbour more craft and more corrupter ends
    Than twenty silly-ducking observants
    That stretch their duties nicely.
KENT Sir, in good faith, in sincere verity,   95
    Under th'allowance of your great aspect,
    Whose influence like the wreath of radiant fire
    On flick'ring Phoebus' front –
CORNWALL   What mean'st by this?
KENT To go out of my dialect, which you discommend so much. I
    know, sir, I am no flatterer. He that beguiled you in a plain   100
    accent was a plain knave, which for my part I will not be,
    though I should win your displeasure to entreat me to't.
CORNWALL What was th'offence you gave him?
OSWALD I never gave him any.
    It pleased the king his master very late   105
    To strike at me upon his misconstruction,
    When he, compact, and flattering his displeasure,
    Tripped me behind; being down, insulted, railed,
    And put upon him such a deal of man
    That worthied him, got praises of the king   110
    For him attempting who was self-subdued,
    And in the fleshment of this dread exploit
    Drew on me here again.
KENT   None of these rogues and cowards
    But Ajax is their fool.
CORNWALL   Fetch forth the stocks!
    You stubborn, ancient knave, you reverend braggart,   115
    We'll teach you.

Kent protests against Cornwall's order to put him in the stocks, but Cornwall is unmoved, despite Gloucester's pleading. Gloucester commiserates with Kent, who accepts his punishment philosophically.

Kent in the stocks. In some productions Oswald seizes the opportunity to get his own back on Kent. For example, in one, Oswald removed Kent's boots, and in another he returned and urinated over Kent. Would Oswald attempt to get his own back on Kent in your production?

1 Kent in the stocks: different perspectives (in groups of five)

Take parts (Regan, Cornwall, Kent, Gloucester and the silent Oswald). Memorise your words between lines 121 and 142 and present to the class your version of how you think this episode should be staged.

respects courtesy		**rubbed** hindered, challenged
selfsame colour same complexion		**entreat** plead
beseech beg		

KENT   Sir, I am too old to learn:
Call not your stocks for me. I serve the king,
On whose employment I was sent to you.
You shall do small respects, show too bold malice
Against the grace and person of my master,   120
Stocking his messenger.
CORNWALL   Fetch forth the stocks!
As I have life and honour, there shall he sit till noon.
REGAN Till noon? Till night, my lord, and all night too.
KENT Why, madam, if I were your father's dog,
You should not use me so.
REGAN   Sir, being his knave, I will.   125
                    Stocks brought out
CORNWALL This is a fellow of the selfsame colour
Our sister speaks of. Come, bring away the stocks.
GLOUCESTER Let me beseech your grace not to do so.
The king his master needs must take it ill
That he, so slightly valued in his messenger,   130
Should have him thus restrained.
CORNWALL   I'll answer that.
REGAN My sister may receive it much more worse
To have her gentleman abused, assaulted.
              [Kent is put in the stocks]
CORNWALL Come, my lord, away.
            [Exeunt all but Gloucester and Kent]
GLOUCESTER I am sorry for thee, friend; 'tis the duke's pleasure,   135
Whose disposition all the world well knows
Will not be rubbed nor stopped. I'll entreat for thee.
KENT Pray do not, sir. I have watched and travelled hard.
Some time I shall sleep out, the rest I'll whistle.
A good man's fortune may grow out at heels.   140
Give you good morrow.
GLOUCESTER The duke's to blame in this; 'twill be ill taken.   *Exit*

In the stocks Kent reads a letter from Cordelia in which she promises to right all wrongs. Wearied, he sleeps. In Scene 3 Edgar plans to disguise himself as a mad beggar in an attempt to escape capture.

1 Cordelia's letter

Kent reads a letter he has received from Cordelia. She has been informed of Kent's disguise and of his activities ('obscurèd course'), and she intends to restore order to the country ('give / Losses their remedies'). Write Cordelia's letter.

2 Is Kent like Edgar?

In many productions Kent remains on stage, sleeping silently as Edgar disguises himself to escape capture by his pursuers. Directors often choose to highlight the similarity between the two men here. After all, Shakespeare deliberately follows a soliloquy from the imprisoned Kent with one from the fugitive Edgar. Make a list of all the similarities between Kent and Edgar that you can identify.

3 Edgar as Tom o'Bedlam

In Shakespeare's time mentally ill people were sent to the hospital of Bethlehem ('Bedlam') in London. When they were discharged, they lived by begging on the streets and wandering the countryside, often sticking sharp objects into their flesh in order to attract attention and charity. Such beggars were given the name 'Tom o'Bedlam'.

Edgar plans to reduce himself to an almost animal-like existence, wearing only a loin-cloth and tangling ('elf'-ing) all his hair. In some productions he removes his clothes and grimes himself with filth as he talks (see p. 97). How would you stage lines 1–21 to show the way in which Edgar plans to adopt a new personality? Try speaking the lines to show Edgar transforming himself from one identity to another. Edgar's 'Poor Turlygod!' (line 20) is his attempt at using the nonsensical language of a mad beggar.

---

saw proverb
Thou ... sun you go from bad to good
thou beacon sun
Nothing ... misery only the most miserable witness miracles
enormous state wicked situation

o'er-watched exhausted
proclaimed publicly declared an outlaw
penury ... man poverty, treating humanity with contempt
mortifièd dead to pain

KENT Good king, that must approve the common saw,
      Thou out of heaven's benediction com'st
      To the warm sun.   145
      Approach, thou beacon to this under globe,
      That by thy comfortable beams I may
      Peruse this letter. Nothing almost sees miracles
      But misery. I know 'tis from Cordelia,
      Who hath most fortunately been informed   150
      Of my obscurèd course, and shall find time
      For this enormous state, seeking to give
      Losses their remedies. All weary and o'er-watched,
      Take vantage, heavy eyes, not to behold
      This shameful lodging. Fortune, goodnight,   155
      Smile once more, turn thy wheel. [*He sleeps*]

Act 2 Scene 3
Open countryside near Gloucester's castle

Enter EDGAR

EDGAR I heard myself proclaimed,
       And by the happy hollow of a tree
       Escaped the hunt. No port is free, no place
       That guard and most unusual vigilance
       Does not attend my taking. Whiles I may 'scape   5
       I will preserve myself, and am bethought
       To take the basest and most poorest shape
       That ever penury in contempt of man
       Brought near to beast. My face I'll grime with filth,
       Blanket my loins, elf all my hairs in knots,   10
       And with presented nakedness outface
       The winds and persecutions of the sky.
       The country gives me proof and precedent
       Of Bedlam beggars, who with roaring voices
       Strike in their numbed and mortifièd arms,   15
       Pins, wooden pricks, nails, sprigs of rosemary;

Lear wonders why Cornwall and Regan were not at home to receive him. Seeing Kent in the stocks, the Fool mocks him, but Lear refuses to believe that Cornwall and Regan were responsible for such punishment.

1 'Edgar I nothing am' (in pairs)

In line 21 of Scene 3, notice that Shakespeare again inserts the word 'nothing'. Just as Cordelia was told 'Nothing will come of nothing', Edgar will come to nothing unless he adopts a new personality. However mean and lowly his disguise as Poor Tom (see colour section, p. vii, top), at least it gives Edgar the chance to survive. The word 'nothing' has been spoken at least ten times so far. Find all those references and talk together about any possible connections or contrasts.

2 How do the Fool and Lear respond?

The Fool jokes cuttingly about Kent's imprisonment, using a pun: 'nether-stocks' are stockings, but the expression also suggests the stocks which shackle Kent. Lear, however, does not seem amused. At the opening of the scene he appears distracted by thoughts of Regan's absence from home – and then he notices Kent. Invent gestures and other stage business which the Fool and Lear could use to accompany lines 5–12 to show how you interpret their differing responses.

3 Outdoing Lear (in pairs)

Take parts and speak lines 11–19. Each person tries to outdo the other, using gesture as appropriate. Lear's words of course can be reinforced by movement, but Kent must remain fixed in the stocks.

Change parts and read again, first quickly, so that the exchange is rapid and quick-fire, then slowly and deliberately. Which version do you prefer? Why?

What similarities are there between Kent's language style here and in Act 2 Scene 2?

---

pelting   paltry
lunatic bans   mad curses
Enforce their charity   beg for money
Mak'st . . . pastime?   is this your idea of a joke?
overlusty at legs   keen to run away, oversexed

thy place mistook   mistaken your status (as my messenger)
Juno   wife of Jupiter, the chief Roman god

And with this horrible object, from low farms,
Poor pelting villages, sheep-cotes, and mills,
Sometimes with lunatic bans, sometime with prayers,
Enforce their charity. 'Poor Turlygod! Poor Tom!'   20
That's something yet: Edgar I nothing am.   *Exit*

Act 2 Scene 4
The entrance to Gloucester's castle

Enter LEAR, FOOL, and GENTLEMAN

LEAR 'Tis strange that they should so depart from home
        And not send back my messenger.
GENTLEMAN   As I learned,
        The night before there was no purpose in them
        Of this remove.
KENT *[Waking]*   Hail to thee, noble master.
LEAR Ha!   5
        Mak'st thou this shame thy pastime?
KENT   No, my lord.
FOOL Ha, ha, he wears cruel garters. Horses are tied by the heads,
        dogs and bears by th'neck, monkeys by th'loins, and men by
        th'legs: when a man's overlusty at legs, then he wears wooden
        nether-stocks.   10
LEAR What's he that hath so much thy place mistook
        To set thee here?
KENT   It is both he and she,
        Your son and daughter.
LEAR No.
KENT Yes.   15
LEAR No, I say.
KENT I say, yea.
LEAR By Jupiter, I swear no.
KENT By Juno, I swear ay.

Lear, angered by Kent's punishment, asks him to explain. Kent describes his cold reception and his recent clash with Oswald. The Fool speaks ominously of fortune favouring the wealthy.

1 Kent tells his story (in small groups)

Lear seems unwilling or unable to accept what Kent has told him. For Regan and Cornwall to put Kent in the stocks is 'worse than murder' as it is blatantly disrespectful to Lear. Choose one of the following activities based on Kent's story. In each, one person reads lines 24–42.

a The others, as Kent, Regan, Cornwall and Oswald, enact Kent's story.

b Another person, as the Fool, mimes all the events which Kent describes. Remember, the Fool may choose to exaggerate or mock whatever he hears.

c Lear makes no verbal response to Kent, but you can imagine what he is thinking as he listens to Kent's story. Later he complains of mounting hysteria, a choking feeling (lines 52–3). Write a 'stream of consciousness' narrative that reflects Lear's growing agitation, hurt and anger at what he hears.

2 True or false? (in small groups)

The Fool continues his role as a chorus, commenting on, interpreting and evaluating what he sees. He expresses his thoughts in puzzling and teasing language, but with obvious reference to Lear's treatment by his daughters. He seems to suggest that fortune never favours ('Ne'er turns the key to') the poor, and that poor fathers ('Fathers that wear rags') will have unkind ('blind') children.

Capture one of the three statements in lines 44–9 as a 'still image' and talk together about how far you agree with the Fool's remarks. What evidence is there in the play so far to support his observations?

Resolve me   explain to me
commend   deliver
reeking post   sweating messenger
spite of intermission   in spite of
 interrupting me
meiny   followers
Displayed   behaved

more man than wit   more courage
 than sense
Winter's . . . way   we're in for more
 bad weather (trouble ahead!)
bear bags   are rich
dolours   griefs, silver coins (dollars)
tell   count

LEAR   They durst not do't:
They could not, would not do't. 'Tis worse than murder,   20
To do upon respect such violent outrage.
Resolve me with all modest haste which way
Thou mightst deserve or they impose this usage,
Coming from us.
KENT   My lord, when at their home
I did commend your highness' letters to them,   25
Ere I was risen from the place that showed
My duty kneeling, came there a reeking post,
Stewed in his haste, half breathless, panting forth
From Gonerill, his mistress, salutations;
Delivered letters spite of intermission,   30
Which presently they read. On those contents
They summoned up their meiny, straight took horse,
Commanded me to follow and attend
The leisure of their answer, gave me cold looks;
And meeting here the other messenger,   35
Whose welcome I perceived had poisoned mine –
Being the very fellow which of late
Displayed so saucily against your highness –
Having more man than wit about me, drew.
He raised the house with loud and coward cries.   40
Your son and daughter found this trespass worth
The shame which here it suffers.
FOOL Winter's not gone yet, if the wild geese fly that way.
       Fathers that wear rags
          Do make their children blind,   45
       But fathers that bear bags
          Shall see their children kind.
       Fortune, that arrant whore,
       Ne'er turns the key to th'poor.
But for all this, thou shalt have as many dolours for thy   50
daughters as thou canst tell in a year.

Lear feels hysteria rising. He goes to find Regan. Kent asks why Lear has come with so few followers. The Fool speaks of the way in which men desert unsuccessful leaders, but claims he will remain faithful.

1 'Mother' – a 'climbing sorrow'

Hysteria was believed to be primarily a female disease originating in the uterus (hence Lear's reference to 'this mother' in line 52) and then rising through the body, affecting one part after another. (Lear calls it 'climbing sorrow' in line 53.) As you read on through Act 2, think about the way in which Lear's rising anger and potential madness might be conveyed.

2 Fair-weather friends

In lines 62–70 the Fool tells Kent of the folly of following a leader in decline. Kent could learn the folly of pointless labour from the proverbial ant, which will not try to seek food in the winter when there is none about. Even a blind man can smell the ill-fortune ('him that's stinking') which accompanies a great man's fall from prosperity. Follow the 'great wheel' as it moves upwards, but get off as it spins downhill. That is the time when a hanger-on ('which serves and seeks for gain') will desert his master.

a The Fool's image is derived from the traditional wheel of fortune. Look out for further uses of the wheel of fortune image as you read through the play. Why do you think it becomes so important?

b If you were playing the Fool, how would you present lines 71–8? Experiment with different versions, maybe even a musical one.

c For all his scepticism about human loyalty, the Fool makes it clear that he will not desert Lear. What does his, and Kent's, devotion say about Lear?

3 Lear's fixations

Lear has received uncomfortable news off stage: his daughter will not speak with him. As his anger intensifies, he resorts to repetitions and imperatives (command sentences). Identify them in his lines 81–4 and explain why you think they are dramatically powerful.

---

mother hysteria (see Activity 1 above)	**perdy** by God
Hysterica passio! hysteria	**fetches** tricks
element's place is	**revolt and flying off** rebellion and
sir (line 71) man, servant	desertion
form show	

LEAR O how this mother swells up toward my heart!
          Hysterica passio! Down, thou climbing sorrow,
          Thy element's below. Where is this daughter?
KENT With the earl, sir, here within.
LEAR   Follow me not, stay here.   55
                                          Exit

GENTLEMAN Made you no more offence but what you speak of?
KENT None.
      How chance the king comes with so small a number?
FOOL And thou hadst been set i'th'stocks for that question,
    thou'dst well deserved it.   60
KENT Why, fool?
FOOL We'll set thee to school to an ant, to teach thee there's no
    labouring i'th'winter. All that follow their noses are led by their
    eyes but blind men, and there's not a nose among twenty but
    can smell him that's stinking. Let go thy hold when a great   65
    wheel runs down a hill, lest it break thy neck with following.
    But the great one that goes upward, let him draw thee after.
    When a wise man gives thee better counsel, give me mine
    again; I would have none but knaves follow it, since a fool gives
    it.   70
            That sir which serves and seeks for gain
                And follows but for form,
            Will pack when it begins to rain
                And leave thee in the storm.
            But I will tarry, the fool will stay,   75
                And let the wise man fly;
            The knave turns fool that runs away,
                The fool no knave, perdy.
KENT Where learned you this, fool?
FOOL Not i'th'stocks, fool.   80

        Enter LEAR *and* GLOUCESTER

LEAR Deny to speak with me? They are sick, they are weary,
          They have travelled all the night? Mere fetches,
          The images of revolt and flying off.
          Fetch me a better answer.

Gloucester tries to excuse Cornwall's refusal to speak to Lear. At first Lear is angry, then hesitant, but finally he demands that Regan and Cornwall appear. He fears the onset of madness.

1 Lear's angry words (in pairs)

To experience Lear's changing moods, try one or more of the following activities on what he says in lines 88–114:

a Read aloud Lear's lines as you walk around the room. Change direction at every punctuation mark.

b One person reads all Lear's lines aloud. After each punctuation mark, the other says 'calmer' or 'angrier' to indicate Lear's changing emotions.

c Decide what movements or gestures Lear could use to accompany his words.

d Rate Lear's moods on a scale of 1–10 (1 for calm, 10 for violently angry). Draw a graph to show the ups and downs of his temper.

2 Gloucester the peacekeeper (in pairs)

Lear's explosive volatility is clearly going to lead to confrontation. Gloucester is naturally keen to preserve harmony in his home. One of you reads Lear's lines 88–114; the other intercuts them with a selection of Gloucester's words from the opposite page. Then talk together about the differences in the two men's language styles.

3 Cockney fools

The Fool gives two examples of acts of foolish kindness. The cockney (a Londoner) cook could not bear to kill eels before cooking them in a pie, so she 'put 'em i'th'paste alive'. She had to hit them on the head ('knapped 'em o'th'coxcombs') when they tried to escape. Her brother put butter on his horse's hay as a treat, without realising that horses dislike grease and fat. Think about why the Fool tells these two stories. Is he trying to cheer Lear up, or to remind him of his folly, or to paint a picture of a world going mad? Or . . .?

Infirmity . . . bound illness makes us neglect our duties
forbear cease my command
fallen . . . will no longer in sympathy with my headstrong impulse
sickly fit ill person
remotion aloofness, refusal
practice trickery
presently instantly
paste pastry

GLOUCESTER   My dear lord,
        You know the fiery quality of the duke,   85
        How unremovable and fixed he is
        In his own course.
LEAR Vengeance, plague, death, confusion!
        'Fiery'? What 'quality'? Why Gloucester, Gloucester,
        I'd speak with the Duke of Cornwall and his wife.   90
GLOUCESTER Well, my good lord, I have informed them so.
LEAR 'Informed them'? Dost thou understand me, man?
GLOUCESTER Ay, my good lord.
LEAR The king would speak with Cornwall, the dear father
        Would with his daughter speak! Commands – tends –
            service!   95
        Are they 'informed' of this? My breath and blood!
        'Fiery'? The 'fiery duke'? Tell the hot duke that –
        No, but not yet; maybe he is not well:
        Infirmity doth still neglect all office
        Whereto our health is bound. We are not ourselves   100
        When nature, being oppressed, commands the mind
        To suffer with the body. I'll forbear,
        And am fallen out with my more headier will,
        To take the indisposed and sickly fit
        For the sound man. – Death on my state! Wherefore   105
        Should he sit here? This act persuades me
        That this remotion of the duke and her
        Is practice only. Give me my servant forth.
        Go tell the duke and's wife I'd speak with them,
        Now, presently: bid them come forth and hear me,   110
        Or at their chamber door I'll beat the drum
        Till it cry sleep to death.
GLOUCESTER I would have all well betwixt you.   *Exit*
LEAR Oh me, my heart! My rising heart! But down.
FOOL Cry to it, nuncle, as the cockney did to the eels when she put   115
        'em i'th'paste alive; she knapped 'em o'th'coxcombs with a stick
        and cried, 'Down, wantons, down!' 'Twas her brother that in
        pure kindness to his horse buttered his hay.

Kent is freed from the stocks. Lear criticises Gonerill's treatment of him. Regan defends her sister, and says that Lear needs guidance in old age. Lear mocks the suggestion that he should apologise to Gonerill.

---

1 A frosty greeting? (in groups of four)

Even very short, simple sentences and clipped, precise language contain a wealth of possibilities for actors to interpret and perform. Using lines 119–20 only, stage the entrance of Cornwall and Regan, and the greetings they exchange with Lear. How does Lear say his five words, Cornwall his four and Regan her seven? Would you dress Cornwall and Regan in their night attire or have them in ceremonial costume? How would this affect the impressions you create?

2 Why is Kent being overlooked?

At the start of this scene Kent's imprisonment in the stocks was of great concern to Lear. Now Kent's release from them draws barely a response from the king. Account for this change in Lear's attitude.

3 Naming Regan

In lines 121–9 Lear uses Regan's name four times. You will find that he continues to use it many times later in the scene. Do you agree with those critics who say that he has recovered a sense of affection for her, or do you think that there are other explanations?

4 'Unsightly tricks'

Regan reminds her father that his natural course of life is near its limit (lines 138–40). She says that he should ask Gonerill's forgiveness. Lear responds sarcastically in lines 144–8.

a Try different ways of performing Lear's lines to discover how his kneeling and language make Regan see his behaviour as the awkward and embarrassing 'unsightly tricks' of an elderly relative.

b Make a note of this episode and look out for a moving repetition of the same 'kneeling' motif later in Act 4.

Sepulch'ring entombing, containing buried within
naught wicked
You less ... duty she appreciates her duty more than you appreciate her worth

confine limit
house family
vouchsafe give
raiment clothes

Enter CORNWALL, REGAN, GLOUCESTER, [*and*] *Servants*

LEAR Good morrow to you both.

CORNWALL   Hail to your grace.

               Kent here set at liberty

REGAN I am glad to see your highness.   120

LEAR Regan, I think you are. I know what reason
        I have to think so. If thou shouldst not be glad,
        I would divorce me from thy mother's tomb,
        Sepulch'ring an adultress. [*To Kent*] O are you free?
        Some other time for that. Belovèd Regan,   125
        Thy sister's naught. Oh Regan, she hath tied
        Sharp-toothed unkindness, like a vulture here –
        I can scarce speak to thee – thou'lt not believe
        With how depraved a quality – oh Regan!

REGAN I pray you, sir, take patience. I have hope   130
        You less know how to value her desert
        Than she to scant her duty.

LEAR   Say? How is that?

REGAN I cannot think my sister in the least
        Would fail her obligation. If, sir, perchance
        She have restrained the riots of your followers,   135
        'Tis on such ground and to such wholesome end
        As clears her from all blame.

LEAR   My curses on her.

REGAN O sir, you are old,
        Nature in you stands on the very verge
        Of his confine. You should be ruled and led   140
        By some discretion that discerns your state
        Better than you yourself. Therefore I pray you
        That to our sister you do make return;
        Say you have wronged her.

LEAR   Ask her forgiveness?
        Do you but mark how this becomes the house?   145
        [*Kneels*] 'Dear daughter, I confess that I am old;
        Age is unnecessary: on my knees I beg
        That you'll vouchsafe me raiment, bed, and food.'

REGAN Good sir, no more: these are unsightly tricks.
        Return you to my sister.

Lear refuses to stay with Gonerill, cursing her ingratitude and ill-treatment of him. Lear says that Regan is a better, more natural daughter than Gonerill. A trumpet heralds Gonerill's arrival.

1 Lear curses Gonerill (individually or in pairs)

Lear rehearses his grievances against Gonerill. She has reduced his followers by half, scowled at him ('Looked black upon me'), and lashed him verbally, striking at his heart and his love.

Identify all the curses which Lear directs at Gonerill in lines 154–60, and speak them as powerfully and dramatically as you can. Concentrate on his use of imperatives (commands) and shocking images of disease. How far do you think Gonerill deserves this vitriolic attack?

2 The arithmetic of love (in pairs)

Lear's language shows how selfishly he quantifies and calculates his love. In Act 1 he demanded of his daughters, 'Which of you shall we say doth love us most?', pitting the daughters against each other in a competitive test of their love. Now his hatred of Gonerill is born of his belief that she has not appropriately acknowledged her debt of love to her father, halving his followers. Even his softer language to Regan, whom he says he will never curse, expresses the arithmetic of love ('grudge', 'cut', 'scant', 'offices', 'bond', 'effects', 'dues', 'half').

Read lines 166–74 (from ''Tis not in thee') to each other, highlighting any words or phrases that express Lear's calculating view of love.

3 Regan's reply: appearance versus reality

Regan responds briefly to Lear's flattering words with: 'Good sir, to th'purpose.' Experiment with different ways of speaking Regan's five words to show her superficial politeness masking a cold and steely determination.

---

abated deprived
top head
young bones unborn child
You taking airs you evil vapours
scant my sizes cut my allowances

oppose the bolt lock the door
offices duties
Effects necessary requirements
approves confirms

LEAR [*Rising*]   Never, Regan.   150
    She hath abated me of half my train,
    Looked black upon me, struck me with her tongue
    Most serpent-like upon the very heart.
    All the stored vengeances of heaven fall
    On her ingrateful top! Strike her young bones,   155
    You taking airs, with lameness.
CORNWALL   Fie, sir, fie.
LEAR You nimble lightnings, dart your blinding flames
    Into her scornful eyes! Infect her beauty,
    You fen-sucked fogs, drawn by the powerful sun
    To fall and blister.   160
REGAN O the blessed gods! So will you wish on me
    When the rash mood is on.
LEAR No, Regan, thou shalt never have my curse.
    Thy tender-hefted nature shall not give
    Thee o'er to harshness. Her eyes are fierce, but thine   165
    Do comfort and not burn. 'Tis not in thee
    To grudge my pleasures, to cut off my train,
    To bandy hasty words, to scant my sizes,
    And in conclusion, to oppose the bolt
    Against my coming in. Thou better know'st   170
    The offices of nature, bond of childhood,
    Effects of courtesy, dues of gratitude.
    Thy half o'th'kingdom hast thou not forgot
    Wherein I thee endowed.
REGAN   Good sir, to th'purpose.
LEAR Who put my man i'th'stocks?
                Tucket within
CORNWALL   What trumpet's that?   175
REGAN I know't, my sister's. This approves her letter
    That she would soon be here.

            Enter OSWALD

            Is your lady come?

Lear is shaken by Regan's warm greeting of Gonerill. Regan advises Lear to return to Gonerill, reducing his followers by half. Lear lists the hardships and ignominies which he would rather endure.

1 Lear's isolation

Stage directors often seize the opportunity to use Gonerill's entrance as a means of emphasising Lear's growing isolation. Characters are 'blocked' (grouped) to show their allegiances.

When Gonerill arrives, Regan takes her by the hand in a show of friendship. Gonerill chooses her words carefully to give offence to Lear, referring to his 'indiscretion' and 'dotage'. Cornwall also lines up against Lear, confirming that Kent was punished on his orders. Kent, the Gentleman, the Fool and Gloucester, all possible allies of Lear, are on stage but do not speak.

Imagine that you are directing the play. Work out how to 'block' Gonerill's entrance in order to underline Lear's vulnerability in the face of his daughters' hostility. How would you costume her in order to support your ideas?

2 Kent's perspective

Kent is a silent observer from the entrance of the king at line 81 to his exit with him at line 279. (See colour section, p. vii, bottom.) Yet his loyalty to Lear has been paramount and it must hurt him to witness his master's torment. Write his version of events and how he responds to what he witnesses as you read through to the end of the scene. Remember that Kent the plain-speaker will not mince his words.

3 'Necessity's sharp pinch'

Lear imagines a life like the wolf and the owl, suffering hostility from exposure to the raw elements. His image in line 204 is of physical pain ('pinch') inflicted upon him by another of his grim, cruel companions, 'Necessity' (the most bare existence). As you read on, you will discover that Lear's imagined ordeal will become all too real.

---

easy-borrowed quickly put on
sway influence
indiscretion lack of judgement
dotage foolish old age
sides chest
abjure reject

enmity o'th'air fierce storms
knee kneel before
squire-like like a servant
afoot intact
sumpter pack-horse

LEAR   This is a slave whose easy-borrowed pride
　　　　Dwells in the sickly grace of her he follows.
　　　　Out, varlet, from my sight!
CORNWALL　　　　　　　　　　What means your grace?　　　　　180

　　　　　　　　　Enter GONERILL

LEAR   Who stocked my servant? Regan, I have good hope
　　　　Thou didst not know on't. Who comes here? O heavens!
　　　　If you do love old men, if your sweet sway
　　　　Allow obedience, if you yourselves are old,
　　　　Make it your cause; send down and take my part.　　　　185
　　　　[*To Gonerill*] Art not ashamed to look upon this beard?
　　　　O Regan, will you take her by the hand?
GONERILL   Why not by th'hand, sir? How have I offended?
　　　　All's not offence that indiscretion finds,
　　　　And dotage terms so.
LEAR　　　　　　　　　　O sides, you are too tough!　　　　190
　　　　Will you yet hold? How came my man i'th'stocks?
CORNWALL   I set him there, sir; but his own disorders
　　　　Deserved much less advancement.
LEAR　　　　　　　　　　　　You? Did you?
REGAN   I pray you, father, being weak, seem so.
　　　　If till the expiration of your month　　　　195
　　　　You will return and sojourn with my sister,
　　　　Dismissing half your train, come then to me.
　　　　I am now from home and out of that provision
　　　　Which shall be needful for your entertainment.
LEAR   Return to her? and fifty men dismissed?　　　　200
　　　　No, rather I abjure all roofs and choose
　　　　To wage against the enmity o'th'air,
　　　　To be a comrade with the wolf and owl,
　　　　Necessity's sharp pinch. Return with her?
　　　　Why, the hot-blooded France, that dowerless took　　　　205
　　　　Our youngest born – I could as well be brought
　　　　To knee his throne and, squire-like, pension beg
　　　　To keep base life afoot. Return with her?
　　　　Persuade me rather to be slave and sumpter
　　　　To this detested groom.
GONERILL　　　　　　　　　At your choice, sir.　　　　210

Lear curses Gonerill and renounces her. He decides to stay with Regan with his hundred followers. Regan gives her reasons for rejecting Lear's proposal, and says that she will accept only twenty-five knights.

---

1 'my daughter . . . a disease' (in pairs)

Although Gonerill is his daughter ('thou art my flesh, my blood, my daughter'), Lear virulently curses her in lines 214–18 using the language of bodily corruption: 'disease', 'boil', 'plague-sore', 'embossèd carbuncle' (swollen tumour). Once again Shakespeare contrasts the natural and healthy order of family life with the corrupt, distorting infection of Gonerill's 'unnatural' behaviour.

Talk together about the way in which Gonerill might react on hearing herself described as a disease. Then compare these lines with lines 155–60 of this scene. What similarities do you find in Lear's language?

2 Like father, like daughter (in groups of three)

Just as Lear's love is measured and calculating, so his sense of self-esteem seems to be in direct proportion to the number of his knights. Now he is experiencing the consequences of his arithmetical way of judging value. Regan and Gonerill cruelly pay their father back in kind, by also measuring their love for him in numbers.

Take parts and speak lines 223–56, emphasising all words connected with numbers. Then talk together about any other similarities you have found between father and daughters.

3 'I gave you all'

Lear's very simple, clear language in line 243 carries huge emotional weight. Try different ways of speaking the line in order to capture a variety of Lear's possible moods. For example, he could be furious, despairing, astonished, disbelieving or full of pathos or . . .

---

thunder-bearer Jupiter (Jove), the Roman god who was armed with thunderbolts
shoot fire thunderbolts
mingle . . . passion think rationally about your impulsive behaviour

avouch it declare it true
sith since
charge expense
slack ye serve you negligently
depositaries trustees

LEAR   I prithee, daughter, do not make me mad.
　　　　I will not trouble thee, my child. Farewell.
　　　　We'll no more meet, no more see one another.
　　　　But yet thou art my flesh, my blood, my daughter,
　　　　Or rather a disease that's in my flesh,　　　　　　　　215
　　　　Which I must needs call mine. Thou art a boil,
　　　　A plague-sore, or embossèd carbuncle
　　　　In my corrupted blood. But I'll not chide thee;
　　　　Let shame come when it will, I do not call it.
　　　　I do not bid the thunder-bearer shoot,　　　　　　　　220
　　　　Nor tell tales of thee to high-judging Jove.
　　　　Mend when thou canst, be better at thy leisure;
　　　　I can be patient, I can stay with Regan,
　　　　I and my hundred knights.
REGAN　　　　　　　　　　　　　Not altogether so.
　　　　I looked not for you yet, nor am provided　　　　　　225
　　　　For your fit welcome. Give ear, sir, to my sister,
　　　　For those that mingle reason with your passion
　　　　Must be content to think you old, and so –
　　　　But she knows what she does.
LEAR　　　　　　　　　　　　　Is this well spoken?
REGAN　I dare avouch it, sir. What, fifty followers?　　　　230
　　　　Is it not well? What should you need of more?
　　　　Yea, or so many, sith that both charge and danger
　　　　Speak 'gainst so great a number? How in one house
　　　　Should many people under two commands
　　　　Hold amity? 'Tis hard, almost impossible.　　　　　　235
GONERILL　Why might not you, my lord, receive attendance
　　　　From those that she calls servants, or from mine?
REGAN　Why not, my lord? If then they chanced to slack ye,
　　　　We could control them. If you will come to me
　　　　(For now I spy a danger) I entreat you　　　　　　　　240
　　　　To bring but five and twenty; to no more
　　　　Will I give place or notice.
LEAR　I gave you all.
REGAN　　　　　　　　And in good time you gave it.
LEAR　Made you my guardians, my depositaries,
　　　　But kept a reservation to be followed　　　　　　　　245
　　　　With such a number. What, must I come to you
　　　　With five and twenty? Regan, said you so?

Lear engages in the arithmetic of love, but his daughters' reductive calculations devastate him. He deliberates on humanity's basic needs, and swears revenge against his daughters. He fears for his sanity.

1 'O reason not the need!' (in groups of five or six)

Lear's final outburst has several elements:

Lines 257–63 Human need cannot be determined by precise calculation. If our requirements are no more than the very basic necessities, then a human life is worth no more than an animal's. Regan's fine clothes are superfluous to her natural needs.

Lines 264–71 Pleading for patience, Lear calls upon the gods to inspire him to noble and manly anger against his daughters.

Lines 271–5 Lear issues a terrifying but confused threat against his daughters.

Lines 275–9 Lear claims that nothing will make him weep. He fears that he will go mad.

a Decide to whom Lear is addressing the lines (e.g. to both sisters, only one sister, the gods, the Fool?).

b Lear identifies his prime need as patience. Share your ideas about what you think is his most pressing need at this moment.

c Take turns at speaking lines 271–5 in different ways. Is Lear's threat terrifying, pathetic, or what?

d Lear's repetitions. Identify the words and phrases that Lear repeats in this speech, then talk together about the effects created.

e At line 276, as Lear begins to speak of his weeping, there are the sounds of a gathering '*Storm and tempest*'. What kind of storm effects would you have to complement Lear's emotional state?

f At the end of Lear's speech he and his companions go out into the storm. Allocate the five parts and a director. Work on how to stage the characters' exits to create a powerful dramatic effect. Notice Lear's final two sentences. How might his companions react to them?

---

tend attend, serve
Our basest . . . superfluous our poorest people, even with the little they have, have more than they need

flaws splinters, fragments
Or ere before

REGAN And speak't again, my lord. No more with me.
LEAR Those wicked creatures yet do look well-favoured
    When others are more wicked. Not being the worst   250
    Stands in some rank of praise. [*To Gonerill*] I'll go with
       thee;
    Thy fifty yet doth double five and twenty,
    And thou art twice her love.
GONERILL   Hear me, my lord:
    What need you five and twenty? ten? or five?
    To follow in a house where twice so many   255
    Have a command to tend you?
REGAN   What need one?
LEAR O reason not the need! Our basest beggars
    Are in the poorest thing superfluous.
    Allow not nature more than nature needs,
    Man's life is cheap as beast's. Thou art a lady;   260
    If only to go warm were gorgeous,
    Why nature needs not what thou gorgeous wear'st,
    Which scarcely keeps thee warm. But for true need –
    You heavens, give me that patience, patience I need.
    You see me here, you gods, a poor old man,   265
    As full of grief as age, wretched in both;
    If it be you that stirs these daughters' hearts
    Against their father, fool me not so much
    To bear it tamely. Touch me with noble anger,
    And let not women's weapons, water drops,   270
    Stain my man's cheeks. No, you unnatural hags,
    I will have such revenges on you both
    That all the world shall – I will do such things –
    What they are, yet I know not, but they shall be
    The terrors of the earth! You think I'll weep;   275
    No, I'll not weep,
             Storm and tempest
    I have full cause of weeping, but this heart
    Shall break into a hundred thousand flaws
    Or ere I'll weep. O fool, I shall go mad.
        Exeunt [Lear, Gloucester, Kent, Gentleman, and Fool]

Regan and Gonerill agree that they will welcome Lear, but not his followers. Gloucester fears for Lear's well-being. Regan and Cornwall insist that Gloucester close his doors against Lear and the storm.

Regan and Cornwall. In many productions Regan and Cornwall are portrayed as physically attractive. Think about why such productions choose to emphasise their good looks, and suggest how you would want to present them.

1 Gloucester: torn loyalty?

Although Gloucester initially follows Lear out into the storm, he quickly returns to his own castle with news of the king's distress. (See also colour section, p. viii, bottom.) Study his lines opposite, then write his thoughts about the situation now facing him. Where do his loyalties lie?

---

bestowed accommodated
put himself from rest deprived
 himself of comfort
For his particular as for him
but will . . . whither but I've no idea
 where he intends to go

ruffle blow, rage
desperate riotous
incense incite, provoke
apt . . . abused susceptible to lies and
 flattery

CORNWALL Let us withdraw; 'twill be a storm.   280
REGAN This house is little. The old man and's people
     Cannot be well bestowed.
GONERILL 'Tis his own blame; hath put himself from rest
     And must needs taste his folly.
REGAN For his particular, I'll receive him gladly,   285
     But not one follower.
GONERILL   So am I purposed.
     Where is my lord of Gloucester?
CORNWALL Followed the old man forth.

         Enter GLOUCESTER

                He is returned.
GLOUCESTER The king is in high rage.
CORNWALL   Whither is he going?
GLOUCESTER He calls to horse, but will I know not whither.   290
CORNWALL 'Tis best to give him way; he leads himself.
GONERILL My lord, entreat him by no means to stay.
GLOUCESTER Alack, the night comes on, and the high winds
     Do sorely ruffle; for many miles about
     There's scarce a bush.
REGAN   O sir, to wilful men,   295
     The injuries that they themselves procure
     Must be their schoolmasters. Shut up your doors.
     He is attended with a desperate train,
     And what they may incense him to, being apt
     To have his ear abused, wisdom bids fear.   300
CORNWALL Shut up your doors, my lord; 'tis a wild night,
     My Regan counsels well: come out o'th'storm.

                   Exeunt

Looking back at Act 2
Activities for groups or individuals

---

1 Storm clouds gather

In Shakespeare's plays a storm often mirrors the disorder within individual minds or society. Identify instances of either individual or social disturbance in each of the four scenes in Act 2. Display your findings in an appropriate way, for example by drawings or a collage of quotations.

2 Old age

Gonerill and Regan find their father's erratic behaviour perplexing and demanding. They are greatly provoked by Lear's capricious and unpredictable ways. Working in groups of four, talk together about whether or not you think that old people can be difficult to handle, especially for young people. Then take roles as Lear, Gonerill, Regan and a family guidance counsellor. The counsellor's task is to interview father and daughters about the disagreements and tensions between them.

3 Goodness

The forces of wickedness gather momentum in Act 2, although a few signs of hope flicker, suggesting that 'goodness' is still at work in Lear's Britain. Find at least one example of goodness – the hope of a better future – in each of the four scenes.

4 The Fool's jingles

Choose any of the Fool's songs or jingles from Act 2. Decide which aspect you want to emphasise, rehearse it, and present it appropriately.

5 Points of view

Talk together about the extent to which you agree with the students who wrote the following statements:

- 'Lear's curses against his daughters are both terrifying and pathetic.'

- 'Regan's line 256 in Scene 4 ('What need one?') is the cruellest line in *King Lear*.'

6 See-sawing power

All of the scenes in Act 2 focus in some way on characters jostling to display and exert authority and control. Explore who holds the power in each section of each scene and display your findings in visual form.

Edgar adopts his disguise as Poor Tom. Remind yourself of lines 9–12 in Act 2 Scene 3, and compare this picture with those on page vii (top) of the colour section and page 120.

The Gentleman describes Lear raging at the storm. Kent recounts the French spies' reports of growing rivalry between Albany and Cornwall. Kent gives the Gentleman a ring to show to Cordelia.

1 What the Gentleman knows

Several anonymous characters (the Gentleman, the Knight and the Captain) make brief appearances in the play. Such characters are often used by Shakespeare to convey information to the audience through what they say and what they are told.

This short scene gives the audience news of Lear, of Albany's and Cornwall's political rivalry and of the French intelligence operation against the British. In the Quarto version (see p. 240) additional lines provide a striking description of Lear in the storm and news of the French invasion.

Write a few lines which the Gentleman could speak to Cordelia, telling her about his encounter with a mysterious well-wisher.

2 'minded like the weather' (in pairs)

The play was written for a theatre that – apart from very basic sound effects like thunder – relied on the actors' words to create setting and atmosphere. The Gentleman's comment that he is 'minded like the weather' is a reminder that the troubled affairs of the kingdom are reflected in people's minds and in the raging storm around them.

In modern productions or film versions, all sorts of special lighting and sound effects are possible, and sometimes 'real' rain.

- One partner argues the advantages and one the disadvantages of using modern special effects to add to the effect of the storm that characters describe in Act 3 Scene 1.
- Plan how you would stage this scene if you were directing it.

Contending with struggling against
fretful elements stormy weather
main mainland
labours to out-jest tries to make a joke of
upon . . . Commend on the evidence of my eyes I trust

speculations / Intelligent secret agents
snuffs huffs, grudges
packings conspiracies
hard rein harsh treatment
furnishings surface details
out-wall appearance

Act 3 Scene 1
Near Gloucester's castle

Storm still. Enter KENT *(disguised) and a* GENTLEMAN, *severally*

KENT Who's there, besides foul weather?

GENTLEMAN One minded like the weather, most unquietly.

KENT I know you. Where's the king?

GENTLEMAN Contending with the fretful elements;
　　　　　Bids the wind blow the earth into the sea,　　　　　　　5
　　　　　Or swell the curlèd waters 'bove the main,
　　　　　That things might change or cease.

KENT　　　　　　　　　　　　　　But who is with him?

GENTLEMAN None but the fool, who labours to out-jest
　　　　　His heart-struck injuries.

KENT　　　　　　　　　　Sir, I do know you,
　　　　　And dare upon the warrant of my note　　　　　　　　10
　　　　　Commend a dear thing to you. There is division,
　　　　　Although as yet the face of it is covered
　　　　　With mutual cunning, 'twixt Albany and Cornwall,
　　　　　Who have – as who have not, that their great stars
　　　　　Throned and set high? – servants, who seem no less,　　15
　　　　　Which are to France the spies and speculations
　　　　　Intelligent of our state. What hath been seen,
　　　　　Either in snuffs and packings of the dukes,
　　　　　Or the hard rein which both of them hath borne
　　　　　Against the old kind king; or something deeper,　　　　20
　　　　　Whereof, perchance, these are but furnishings –

GENTLEMAN I will talk further with you.

KENT　　　　　　　　　　　　　　No, do not.
　　　　　For confirmation that I am much more
　　　　　Than my out-wall, open this purse and take
　　　　　What it contains. If you shall see Cordelia –　　　　　25
　　　　　As fear not but you shall – show her this ring,
　　　　　And she will tell you who that fellow is
　　　　　That yet you do not know. Fie on this storm!
　　　　　I will go seek the king.

Kent and the Gentleman separate to find Lear. Lear rages furiously with the storm, demanding that it destroy humankind. He ignores the Fool's request for shelter, and accuses the storm of joining forces with his daughters.

1 The storm (in small groups)

Lear is an old man in an exposed place facing a terrible storm. He may seem to be a vulnerable victim of the weather, but his words in lines 1–9 are a defiant sequence of imperatives commanding the storm to become even more violent and thus bring about the destruction of the entire human race.

- Create the storm. Share out lines 1–9 and memorise them. Experiment with voices and movement to present your own interpretation of the chaos and confusion of the storm.
- Repeat your reading of lines 1–9, but allow a pause after each group member's part to share ideas about the pictures created in your head by the words.
- The violent weather reflects not only events in the story, but also the state of Lear's mind. Identify the lines which suggest that Lear may now have descended into madness.

2 Master and Fool (in pairs)

The Fool says 'Here's a night that pities neither wise men nor fools.'

a Look at the Fool's words in lines 10–12 and Lear's in lines 19–23. Talk together about how far you feel an audience might feel sympathy or pity for Lear and his Fool.

b If you were directing the play, where in lines 19–23 would you want Lear to switch from defiance to self-pity? Give your reasons.

---

to effect in importance
cataracts and hurricanoes waterfalls and waterspouts
cocks weather-cocks
thought-executing mind-numbing, swifter than thought

Vaunt-couriers forerunners
thick rotundity round-belliedness
court holy water flattery
subscription loyalty
high-engendered sky-born

GENTLEMAN Give me your hand. Have you no more to say?   30
KENT Few words, but to effect more than all yet:
      That when we have found the king – in which your pain
      That way, I'll this – he that first lights on him
      Holla the other.

Exeunt

Act 3 Scene 2
The heath near Gloucester's castle

Storm still. Enter LEAR and FOOL

LEAR Blow, winds, and crack your cheeks! Rage, blow,
      You cataracts and hurricanoes, spout
      Till you have drenched our steeples, drowned the cocks!
      You sulph'rous and thought-executing fires,
      Vaunt-couriers of oak-cleaving thunderbolts,   5
      Singe my white head; and thou all-shaking thunder,
      Strike flat the thick rotundity o'th'world,
      Crack nature's moulds, all germens spill at once
      That makes ingrateful man.
FOOL O nuncle, court holy water in a dry house is better than this   10
    rain-water out o'door. Good nuncle, in, ask thy daughters
    blessing. Here's a night pities neither wise men nor fools.
LEAR Rumble thy bellyful; spit, fire; spout, rain!
      Nor rain, wind, thunder, fire are my daughters.
      I tax not you, you elements, with unkindness.   15
      I never gave you kingdom, called you children.
      You owe me no subscription. Then let fall
      Your horrible pleasure. Here I stand your slave,
      A poor, infirm, weak, and despised old man;
      But yet I call you servile ministers,   20
      That will with two pernicious daughters join
      Your high-engendered battles 'gainst a head
      So old and white as this. O, ho! 'tis foul.

The Fool sings of the foolishness of sexual excess. Kent fears for Lear's safety in this worst-ever storm. Lear calls on the gods to use the storm to reveal all hidden crimes.

1 The Fool's gibes

The Fool picks up on Lear's use of the word 'head' and his lack of shelter, singing a song that gives both 'house' and 'head' a sexual double meaning. Many of the sexual innuendoes involve slang words for 'penis': 'codpiece', 'head', 'headpiece' and 'toe'. The Fool is satirising irresponsible behaviour and its consequences. Uncontrolled sex results in disease; Lear's foolishness results in homelessness. Lear responds to the Fool's teasing by promising patience and again saying 'nothing'.

Identify the gibes in lines 24–34 which you think would pierce Lear's conscience most sharply.

2 Kent and the storm (in small groups)

Kent's sane description of the storm's force provides a marked contrast to the Fool's babbling and Lear's near-insane ravings.

Share a group reading of Kent's speech (lines 40–7), stressing the words which most powerfully convey the power of a storm at night.

3 More sinned against?

In lines 47–57 Lear lists those wrong-doers who should fear the storm's ferocity, because it will leave them exposed to the anger of the gods: unpunished criminals, liars, sex hypocrites and murderers.

How accurate do you think Lear's subsequent assessment of himself is in lines 57–8? Compile two lists to show Lear's sins and the sins against him, and make your own judgement about whether you think he is 'more sinned against than sinning'.

---

louse catch a sexually transmitted disease
made mouths in a glass practised smiling in a mirror
grace majesty
affliction effect
pudder turmoil

Caitiff wretch
seeming hypocrisy
Rive . . . continents burst out of your bodies
cry . . . grace beg for mercy
(a summoner was a court official)

FOOL He that has a house to put 's head in has a good head-piece.
      [*Sings*] The codpiece that will house   25
          Before the head has any,
         The head and he shall louse;
          So beggars marry many.
         The man that makes his toe
          What he his heart should make,   30
         Shall of a corn cry woe,
          And turn his sleep to wake.
  For there was never yet fair woman but she made mouths in
a glass.

         Enter KENT [*disguised*]

LEAR No, I will be the pattern of all patience.   35
      I will say nothing.
KENT Who's there?
FOOL Marry, here's grace and a codpiece; that's a wise man and a
  fool.
KENT Alas, sir, are you here? Things that love night   40
      Love not such nights as these. The wrathful skies
      Gallow the very wanderers of the dark
      And make them keep their caves. Since I was man
      Such sheets of fire, such bursts of horrid thunder,
      Such groans of roaring wind and rain I never   45
      Remember to have heard. Man's nature cannot carry
      Th'affliction nor the fear.
LEAR   Let the great gods,
      That keep this dreadful pudder o'er our heads,
      Find out their enemies now. Tremble, thou wretch,
      That hast within thee undivulgèd crimes   50
      Unwhipped of justice. Hide thee, thou bloody hand,
      Thou perjured and thou simular of virtue
      That art incestuous. Caitiff, to pieces shake,
      That under covert and convenient seeming
      Has practised on man's life. Close pent-up guilts,   55
      Rive your concealing continents and cry
      These dreadful summoners grace. I am a man
      More sinned against than sinning.

Kent urges Lear to rest in a nearby hovel. Kent plans to return to the castle to ask for shelter for the king. The Fool's prophecy promises mixed fortunes for Britain.

1 The magic of poverty (in pairs)

In lines 67–9 Lear remarks on the way in which the most ordinary, basic needs of shelter and warmth are made precious by poverty. But will he truly learn from having to manage with the meanest of comforts when he is in the hovel? Talk together about any occasion on which you were especially grateful for food, warmth or shelter.

2 A song in the storm

In one film version, as the Fool sang lines 72–5 the camera cut to Lear's daughters feasting in front of a blazing fire. They sat in silence, listening to the Fool's plaintive voice coming to them from outside in the storm. Suggest what reasons the director may have had for intercutting this scene while the Fool is singing.

3 A Fool's prophecy (in groups of three or four)

The Fool, alone on stage, makes a strange prediction (lines 77–93): that corruption, immorality and unhappiness will come to Britain ('Albion'), but then be followed by a golden age in which customary evils will be reversed.

- Plan how you would stage this episode if you were directing the play. Should the Fool speak seriously, optimistically, humorously, satirically? Should he appear to talk to himself about some longed-for ideal world or perhaps step outside his role in the play to engage directly with the audience?
- Experiment with at least two different ways of delivering the lines. Consider in particular how the Fool should deliver his final line. Should he use it to draw attention deliberately to the artificiality of the theatrical experience or not? Give your reasons.

---

scanted mean, neglected
courtesan prostitute
matter deed
cutpurses pickpockets
throngs crowded places
usurers . . . field money-lenders do business in public

bawds pimps
That going . . . feet everything will be normal
Merlin wizard to the legendary King Arthur

KENT   Alack, bare-headed?
        Gracious my lord, hard by here is a hovel.
        Some friendship will it lend you 'gainst the tempest.   60
        Repose you there, while I to this hard house –
        More harder than the stones whereof 'tis raised,
        Which even but now, demanding after you,
        Denied me to come in – return and force
        Their scanted courtesy.
LEAR   My wits begin to turn.   65
        Come on, my boy. How dost, my boy? Art cold?
        I am cold myself. – Where is this straw, my fellow?
        The art of our necessities is strange,
        And can make vile things precious. Come, your hovel. –
        Poor fool and knave, I have one part in my heart   70
        That's sorry yet for thee.
FOOL [*Sings*] He that has and a little tiny wit,
                With heigh-ho, the wind and the rain,
                Must make content with his fortunes fit,
                Though the rain it raineth every day.   75
LEAR True, boy. – Come, bring us to this hovel.
                              [*Exeunt Lear and Kent*]
FOOL This is a brave night to cool a courtesan. I'll speak a pro-
        phecy ere I go:
                When priests are more in word than matter;
                When brewers mar their malt with water;   80
                When nobles are their tailors' tutors,
                No heretics burned, but wenches' suitors,
                Then shall the realm of Albion
                Come to great confusion.
                When every case in law is right;   85
                No squire in debt nor no poor knight;
                When slanders do not live in tongues,
                Nor cutpurses come not to throngs;
                When usurers tell their gold i'th'field,
                And bawds and whores do churches build,   90
                Then comes the time, who lives to see't,
                That going shall be used with feet.
        This prophecy Merlin shall make, for I live before his time.
                                                        Exit

Gloucester has been forbidden to help Lear. He tells of a secret letter about an armed invasion to support the king, and proposes to go to Lear. But the treacherous Edmond plans to betray his father.

1 Edmond's irony (in pairs)

Some members of the audience might smile knowingly at Edmond's outrage in line 6 at the way Lear has been treated by his daughters. How could the actor playing Edmond emphasise the word 'unnatural' (i.e. against natural feeling, not in accord with kinship) so as to create an ironic echo of Gloucester's opening sentence?

Take a part each and see if you can demonstrate how you think lines 1–6 should be delivered.

2 The language of father and son (in small groups)

a Gloucester's lines 7–17 are a disjointed succession of short sentences and broken phrases. Read the lines around the group, changing over at each punctuation mark. Repeat the reading, trying to bring out the urgency of the situation by adding gesture and different tones of voice. Talk together about what Gloucester's style of speaking suggests about his emotions and state of mind.

b Edmond's words at the end of the scene (lines 18–22) show a side to his character of which Gloucester seems dangerously unaware. Talk about the ways his language use contrasts with his father's. What is the effect of Edmond's sudden switch from prose to verse? (See p. 235 for more detail on the use of verse and prose in the play.)

c Edmond talks of betraying his father to the Duke of Cornwall as a 'fair deserving' (line 20). Should he speak the term as if he sincerely believes his father deserves to be betrayed, as a cynical ironic comment or in some other way?

---

leave permission
perpetual everlasting
sustain help
footed landed
incline to side with

privily secretly
perceived noticed
toward to come
deserving reward
draw win

Act 3 Scene 3
A room in Gloucester's castle

Enter GLOUCESTER *and* EDMOND

GLOUCESTER Alack, alack, Edmond, I like not this unnatural
dealing. When I desired their leave that I might pity him, they
took from me the use of mine own house, charged me on pain
of perpetual displeasure neither to speak of him, entreat for
him, or any way sustain him.   5
EDMOND Most savage and unnatural!
GLOUCESTER Go to, say you nothing. There is division between
the dukes, and a worse matter than that. I have received a letter
this night – 'tis dangerous to be spoken – I have locked the
letter in my closet. These injuries the king now bears will be   10
revenged home. There is part of a power already footed. We
must incline to the king. I will look him and privily relieve him.
Go you and maintain talk with the duke, that my charity be not
of him perceived. If he ask for me, I am ill and gone to bed. If I
die for it – as no less is threatened me – the king my old master   15
must be relieved. There is strange things toward, Edmond;
pray you be careful.   *Exit*
EDMOND This courtesy, forbid thee, shall the duke
    Instantly know, and of that letter too.
    This seems a fair deserving, and must draw me   20
    That which my father loses: no less than all.
    The younger rises when the old doth fall.   *Exit*

Kent urges Lear to shelter in a hovel. Lear refuses, saying that he cannot feel the storm because the mental pain caused by his daughters is more severe. He insists the Fool goes in before him.

1 Lear's real source of suffering (in large groups)

In lines 6–21 Lear explains why the storm does not torment him as much as the hurt caused by his daughters' 'filial ingratitude'. He is so obsessed by the extent of their hostility and disrespect that he is numb to the effects of the 'contentious storm'. Only someone free of mental worries has the time to think about bodily discomforts ('When the mind's free / The body's delicate').

To explore Lear's feelings, one student plays Kent. All the others represent Lear and stand in a circle around Kent. Kent asks each Lear to enter speaking line 22 ('Good my lord, enter here'). Each Lear refuses, using any one of the remarks from lines 6–22. The Lears should vary their tone and add gestures, deciding whether they reply to Kent, address Gonerill and Regan, or speak to the storm. Which responses does Kent have most difficulty in understanding?

2 'In, boy, go first' (in pairs)

Over the years Lear must have become accustomed to unthinking acceptance of respectful treatment, but in lines 23–7 he refuses the chance to go first into the hut, considering instead the needs and feelings of those around him.

Compare lines 26–7 with lines 66–71 of Act 3 Scene 2. What do these two brief episodes tell you about Lear's growth of concern for others?

Wilt will you
contentious angry
malady illness, torment
scarce hardly
shun avoid
filial daughterly

frank honest
Prithee please
ease rest
leave . . . more the chance to think about more painful things

Act 3 Scene 4
Outside a hovel on the heath

Enter LEAR, KENT *(disguised), and* FOOL

KENT Here is the place, my lord. Good my lord, enter.
    The tyranny of the open night's too rough
    For nature to endure.
                 Storm still
LEAR   Let me alone.
KENT Good my lord, enter here.
LEAR   Wilt break my heart?
KENT I had rather break mine own. Good my lord, enter.   5
LEAR Thou think'st 'tis much that this contentious storm
    Invades us to the skin: so 'tis to thee.
    But where the greater malady is fixed,
    The lesser is scarce felt. Thou'dst shun a bear,
    But if thy flight lay toward the roaring sea,   10
    Thou'dst meet the bear i'th'mouth. When the mind's free,
    The body's delicate. This tempest in my mind
    Doth from my senses take all feeling else,
    Save what beats there: filial ingratitude.
    Is it not as this mouth should tear this hand   15
    For lifting food to't? But I will punish home.
    No, I will weep no more. In such a night
    To shut me out? Pour on, I will endure.
    In such a night as this! O Regan, Gonerill,
    Your old kind father, whose frank heart gave all –   20
    O that way madness lies; let me shun that;
    No more of that.
KENT   Good my lord, enter here.
LEAR Prithee, go in thyself, seek thine own ease.
    This tempest will not give me leave to ponder
    On things would hurt me more; but I'll go in.   25
    In, boy, go first. You houseless poverty –
    Nay, get thee in; I'll pray, and then I'll sleep.
                        Exit [*Fool*]

Lear prays for the homeless and starving, whose plight he has previously ignored. The Fool rushes from the hovel, frightened and crying for help. Edgar, as Poor Tom, speaks madly of being tormented by the devil.

1 Lear feels compassion (in pairs)

Many people believe that lines 28–36 mark a turning point in Lear's spiritual development. After years of absolute rule, he now begins to pity the poor and homeless and to regret his neglect ('O I have ta'en / Too little care of this.').

a Experiment with appropriate ways of staging lines 28–36. It could be an elaborate ceremony with Kent joining in, a private prayer heard only by the audience, or a way of your choosing.

b Collect newspaper photographs of the poor and homeless for a montage wall display under the title of 'Poor naked wretches'. Select suitable phrases from Lear's lines to use as captions.

2 Poor Tom's mad words (in groups of four)

As Poor Tom, pretending madness, Edgar uses language which mixes sense and nonsense. Don't feel you have to understand it all. (No one knows what 'do, de, do, de, do de' means.) His dislocated language adds to the chaotic atmosphere, and his appearance may shock the audience. Lear, for example, assumes in his confusion that Poor Tom must have given everything away to his daughters to be reduced to such a state.

In lines 49–58 Edgar begs for charity and describes how he has been tempted and tormented by a devilish 'foul fiend'. He could be addressing his words to a specific character on stage, to Lear, Kent and the Fool as a group, or to an imaginary person.

Take a part each and decide amongst yourselves to whom Edgar is addressing each sentence and the kind of reaction he gets. Present your version to the rest of the class.

---

bide endure
looped and windowed tattered
physic medicine
pomp royalty
shake the superflux discard unnecessary possessions
pew porch, balcony

ratsbane rat poison
ride . . . bridges ride over narrow bridges
five wits intelligence, senses
star-blasting diseases caused by the stars

Poor naked wretches, wheresoe'er you are
That bide the pelting of this pitiless storm,
How shall your houseless heads and unfed sides, 30
Your looped and windowed raggedness defend you
From seasons such as these? O I have ta'en
Too little care of this. Take physic, pomp,
Expose thyself to feel what wretches feel,
That thou mayst shake the superflux to them 35
And show the heavens more just.

Enter FOOL

EDGAR [*Within*] Fathom and half; fathom and half; poor Tom!
FOOL Come not in here, nuncle! Here's a spirit! Help me, help
me!
KENT Give me thy hand. Who's there? 40
FOOL A spirit, a spirit! He says his name's Poor Tom.
KENT What art thou that dost grumble there i'th'straw? Come
forth.

[*Enter* EDGAR, *disguised as a madman*]

EDGAR Away, the foul fiend follows me. Through the sharp
hawthorn blow the winds. Humh! Go to thy bed and warm 45
thee.
LEAR Didst thou give all to thy daughters? And art thou come to
this?
EDGAR Who gives anything to Poor Tom, whom the foul fiend
hath led through fire and through flame, through ford and 50
whirlpool, o'er bog and quagmire; that hath laid knives under
his pillow and halters in his pew; set ratsbane by his porridge;
made him proud of heart to ride on a bay trotting-horse over
four-inched bridges, to course his own shadow for a traitor.
Bless thy five wits, Tom's a-cold! O do, de, do, de, do de. Bless 55
thee from whirlwinds, star-blasting, and taking. Do Poor Tom
some charity, whom the foul fiend vexes. There could I have
him now, and there, and there again, and there.
Storm still

Lear assumes that Tom's madness has been caused by unkind daughters. Tom offers a mangled version of the ten commandments, and then parodies the seven deadly sins in his story of his past life as a lustful serving-man.

1 Lear blames daughters (in groups of three)

Lear explains Tom's condition as the result of his experience as the father of 'pelican daughters'. It was believed that the pelican fed on the flesh of its parents. Take parts and read aloud lines 59–70. Echo or repeat every mention of fathers or daughters.

Audiences often find Lear's obsession with daughters amusing, even in this grim situation. Talk about whether you would want to encourage or discourage such a response if you were directing the play.

2 Poor Tom's story (in groups of four or five)

There is a danger of reading too much into the disjointed thoughts in lines 77–90. For example, some critics suggest that Tom is imitating the sound of the wind at 'suum' and 'mun', and pretending to ride an imaginary horse at 'Dauphin . . . *cessez!*'. But who really knows?

However, his story may illuminate the themes and situations in the play. Tom appears to parody the biblical ten commandments (see Exodus 20:2–17 and Deuteronomy 5:6–21) and the seven deadly sins: lust, gluttony, greed, sloth, wrath, envy and pride.

a One person reads aloud lines 77–90, pausing frequently for the others to illustrate the tale with a series of tableaux.

b Much of Tom's story of his life as a lecherous serving-man is concerned with illicit sexual behaviour, sleeping with his mistress and using prostitutes. Why do you think Edgar has Tom show so much sexual disgust? Talk together about Edgar's possible motives for this aspect of Tom's character.

---

pass predicament
Nay . . . shamed no, he kept a blanket to save our blushes
plagues . . . air diseases in the atmosphere
light land

commit . . . array don't commit adultery or desire fine clothing
outparamoured outwhored, had more lovers than
sloth idleness
plackets slits in petticoats

LEAR What, has his daughters brought him to this pass?
      Couldst thou save nothing? Wouldst thou give 'em all?   60
FOOL Nay, he reserved a blanket, else we had been all shamed.
LEAR Now all the plagues that in the pendulous air
      Hang fated o'er men's faults, light on thy daughters!
KENT He hath no daughters, sir.
LEAR Death, traitor! Nothing could have subdued nature   65
      To such a lowness but his unkind daughters.
      Is it the fashion that discarded fathers
      Should have thus little mercy on their flesh?
      Judicious punishment: 'twas this flesh begot
      Those pelican daughters.   70
EDGAR Pillicock sat on Pillicock Hill; alow, alow, loo, loo.
FOOL This cold night will turn us all to fools and madmen.
EDGAR Take heed o'th'foul fiend, obey thy parents, keep thy
      words' justice, swear not, commit not with man's sworn spouse,
      set not thy sweet heart on proud array. Tom's a-cold.   75
LEAR What hast thou been?
EDGAR A servingman, proud in heart and mind, that curled my
      hair, wore gloves in my cap, served the lust of my mistress'
      heart, and did the act of darkness with her. Swore as many
      oaths as I spake words, and broke them in the sweet face of   80
      heaven. One that slept in the contriving of lust and waked to
      do it. Wine loved I dearly, dice dearly, and in woman out-
      paramoured the Turk. False of heart, light of ear, bloody of
      hand; hog in sloth, fox in stealth, wolf in greediness, dog in
      madness, lion in prey. Let not the creaking of shoes nor the   85
      rustling of silks betray thy poor heart to woman. Keep thy foot
      out of brothels, thy hand out of plackets, thy pen from lender's
      books, and defy the foul fiend. Still through the hawthorn
      blows the cold wind, says suum, mun, nonny. Dauphin, my boy,
      boy, *cessez!* let him trot by.   90
                    Storm still

Lear believes that poor naked Tom represents humankind's essential nature and tries to remove his own clothes in imitation. Edgar, as Tom, speaks of demons and nightmares, and tells Gloucester of his suffering.

1 'The thing itself' (in pairs)

Lear in his madness continues to be preoccupied with 'poor Tom': the greatest in the kingdom is learning from the least of his subjects. Tom, 'the thing itself', demonstrates humanity's fundamental nature. 'Unaccommodated man' (i.e. man stripped of the material trappings of life) is just a 'poor, bare, forked animal'.

Take turns to speak lines 91–7 to each other, then suggest why the traumatised king should wish to remove his clothes, and how you imagine the other characters would react to Lear's attempts to undress.

2 Poor Tom's language (in groups of five)

Shakespeare probably borrowed much of Tom's language from Samuel Harsnett's book on witchcraft, *A Declaration of Egregious Popish Impostures* (1603; see p. 204). For example, Edgar calls Gloucester 'Flibbertigibbet', a dancing devil that stalks the earth at night, spreading disease and deformity. He chants about St Swithin meeting the nightmare, a female monster who suffocated her victims. St Swithin orders her to 'alight' (get off), makes her 'troth plight' (promise not to do it again) and tells her to clear off ('aroint thee').

Prepare a performance of lines 102–25. Consider the following.

- In what ways might the disguised Edgar speak or sing his words?
- How might each of the other characters respond to the deranged beggar? Do they listen attentively, ignore him or what?
- What kind of dramatic tension can you create between Edgar and his father when they see each other?

---

ow'st owe
on's of us (line 95), of his (line 100)
forked two-legged
lendings clothes
naughty wicked
old lecher dirty old man
web and the pin cataracts in the eye

mildews the white rots the ripe
creature creatures
Swithold . . . wold St Swithin walks over open country three times
mantle slime
tithing parish
Smulkin devil

LEAR Thou wert better in a grave than to answer with thy uncovered body this extremity of the skies. Is man no more than
this? Consider him well. Thou ow'st the worm no silk, the beast
no hide, the sheep no wool, the cat no perfume. Ha! Here's
three on's are sophisticated; thou art the thing itself. Unaccom-   95
modated man is no more but such a poor, bare, forked animal
as thou art. Off, off, you lendings! Come, unbutton here.

FOOL Prithee, nuncle, be contented; 'tis a naughty night to swim
in. Now a little fire in a wild field were like an old lecher's heart
– a small spark, all the rest on's body cold. Look, here comes a   100
walking fire.

Enter GLOUCESTER *with a torch*

EDGAR This is the foul Flibbertigibbet; he begins at curfew and
walks till the first cock. He gives the web and the pin, squints
the eye, and makes the harelip; mildews the white wheat, and
hurts the poor creature of earth.   105
[*Chants*] Swithold footed thrice the wold,
　　　He met the nightmare and her ninefold;
　　　　Bid her alight
　　　　And her troth plight,
　　　And aroint thee, witch, aroint thee!   110

KENT How fares your grace?

LEAR What's he?

KENT Who's there? What is't you seek?

GLOUCESTER What are you there? Your names?

EDGAR Poor Tom, that eats the swimming frog, the toad, the   115
tadpole, the wall-newt, and the water; that in the fury of his
heart, when the foul fiend rages, eats cowdung for salads,
swallows the old rat and the ditch-dog, drinks the green mantle
of the standing pool; who is whipped from tithing to tithing,
and stocked, punished, and imprisoned; who hath had three   120
suits to his back, six shirts to his body,
　　　Horse to ride, and weapon to wear;
　　　But mice and rats and such small deer
　　　Have been Tom's food for seven long year.
Beware my follower. Peace, Smulkin; peace, thou fiend!   125

Gloucester tries to persuade Lear to leave for a place of safety, but Lear wants to learn wisdom from Poor Tom. Gloucester speaks of his love for Edgar. Lear shows compassion for Poor Tom.

1 Tom the philosopher

In lines 127–8 Poor Tom speaks of more of Harsnett's devils (see p. 114). Modo is the devil, and Mahu the organiser of hell. Tom twice complains of the cold, perhaps to avoid (or attract?) his father's attention. Despite the poor naked man's bizarre language and behaviour, Lear's preoccupation with Tom continues.

On three occasions Lear calls Tom a philosopher. Find these moments and suggest reasons why he attributes such great wisdom to a down-and-out.

2 Dramatic irony (in groups of six)

Lear could not recognise the true nature of his own daughters until they turned on him, and Gloucester displays similar blindness. He laments the loss of Kent and Edgar, but fails to recognise them when they are right in front of him and, of course, remains completely unaware of Edmond's scheming.

Four of the group take parts as Lear, Kent, Edgar and Gloucester and prepare to read aloud lines 126–60. The remaining two group members should prepare themselves to speak what they think Edgar and Kent's reactions and private thoughts might be at significant moments. The four character readers should pause at the end of each of their character's sets of lines to allow the 'other' Edgar and Kent to interject their private thoughts and comments on what has been said.

---

flesh . . . it our children have become wicked and hate us, their parents
injunction order
Theban Greek scholar (the ancient Greeks were famous for their learning)

Importune implore
His wits . . . unsettle he's cracking up
outlawed from my blood declared an outlaw and disinherited

GLOUCESTER What, hath your grace no better company?
EDGAR The Prince of Darkness is a gentleman. Modo he's called,
    and Mahu.
GLOUCESTER Our flesh and blood, my lord, is grown so vile,
    That it doth hate what gets it.   130
EDGAR Poor Tom's a-cold.
GLOUCESTER Go in with me. My duty cannot suffer
    T'obey in all your daughters' hard commands.
    Though their injunction be to bar my doors
    And let this tyrannous night take hold upon you,   135
    Yet have I ventured to come seek you out
    And bring you where both fire and food is ready.
LEAR First let me talk with this philosopher.
    What is the cause of thunder?
KENT Good my lord, take his offer; go into th'house.   140
LEAR I'll talk a word with this same learnèd Theban.
    What is your study?
EDGAR How to prevent the fiend, and to kill vermin.
LEAR Let me ask you one word in private.
KENT Importune him once more to go, my lord.   145
    His wits begin t'unsettle.
GLOUCESTER   Canst thou blame him?
                  Storm still
    His daughters seek his death. Ah, that good Kent,
    He said it would be thus, poor banished man!
    Thou sayst the king grows mad; I'll tell thee, friend,
    I am almost mad myself. I had a son,   150
    Now outlawed from my blood; he sought my life
    But lately, very late. I loved him, friend;
    No father his son dearer. True to tell thee,
    The grief hath crazed my wits. What a night's this!
    I do beseech your grace –
LEAR   O, cry you mercy, sir. –   155
    Noble philosopher, your company.
EDGAR Tom's a-cold.
GLOUCESTER In, fellow, there, in t'hovel; keep thee warm.
LEAR Come, let's in all.
KENT   This way, my lord.
LEAR   With him;
    I will keep still with my philosopher.   160

The king's party enters the hovel. Edmond shows Cornwall the letter implicating Gloucester in the French invasion plans. Cornwall promises Edmond his father's title and orders him to help in Gloucester's arrest.

1 Out of the storm

Stage directors often end a scene with exits which express the mood that has been developed in that scene. Decide how you would stage the exit of Lear and his followers. For each character suggest the movements and expressions which you think convey their feelings most dramatically.

2 Tom the story-teller (in pairs)

Edgar's final lines refer to two medieval stories. Child Roland ('Child' here means an untested knight) is the hero of a twelfth-century tale, *Chanson de Roland*, and may also have featured in a version of *Jack the Giant-killer*. The 'dark tower' in Poor Tom's story could be Gloucester's castle. Lines 167–8 are still well known and much used.

Talk together about what Tom's parting words suggest might happen in the play. Also decide how and to whom Edgar speaks: to his father, to the audience, to himself in his own voice, or . . .?

3 Edmond the manipulator (in pairs)

Edmond deliberately betrays his father under the pretence of feeling torn between family obligation and loyalty to Cornwall.

Take parts and try reading lines 1–21 in various tones to bring out Edmond's deceitful nature. Don't forget that his Aside to the audience (lines 17–18) is the only moment in which he expresses his true thoughts and feelings.

censured judged
nature family love
something fears somewhat frightens
a provoking . . . himself an understandable fault caused by Gloucester's evil
approves him . . . party proves him a spy
apprehension arrest
stuff his increase Cornwall's
persever continue, persevere
blood family ties

KENT Good my lord, soothe him; let him take the fellow.
GLOUCESTER Take him you on.
KENT Sirrah, come on. Go along with us.
LEAR Come, good Athenian.
GLOUCESTER No words, no words. Hush.   165
EDGAR Child Roland to the dark tower came.
    His word was still 'Fie, fo, and fum;
    I smell the blood of a British man.'

                Exeunt

Act 3   Scene 5
A room in Gloucester's castle

Enter CORNWALL and EDMOND

CORNWALL I will have my revenge ere I depart his house.
EDMOND How, my lord, I may be censured, that nature thus gives
  way to loyalty, something fears me to think of.
CORNWALL I now perceive it was not altogether your brother's evil
  disposition made him seek his death, but a provoking merit set   5
  a-work by a reprovable badness in himself.
EDMOND How malicious is my fortune, that I must repent to be
  just! This is the letter which he spoke of, which approves him
  an intelligent party to the advantages of France. O heavens, that
  this treason were not, or not I the detector!   10
CORNWALL Go with me to the duchess.
EDMOND If the matter of this paper be certain, you have mighty
  business in hand.
CORNWALL True or false, it hath made thee Earl of Gloucester.
  Seek out where thy father is, that he may be ready for our   15
  apprehension.
EDMOND [*Aside*] If I find him comforting the king, it will stuff his
  suspicion more fully. – I will persever in my course of loyalty,
  though the conflict be sore between that and my blood.
CORNWALL I will lay trust upon thee, and thou shalt find a dearer   20
  father in my love.

                Exeunt

Gloucester leaves to find provisions for Lear and his followers. Edgar continues his talk of devils, but briefly drops his disguise. The Fool poses a puzzling question. In his mental anguish, Lear imagines revenge.

Madness on the heath. The Fool is seated, then from left to right Kent, Edgar as Poor Tom and Lear. In the Quarto version of the play Lear stages a mock trial of Gonerill and Regan after line 14. Turn to page 240 and read the additional lines. If you were putting on the play, would you include the trial scene in your production? Give reasons for your decision.

piece out the comfort make it more comfortable
Frateretto a dancing devil
Nero . . . darkness Nero, the villainous Roman emperor, is damned in hell

yeoman small landowner or farmer (this might be a private joke about Shakespeare's own family)
spits spikes for roasting meat
mar . . . counterfeiting spoil my acting

Act 3 Scene 6
Inside the hovel on the heath

Enter KENT *(disguised) and* GLOUCESTER

GLOUCESTER Here is better than the open air; take it thankfully. I
will piece out the comfort with what addition I can. I will not be
long from you.

KENT All the power of his wits have given way to his impatience;
the gods reward your kindness!   5

Exit [Gloucester]

Enter LEAR, EDGAR *[disguised as a madman], and* FOOL

EDGAR Frateretto calls me, and tells me Nero is an angler in the
lake of darkness. Pray, innocent, and beware the foul fiend.

FOOL Prithee, nuncle, tell me whether a madman be a gentleman
or a yeoman.

LEAR A king, a king!   10

FOOL No, he's a yeoman that has a gentleman to his son; for he's a
mad yeoman that sees his son a gentleman before him.

LEAR To have a thousand with red burning spits
    Come hizzing in upon 'em!

EDGAR Bless thy five wits.   15

KENT O pity! Sir, where is the patience now
    That you so oft have boasted to retain?

EDGAR *[Aside]* My tears begin to take his part so much
    They mar my counterfeiting.

LEAR The little dogs and all,   20
    Tray, Blanch, and Sweetheart – see, they bark at me.

Tom speaks a verse of warning to all dogs. Lear broods on Regan's ingratitude, then falls asleep. Gloucester warns Kent of a plot to assassinate the king. He urges him to take Lear to safety at Dover.

---

1 Tom's rhyme (in pairs)

Lines 22–30 are Tom's response to Lear's vision of his pet dogs. Experiment with ways of reading the lines to make them sound like a nursery rhyme, a charm or an incantation.

How do you think Lear could react? Does he 'see' Tom's dogs in the way he seems to have seen his own dogs, Tray, Blanch and Sweetheart, in line 21?

2 The Fool's last words (in pairs)

'And I'll go to bed at noon' (line 41) are the Fool's last words. Some productions use wordless stage action later in the play to explain his disappearance. One production, however, showed Lear accidentally inflicting a fatal wound at line 33 of this scene. As the king said 'Let them anatomise Regan', he pretended to be carrying out a dissection with his sword and unwittingly stabbed the Fool through a cushion which the Fool was holding across his stomach.

Decide how you would have the Fool speak his last line.

3 Gloucester to the rescue (in groups of three)

Gloucester is, as Edmond suspected, 'comforting the king'. He is anxious for Lear to escape quickly, since he has overheard a plan to kill the king.

Share a reading of lines 44–53, changing readers at each punctuation mark. Try to emphasise the urgency in Gloucester's words.

4 A soliloquy for Edgar?

The Quarto version of the play includes a soliloquy for Edgar to end Scene 6. Turn to page 241 and decide whether or not you would include these lines in your own production. Give reasons for your decision.

Avaunt be gone
brach bitch
Bobtail tyke dog with no tail
trundle-tail dog with curly tail
hatch door
wakes festivals

horn begging cup
Persian fancy, exotic
litter coach with closed curtains
Stand . . . loss are bound to die
that . . . conduct who will quickly lead
you to safety

EDGAR Tom will throw his head at them. – Avaunt, you curs!
    Be thy mouth or black or white,
    Tooth that poisons if it bite,
    Mastiff, greyhound, mongrel grim,   25
    Hound or spaniel, brach or him,
    Bobtail tyke or trundle-tail,
    Tom will make him weep and wail;
    For with throwing thus my head,
    Dogs leap the hatch, and all are fled.   30
  Do, de, de, de. *Cessez!* Come, march to wakes and fairs and
market towns. Poor Tom, thy horn is dry.
LEAR Then let them anatomise Regan; see what breeds about her
heart. Is there any cause in nature that makes these hard-
hearts? [*To Edgar*] You, sir, I entertain for one of my hundred, 35
only I do not like the fashion of your garments. You will say
they are Persian; but let them be changed.
KENT Now, good my lord, lie here and rest a while.
LEAR Make no noise, make no noise. Draw the curtains: so, so.
  We'll go to supper i'th'morning. [*He sleeps*]   40
FOOL And I'll go to bed at noon.

      Enter GLOUCESTER

GLOUCESTER Come hither, friend. Where is the king my master?
KENT Here, sir, but trouble him not; his wits are gone.
GLOUCESTER Good friend, I prithee take him in thy arms.
  I have o'erheard a plot of death upon him.   45
  There is a litter ready. Lay him in't
  And drive toward Dover, friend, where thou shalt meet
  Both welcome and protection. Take up thy master;
  If thou shouldst dally half an hour, his life
  With thine and all that offer to defend him   50
  Stand in assurèd loss. Take up, take up,
  And follow me, that will to some provision
  Give thee quick conduct. Come, come away.
                Exeunt

Cornwall reports that the French army has invaded. He instructs Edmond to leave to avoid witnessing his father's harsh punishment. Oswald reports that some of Gloucester's followers have gone to Dover with Lear.

---

1 'Pluck out his eyes'

In Shakespeare's time punishment depended on rank: a duke guilty of treason could expect to be beheaded rather than hanged, drawn and quartered. Both Regan and Gonerill are keen to say how Gloucester should be punished. As you read on, note how quickly and terrifyingly Gonerill's suggestion becomes reality.

2 Edmond reflects on his success (in pairs)

Edmond says nothing in this scene. He has manoeuvred himself into a powerful position (and close to Gonerill). He now hears Cornwall call him 'my lord of Gloucester'.

Remind yourselves of Edmond's first soliloquy at the start of Act 1 Scene 2, in which he declared his will to succeed. Then write an Aside (of four to six lines) for him to speak after line 12 of this scene.

3 The language of action (in groups of three)

The language of this scene contrasts sharply with the preceding scene on the heath. For example, Cornwall and the two sisters both employ frequent imperatives giving instructions and commands, thereby reflecting their control of fast-moving events.

Plan and rehearse a reading of lines 1–12 that emphasises this sense of power and activity. Experiment in particular with the way lines 4 and 5 could be delivered in order to highlight contrasting facets of Regan's and Gonerill's characters.

Post ride
sister sister-in-law
beholding sight
festinate preparation hasty gearing-up for war

bound to the like going to do the same
posts messengers
Hot questrists fast riders

Act 3 Scene 7
The Great Hall of Gloucester's castle

Enter CORNWALL, REGAN, GONERILL, EDMOND *and Servants*

CORNWALL [*To Gonerill*] Post speedily to my lord your husband;
show him this letter. The army of France is landed. – Seek out
the traitor Gloucester.

            [*Exeunt some Servants*]

REGAN Hang him instantly.
GONERILL Pluck out his eyes.   5
CORNWALL Leave him to my displeasure. Edmond, keep you our
sister company. The revenges we are bound to take upon your
traitorous father are not fit for your beholding. Advise the
duke, where you are going, to a most festinate preparation:
we are bound to the like. Our posts shall be swift and intel- 10
ligent betwixt us. Farewell, dear sister; farewell, my lord of
Gloucester.

    [*Gonerill and Edmond start to leave*]

      Enter OSWALD

How now, where's the king?
OSWALD My lord of Gloucester hath conveyed him hence.
  Some five or six and thirty of his knights,   15
  Hot questrists after him, met him at gate,
  Who, with some other of the lord's dependants,
  Are gone with him toward Dover, where they boast
  To have well-armèd friends.
CORNWALL Get horses for your mistress.   20

         [*Exit Oswald*]

Cornwall plans to punish Gloucester without reference to the law. Gloucester is brought in and tied to a chair. He protests that his captors are breaking the customs of hospitality, but his interrogation begins.

1 Power without responsibility

In lines 24–7 Cornwall admits that he should not execute Gloucester without a proper trial, but knows he has the power to do so without others preventing him. His anger overrides all other considerations ('our power / Shall do a curtsy to our wrath'). Make a list of examples from history or current affairs when the abuse of power has produced similar atrocities.

2 Unnatural behaviour (in pairs)

Regan and Cornwall should show respect to Gloucester as their host, as their elder and as a high-ranking nobleman. Instead they delight in inflicting cruelty on him.

Cornwall orders Gloucester to be bound to a chair, and Regan insultingly pulls hairs out of the old man's beard. Gloucester twice protests about his guests' abuse of his hospitality, but Cornwall's and Regan's malice and threats continue unabated as they accuse him of treachery.

a Discuss the various ways in which Gloucester would regard Regan's behaviour as 'unnatural'.

b Think back to earlier events and select three situations experienced by Gloucester which he might regard as 'unnatural'.

Pinion bind
pass . . . justice sentence him to death without trial
do a curtsy . . . wrath bow down to our anger
corky dry and withered

ravish pluck
quicken come to life
ruffle molest
confederacy conspiracy
Late footed recently landed

GONERILL Farewell, sweet lord, and sister.

CORNWALL Edmond, farewell.

> [*Exeunt Gonerill and Edmond*]

[*To Servants*] Go seek the traitor Gloucester.

Pinion him like a thief; bring him before us.

> [*Exeunt other Servants*]

Though well we may not pass upon his life

Without the form of justice, yet our power   25

Shall do a curtsy to our wrath, which men

May blame but not control.

> *Enter* GLOUCESTER *and Servants*

Who's there – the traitor?

REGAN Ingrateful fox! 'tis he.

CORNWALL Bind fast his corky arms.

GLOUCESTER What means your graces? Good my friends, consider   30

You are my guests. Do me no foul play, friends.

CORNWALL Bind him, I say.

REGAN   Hard, hard! O filthy traitor!

GLOUCESTER Unmerciful lady as you are, I'm none.

CORNWALL To this chair bind him. Villain, thou shalt find –

> [*Regan plucks Gloucester's beard*]

GLOUCESTER By the kind gods, 'tis most ignobly done,   35

To pluck me by the beard.

REGAN So white, and such a traitor?

GLOUCESTER   Naughty lady,

These hairs which thou dost ravish from my chin

Will quicken and accuse thee. I am your host.

With robbers' hands my hospitable favours   40

You should not ruffle thus. What will you do?

CORNWALL Come, sir, what letters had you late from France?

REGAN Be simple-answered, for we know the truth.

CORNWALL And what confederacy have you with the traitors

Late footed in the kingdom?

REGAN   To whose hands   45

You have sent the lunatic king. Speak.

Gloucester admits that he sent Lear to safety in Dover. He hopes to see Lear's enemies receive just punishment. Cornwall gouges out one of Gloucester's eyes. A servant challenges Cornwall.

---

1 Gloucester tied to the stake

The image in line 53 is of the popular Elizabethan 'sport' of bear-baiting. There was a bear-baiting pit next to the Globe Theatre and a nearby street is still called Bear Gardens. Research bear-baiting in Shakespeare's time, then consider how audiences might have reacted to the use of the image here and what it tells us of Gloucester's mood and his fears for his safety.

2 Gloucester's words of defiance (in small groups)

In lines 55–65 Gloucester bravely justifies his actions. His words are rich in imagery of holiness, biting, sea storms, tears, wolf howls and 'wingèd vengeance'. Strangely, Cornwall and Regan do not interrupt him.

Talk about why you think Shakespeare chose to give Gloucester eleven uninterrupted lines. Consider their dramatic purpose: how they recall central themes in the play, help establish the mood of the scene, and prepare for Gloucester's own tragedy.

3 Creating dramatic tension (in groups of three)

In the midst of this horrific scene of torture, an audience may well momentarily experience a sense of relief when one of Cornwall's servants defies the duke, risking his life to protest at such an appalling act.

- Look back at the lines building up to the blinding (lines 49–71) and pick out words and phrases that develop the dramatic tension.
- Consider ways in which the scene could be staged that would increase the audience's awareness of the horror to come.

---

guessingly set down written without knowing the facts
anointed holy, kingly
boarish pig-like
buoyed risen
stellèd starry

holp helped (by weeping)
All cruels else subscribe let dangerous animals in, but not Lear
wingèd vengeance the revenge of the gods

GLOUCESTER I have a letter guessingly set down,
          Which came from one that's of a neutral heart,
          And not from one opposed.
CORNWALL   Cunning.
REGAN   And false.
CORNWALL Where hast thou sent the king?
GLOUCESTER   To Dover.   50
REGAN Wherefore to Dover? Wast thou not charged at peril –
CORNWALL Wherefore to Dover? Let him answer that.
GLOUCESTER I am tied to th'stake, and I must stand the course.
REGAN Wherefore to Dover?
GLOUCESTER Because I would not see thy cruel nails   55
          Pluck out his poor old eyes, nor thy fierce sister
          In his anointed flesh stick boarish fangs.
          The sea, with such a storm as his bare head
          In hell-black night endured, would have buoyed up
          And quenched the stellèd fires.   60
          Yet, poor old heart, he holp the heavens to rain.
          If wolves had at thy gate howled that stern time,
          Thou shouldst have said, 'Good porter, turn the key:
          All cruels else subscribe.' But I shall see
          The wingèd vengeance overtake such children.   65
CORNWALL See't shalt thou never. Fellows, hold the chair.
          Upon these eyes of thine I'll set my foot.
GLOUCESTER He that will think to live till he be old,
          Give me some help! – O cruel! O you gods!
          [*Cornwall puts out one of Gloucester's eyes*]
REGAN One side will mock another: th'other, too.   70
CORNWALL If you see vengeance –
SERVANT   Hold your hand, my lord.
          I have served you ever since I was a child,
          But better service have I never done you
          Than now to bid you hold.
REGAN   How now, you dog!

Regan kills the servant. Cornwall blinds Gloucester's other eye. Regan tauntingly informs Gloucester of Edmond's treachery. She orders Gloucester to be thrown out. Cornwall says he is badly wounded.

1 'Tender-hefted' Regan? (in groups of four)

In Act 2 Scene 4, line 164, Lear described Regan as 'tender-hefted' (soft-hearted or easily moved) and she is sometimes portrayed on stage as very feminine. Yet she urges Cornwall on in his barbaric maiming of Gloucester, kills the servant who protests and further tortures Gloucester by telling him that it was Edmond who betrayed him. Take parts and work together to decide exactly how Regan should be played from the putting out of Gloucester's eyes (line 66) to the end of this scene.

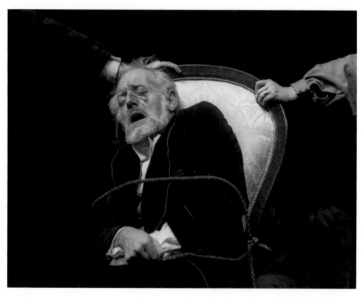

Out, vile jelly! Some productions shift the blinding off stage altogether. Some play the blinding in total darkness. Others heighten the agony with realistic presentations, and show Gloucester shrieking in unbearable pain (see colour section, p. ix, bottom). Write detailed notes on how you would stage the blinding, identifying what the audience would see. (See also p. 132, Activities 1 and 2.)

If you did wear . . . quarrel if you were a man, I'd fight you
stand up defy us
enkindle set alight

nature natural justice
quit punish, repay
made the overture . . . us told us of your treachery

SERVANT If you did wear a beard upon your chin   75
        I'd shake it on this quarrel. What do you mean?
CORNWALL My villain!
SERVANT Nay then, come on, and take the chance of anger.
                        [*They draw and fight*]
REGAN [*To another Servant*] Give me thy sword. A peasant stand up
        thus!
                        Kills him
SERVANT Oh, I am slain. My lord, you have one eye left   80
        To see some mischief on him. Oh!   [*He dies*]
CORNWALL Lest it see more, prevent it. Out, vile jelly!
                [*He puts out Gloucester's other eye*]
        Where is thy lustre now?
GLOUCESTER All dark and comfortless. Where's my son Ed-
        mond?
        Edmond, enkindle all the sparks of nature   85
        To quit this horrid act.
REGAN   Out, treacherous villain!
        Thou call'st on him that hates thee. It was he
        That made the overture of thy treasons to us,
        Who is too good to pity thee.
GLOUCESTER O, my follies! Then Edgar was abused.   90
        Kind gods, forgive me that, and prosper him.
REGAN Go thrust him out at gates, and let him smell
        His way to Dover.
                        Exit [*a Servant*] *with Gloucester*
        How is't, my lord? How look you?
CORNWALL I have received a hurt. Follow me, lady.
        [*To Servants*] Turn out that eyeless villain. Throw this
        slave   95
        Upon the dunghill. Regan, I bleed apace.
        Untimely comes this hurt. Give me your arm.
                                        Exeunt

Looking back at Act 3
Activities for groups or individuals

1 Staging extreme violence

The blinding of Gloucester is often cited by those for and against showing violence on stage, television or film. Some argue that if Shakespeare can include horrific brutality in his plays, why can't modern script writers?

Imagine that a school or college drama club wants to mount a production of *King Lear*, but the principal insists the blinding should be done off stage, unseen by the audience. Role-play a meeting between the principal and protesting members of the production team.

2 Signs of goodness

Some hope is provided in Scene 7 in the actions of the brave servant who attempts to defend Gloucester. He is a reminder that goodness could reign again in Lear's kingdom. In the Quarto version of the play (see p. 240) Scene 7 closes with two other servants who decide to assist the blinded Gloucester. They express revulsion at Cornwall's and Regan's evil, and plan to soothe Gloucester's pain ('I'll fetch some flax and whites of eggs / To apply to his bleeding face'), and call on heaven to help him.

In the theatre, the interval is sometimes placed at the end of this scene. Decide, with reasons, whether you would include the two kind servants from the Quarto version to conclude the first half of the play, end it at line 97 as in the Folio version, or place the interval before the blinding scene.

3 The Fool disappears

The Fool says and does less and less as Act 3 progresses, especially after the appearance of Poor Tom. Indeed, he disappears altogether after Scene 6. Think of reasons why Shakespeare chose to reduce the Fool's role in Act 3, and to have him play no further part in the action. Consider whether directors should seek some way to explain his disappearance or just leave it unexplained.

4 Building an act

The scenes in Act 3 are set either in or near Gloucester's castle or on the heath outside. Note down where each of the seven scenes is set and who is involved, and then decide whether it advances Lear's story, Gloucester's story or the story of the invasion. From the point of view of the audience, what is gained by moving between the scenes of Lear's madness and the events in the castle?

Suggest a suitable caption for this picture of Lear and the Fool in Scene 2.

Edgar reflects on the advantages of being destitute. He is shocked by the sight of his blinded father. In despair, Gloucester acknowledges his past errors. He regrets his treatment of Edgar.

___

1 At the bottom of Fortune's wheel? (in pairs)

Using the image of the wheel of fortune (see p. 80), Edgar reflects that pretending to be an insane beggar brings advantages. He prefers life as an outcast and the knowledge that he is despised to the illusions involved when people are admired insincerely. He feels safe as 'the low'st' on Fortune's wheel because he can hope for improvement.

Some modern productions choose this scene as the first one after the interval. The storm has passed and, although Act 3 ends savagely with torture and violence, Edgar's lines 1–9 present an opportunity to strike a different note. Take turns to read them to each other and then decide what impression you would seek to create in the audience's minds at the start of Act 4.

2 'I stumbled when I saw'

Gloucester expresses regret at his past mistakes. As Gloucester, identify the earlier events in the play which you now feel involved stumbling and error. Write a short paragraph on each of these mistakes, commenting on how suffering has given you new understanding of each event.

3 A son sees his blinded father (in groups of three)

Edgar seems calm and resigned in lines 1–9, but then endures the shock of seeing his blinded father and hearing himself lovingly described. He also has the strange experience of hearing his own feelings echoed when Gloucester says that there are advantages in suffering (lines 20–1).

Two people read aloud lines 12–24, pausing at the end of each line to allow the third to say what Edgar might be thinking as he listens.

___

esperance hope
parti-eyed with bleeding eyes
But that except that
mutations changes
yield to age accept age and death
fourscore eighty

means goods, property
secure us give us a false sense of security
our mere defects the things we lack
commodities opportunities, advantages

Act 4 Scene 1
Near Gloucester's castle

Enter EDGAR *(disguised as a madman)*

EDGAR Yet better thus, and known to be condemned,
    Than still condemned and flattered. To be worst,
    The low'st and most dejected thing of fortune,
    Stands still in esperance, lives not in fear.
    The lamentable change is from the best;   5
    The worst returns to laughter. Welcome, then,
    Thou unsubstantial air that I embrace:
    The wretch that thou hast blown unto the worst
    Owes nothing to thy blasts.

Enter GLOUCESTER *and an* OLD MAN

                                But who comes here?
    My father, parti-eyed? World, world, O world!   10
    But that thy strange mutations make us hate thee,
    Life would not yield to age.
OLD MAN   O my good lord,
    I have been your tenant and your father's tenant
    These fourscore –
GLOUCESTER Away, get thee away; good friend, be gone.   15
    Thy comforts can do me no good at all;
    Thee they may hurt.
OLD MAN   You cannot see your way.
GLOUCESTER I have no way, and therefore want no eyes:
    I stumbled when I saw. Full oft 'tis seen,
    Our means secure us, and our mere defects   20
    Prove our commodities. Oh, dear son Edgar,
    The food of thy abusèd father's wrath:
    Might I but live to see thee in my touch,
    I'd say I had eyes again.
OLD MAN   How now? Who's there?

Edgar fears that worse events may follow. Gloucester recalls that Poor Tom reminded him of Edgar, and reflects that humans are the playthings of the gods. He asks if Edgar knows the way to Dover.

---

1 Edgar's Asides (in pairs)

In lines 1–9 Edgar took comfort in the security of being at the bottom of Fortune's wheel. Seeing and overhearing his blinded father, he finds that he was mistaken, and that his suffering is now even more acute.

Edgar's five Asides express his private thoughts, and are not heard by the others on stage. One of you tries running all of the Asides together to create a continuous flow of thoughts whilst the other repeats and echoes their words to make them as mesmerising and powerful as possible. What do his words suggest is the state of Edgar's mind?

2 'As flies to wanton boys' (in groups of six or more)

Edgar hears his father say that, just as irresponsible boys torment and kill flies, so human life merely provides casual entertainment for the gods.

Stand or sit in a circle. One person speaks Gloucester's lines 36–7, deciding whether to make them sound desperate, accepting, enraged or depressed. The next person in the circle replies with Edgar's words 'How should this be?', varying their tone of voice to suit the tone taken by the first speaker.

Repeat the activity around the circle until everyone has had the opportunity to speak as both Edgar and Gloucester. Afterwards talk together about the extent to which you share Gloucester's opinions.

3 'Bad is the trade'

Edgar appears to decide to continue deceiving his father into thinking he is both 'Madman and beggar' in spite of criticising such behaviour in lines 38–9. Do you think he is justified in choosing to 'play fool to sorrow' with his blind and grief-stricken father? What reasons can you give for his potentially puzzling decision?

---

reason sense
scarce barely
wanton unthinking
twain two
ancient love old loyalty (the man's eighty-year tenancy)

time's plague curse of our time
'parel apparel (clothing)
daub it further pretend any longer

EDGAR [*Aside*] O gods! Who is't can say 'I am at the worst'?   25
    I am worse than e'er I was.

OLD MAN   'Tis poor mad Tom.

EDGAR [*Aside*] And worse I may be yet. The worst is not
    So long as we can say 'This is the worst.'

OLD MAN Fellow, where goest?

GLOUCESTER   Is it a beggarman?

OLD MAN Madman and beggar too.   30

GLOUCESTER He has some reason, else he could not beg.
    I'th'last night's storm I such a fellow saw,
    Which made me think a man a worm. My son
    Came then into my mind, and yet my mind
    Was then scarce friends with him. I have heard more
        since.   35
    As flies to wanton boys are we to th'gods;
    They kill us for their sport.

EDGAR [*Aside*]   How should this be?
    Bad is the trade that must play fool to sorrow,
    Ang'ring itself and others. – Bless thee, master.

GLOUCESTER Is that the naked fellow?

OLD MAN   Ay, my lord.   40

GLOUCESTER Get thee away. If for my sake
    Thou wilt o'ertake us hence a mile or twain
    I'th'way toward Dover, do it for ancient love,
    And bring some covering for this naked soul,
    Which I'll entreat to lead me.   45

OLD MAN Alack, sir, he is mad.

GLOUCESTER 'Tis the time's plague when madmen lead the
    blind.
    Do as I bid thee; or rather do thy pleasure.
    Above the rest, be gone.

OLD MAN I'll bring him the best 'parel that I have,   50
    Come on't what will.   *Exit*

GLOUCESTER   Sirrah, naked fellow.

EDGAR Poor Tom's a-cold. [*Aside*] I cannot daub it further.

GLOUCESTER Come hither, fellow.

EDGAR [*Aside*] And yet I must. – Bless thy sweet eyes, they bleed.

GLOUCESTER Know'st thou the way to Dover?   55

Gloucester hopes for a more just society. Edgar, as Poor Tom, agrees to guide Gloucester to Dover. Oswald tells Gonerill that Albany welcomes the French invasion and criticises Gonerill's and Edmond's actions.

1 The naming of fiends

In the Quarto version of the play (see p. 240) Edgar adds, after line 58:

> Five fiends have been in poor Tom at once: of lust, as Obidicut; Hobbididence Prince of dumbness; Mahu, of stealing; Modo, of murder; Flibbertigibbet, of mopping and mowing, who since possesses chambermaids and waiting-women. So, bless thee, master!

How do you think these lines should be spoken: comically, or threateningly, or . . .? Think about why Edgar might have been given these devil-words to speak at this point and provide reasons whether or not you would include the Quarto lines in your own production.

2 Was Regan's observation right? (in small groups)

Gloucester's blinding has brought him new insight into human problems. His traumatic experience has produced a sharp awareness of issues that he seemed happy to ignore before. He calls on the gods to punish people whose rich lifestyle 'blinds' them to the needs of others. Wealth should be redistributed fairly 'So distribution should undo excess'. Gloucester of course was until recently a wealthy aristocrat.

Gloucester's journey towards self-knowledge is beginning to shadow Lear's. Regan had observed earlier of Lear that headstrong men must learn through bitter experience ('to wilful men / The injuries that they themselves procure / Must be their schoolmasters.' Act 2 Scene 4, lines 295–7).

Talk together about how perceptive you think Regan's assessment of 'headstrong men' is and how closely aligned Gloucester's 'bitter experience' is to Lear's.

---

goodman householder, yeoman
humbled to all strokes made victim of all hardships
superfluous and lust-dieted man excessively rich and lustful man
slaves your ordinance makes the law serve his own desires

confinèd deep narrow sea (the Straits of Dover)
sot fool
turned the wrong side out got things the wrong way round (by mistaking loyalty for treachery)

EDGAR Both stile and gate, horseway and footpath. Poor Tom hath
    been scared out of his good wits. Bless thee, goodman's son,
    from the foul fiend.

GLOUCESTER Here, take this purse, thou whom the heavens'
              plagues
    Have humbled to all strokes. That I am wretched   60
    Makes thee the happier. Heavens deal so still.
    Let the superfluous and lust-dieted man
    That slaves your ordinance, that will not see
    Because he does not feel, feel your power quickly.
    So distribution should undo excess,   65
    And each man have enough. Dost thou know Dover?

EDGAR Ay, master.

GLOUCESTER There is a cliff whose high and bending head
    Looks fearfully in the confinèd deep.
    Bring me but to the very brim of it,   70
    And I'll repair the misery thou dost bear
    With something rich about me. From that place
    I shall no leading need.

EDGAR   Give me thy arm.
    Poor Tom shall lead thee.

                              Exeunt

Act 4   Scene 2
A room in the castle of Gonerill and Albany

Enter GONERILL with EDMOND and OSWALD, severally

GONERILL Welcome, my lord. I marvel our mild husband
    Not met us on the way. – Now, where's your master?

OSWALD Madam, within; but never man so changed.
    I told him of the army that was landed;
    He smiled at it. I told him you were coming;   5
    His answer was, 'The worse'. Of Gloucester's treachery,
    And of the loyal service of his son
    When I informed him, then he called me sot,
    And told me I had turned the wrong side out.
    What most he should dislike seems pleasant to him;   10
    What like, offensive.

Gonerill criticises Albany's cowardice and bids Edmond an affectionate farewell. She reflects on how much she prefers Edmond to her husband. Albany and Gonerill exchange vicious insults.

Gonerill with Edmond in Act 4 Scene 2. Which line from the opposite page might she be speaking here?

1 A formidable woman (in pairs)

Take parts as Gonerill and Edmond and experiment with reading lines 12–29 to bring out Gonerill's contempt for her husband and her admiration for the new Earl of Gloucester. Then:

- discuss the way Gonerill uses sexually suggestive language and behaviour and what this adds to her characterisation
- suggest reasons why Shakespeare might have chosen to put Gonerill and Albany's relationship under the spotlight at this stage in the play.

He'll not feel . . . answer he will ignore insults which demand a response
May prove effects may be fulfilled
musters gathering of soldiers
conduct his powers escort his forces
distaff stick for spinning wool

My fool usurps my body my husband undeservingly possesses me
Who hast not . . . suffering you cannot see the difference between honour and disgrace
Proper natural

GONERILL [*To Edmond*] Then shall you go no further.
 It is the cowish terror of his spirit
 That dares not undertake. He'll not feel wrongs
 Which tie him to an answer. Our wishes on the way   15
 May prove effects. Back, Edmond, to my brother.
 Hasten his musters and conduct his powers.
 I must change names at home and give the distaff
 Into my husband's hands. This trusty servant
 Shall pass between us. Ere long you are like to hear   20
 (If you dare venture in your own behalf)
 A mistress's command. Wear this; spare speech.
 Decline your head. This kiss, if it durst speak,
 Would stretch thy spirits up into the air.
 Conceive, and fare thee well.   25
EDMOND Yours in the ranks of death.
GONERILL   My most dear Gloucester.
             Exit [*Edmond*]
 Oh, the difference of man and man.
 To thee a woman's services are due;
 My fool usurps my body.
OSWALD Madam, here comes my lord.   [*Exit*] 30

      Enter ALBANY

GONERILL I have been worth the whistle.
ALBANY   O Gonerill,
 You are not worth the dust which the rude wind
 Blows in your face.
GONERILL   Milk-livered man,
 That bear'st a cheek for blows, a head for wrongs;
 Who hast not in thy brows an eye discerning   35
 Thine honour from thy suffering –
ALBANY   See thyself, devil:
 Proper deformity shows not in the fiend
 So horrid as in woman.
GONERILL   O vain fool!

A messenger brings news of Cornwall's death and of Gloucester's blinding. Gonerill fears Regan as a rival who could destroy her plans for a life with Edmond. Albany vows to avenge Gloucester's blinding.

1 Married to a woman or a monster? (in pairs)

Gonerill clearly despises her 'Milk-livered' husband (line 33), but exactly how does Albany regard *her*? Is he afraid of her, fascinated, disgusted, horrified? Use the following activities to explore how you think the duke could be played in Act 4 Scene 2.

- Look back through Act 1 Scene 4, the only other scene so far where Albany features significantly. Discuss together the initial impression he might make on the audience and the relationship he appears to have with his wife.
- Read all of Act 4 Scene 2 and the additional lines to this scene in the Quarto version of the play (see p. 241). In what ways do the extra Quarto lines alter your perception of Albany, Gonerill and the relationship between them? Focus in particular on Albany's accusations/insults and Gonerill's responses.
- Take roles as a director and an actor cast to play Albany. The director does not wish to include the extra Quarto lines but the actor playing Albany does. Try to persuade your partner that your preference has more merit.

2 Proof of the existence of the gods?

Albany reacts to the news of Cornwall's death by claiming it as proof of the existence of divine 'justicers' who punish crime in the human world. Do you see Cornwall's death as the result of action by the gods or as the result of natural human goodness on the part of the servant who attacked him, or would you suggest other reasons?

---

bred brought up
thrilled with remorse driven by pity
plucked him after dragged him
 following (to death)
justicers judges
nether earthly

my Gloucester Edmond
all the building . . . hateful life
 demolish all my dreams of Edmond
 and condemn me to continued life with
 Albany
tart sour

Enter a MESSENGER

MESSENGER O my good lord, the Duke of Cornwall's dead,
　　　　　Slain by his servant going to put out   40
　　　　　The other eye of Gloucester.
ALBANY　　　　　　　　　　　Gloucester's eyes?
MESSENGER A servant that he bred, thrilled with remorse,
　　　　　Opposed against the act, bending his sword
　　　　　To his great master; who, thereat enraged,
　　　　　Flew on him and amongst them felled him dead,   45
　　　　　But not without that harmful stroke which since
　　　　　Hath plucked him after.
ALBANY　　　　　　　　　　This shows you are above,
　　　　　You justicers, that these our nether crimes
　　　　　So speedily can venge. But O, poor Gloucester!
　　　　　Lost he his other eye?
MESSENGER　　　　　　　Both, both, my lord.   50
　　　　　This letter, madam, craves a speedy answer:
　　　　　'Tis from your sister.
GONERILL [*Aside*]　　　　　One way I like this well;
　　　　　But being widow, and my Gloucester with her,
　　　　　May all the building in my fancy pluck
　　　　　Upon my hateful life. Another way   55
　　　　　The news is not so tart. – I'll read, and answer.   *Exit*
ALBANY Where was his son when they did take his eyes?
MESSENGER Come with my lady hither.
ALBANY　　　　　　　　　　　He is not here.
MESSENGER No, my good lord; I met him back again.
ALBANY Knows he the wickedness?   60
MESSENGER Ay, my good lord; 'twas he informed against him
　　　　　And quit the house on purpose that their punishment
　　　　　Might have the freer course.
ALBANY　　　　　　　　　　Gloucester, I live
　　　　　To thank thee for the love thou showed'st the king,
　　　　　And to revenge thine eyes. – Come hither, friend.   65
　　　　　Tell me what more thou know'st.
　　　　　　　　　　　　　　　　　　　Exeunt

Cordelia grieves for Lear's madness. She sends soldiers to search for Lear, who has wandered off wearing a crown of wild flowers. The Gentleman says Lear's sanity can be restored by rest.

---

1 Keeping Cordelia in mind

The Quarto includes an extra scene after the end of Act 4 Scene 2 (see p. 242). Cordelia does not appear in it, but a conversation between Kent and a Gentleman reminds the audience of Cordelia's sensitive and compassionate nature. The Gentleman speaks of her 'Patience and sorrow', her smiles and tears are like 'Sunshine and rain', she shakes 'holy water from her heavenly eyes'.

Read quickly through the additional Quarto scene, jotting down any other key words that you feel define Cordelia's nature, especially in the ways she responds to news of what has happened to her father. Then look back to the way in which Gonerill was presented in Act 4 Scene 2. How many contrasts can you find?

2 Cordelia the warrior?

Act 4 Scene 3 begins with the dramatic reappearance of Cordelia at the head of an invading French army. Like her sisters, she has assumed a 'masculine' role as conflict approaches. But, unlike her sisters, she is also strongly associated with natural goodness and healing: 'blest', 'virtues', 'Spring', 'tears', 'aidant and remediate' (helpful and remedial).

Directors have to choose how she will be dressed for this scene. Some productions use simple costume to bring out her humility; others stress her regality as queen of France; yet more costume her as a woman prepared for military combat. What decision would you make and why?

---

colours military flags
rank fumitor . . . Darnel various weeds growing in ploughed land
century hundred soldiers
What . . . wisdom what can knowledge achieve
bereavèd impaired, lost

simples operative effective medicinal herbs
unpublished virtues secret strengths (herbs)
wants the means to lead it lacks reason to control his rage

Act 4 Scene 3
The French camp near Dover

Enter with drum and colours, CORDELIA, GENTLEMAN,
and Soldiers

CORDELIA Alack, 'tis he: why, he was met even now,
　　　　As mad as the vexed sea, singing aloud,
　　　　Crowned with rank fumitor and furrow-weeds,
　　　　With burdocks, hemlock, nettles, cuckoo-flowers,
　　　　Darnel, and all the idle weeds that grow　　　　　　5
　　　　In our sustaining corn. A century send forth.
　　　　Search every acre in the high-grown field,
　　　　And bring him to our eye.
　　　　　　　　　　　　　　　　　　[*Exit an Officer*]
　　　　　　　　　　　　What can man's wisdom
　　　　In the restoring his bereavèd sense?
　　　　He that helps him take all my outward worth.　　　10
GENTLEMAN There is means, madam.
　　　　Our foster-nurse of nature is repose,
　　　　The which he lacks. That to provoke in him
　　　　Are many simples operative, whose power
　　　　Will close the eye of anguish.
CORDELIA　　　　　　　　　　All blest secrets,　　　　15
　　　　All you unpublished virtues of the earth,
　　　　Spring with my tears; be aidant and remediate
　　　　In the good man's distress. – Seek, seek for him,
　　　　Lest his ungoverned rage dissolve the life
　　　　That wants the means to lead it.

Enter MESSENGER

MESSENGER　　　　　　　　　　News, madam.　　　　20
　　　　The British powers are marching hitherward.

Cordelia declares that love, not political ambition, makes her fight. In Scene 4 Regan questions Oswald closely, and says that Edmond has gone in search of Gloucester in order to kill him.

---

1 Cordelia's motivation (in small groups)

At the end of Scene 4 Cordelia claims that she is leading an invading French army to Britain, not out of a desire for power but in order to rescue and support her father. Her lines 23–4 echo words spoken by Jesus in the New Testament (Luke 2:49). This has led some people to see her as a Christ-like figure, someone capable of great self-sacrifice in order to redeem and to relieve suffering.

Take turns to read lines 22–9. Explore different readings in which you try to create a range of possible states of mind for Cordelia. Is she, for example, humble, determined, nervous, tearful or . . .?

2 A consistent picture?

Quickly remind yourself of what happens to Cordelia in Act 1 Scene 1. Make brief notes on her behaviour towards her father in this scene up to the point of her banishment. Then look at how she is presented in Act 4 Scene 3. Is Cordelia's characterisation consistent between these two points in the play, or is Shakespeare now showing a different side to her?

3 Albany's dilemma

In Scene 4 Cordelia brings a French army to Britain to help her father. Her action has put Albany in a difficult situation, torn between loyalty to his king and the wish to defend Britain from a foreign invasion. Such divided loyalties may account for Albany's reluctance (his 'much ado', line 4) to go to war.

Draw a sketch of Albany trying to decide on his course of action. Include speech bubbles all around your Albany figure, each containing a few words about one of the many different pressures and dilemmas which are influencing him as he decides what to do (e.g. his domestic difficulties, the death of his co-general Cornwall).

---

importuned persistent, beseeching
No blown . . . incite we don't fight because of puffed-up ambition
brother's powers Albany's army
import signify, mean

posted hence ridden away speedily
ignorance foolishness
'nighted benighted (ignorant) or blinded (plunged into darkness)
descry establish, find out

CORDELIA 'Tis known before. Our preparation stands
    In expectation of them. – O dear father,
    It is thy business that I go about:
    Therefore great France   25
    My mourning and importuned tears hath pitied.
    No blown ambition doth our arms incite,
    But love, dear love, and our aged father's right.
    Soon may I hear and see him.

                   Exeunt

Act 4 Scene 4
A room in Gloucester's castle

Enter REGAN *and* OSWALD

REGAN But are my brother's powers set forth?
OSWALD Ay, madam.
REGAN Himself in person there?
OSWALD Madam, with much ado.
    Your sister is the better soldier.   5
REGAN Lord Edmond spake not with your lord at home?
OSWALD No, madam.
REGAN What might import my sister's letter to him?
OSWALD I know not, lady.
REGAN Faith, he is posted hence on serious matter.   10
    It was great ignorance, Gloucester's eyes being out,
    To let him live. Where he arrives he moves
    All hearts against us. Edmond, I think, is gone,
    In pity of his misery, to dispatch
    His 'nighted life, moreover to descry   15
    The strength o'th'enemy.
OSWALD I must needs after him, madam, with my letter.
REGAN Our troops set forth tomorrow. Stay with us.
    The ways are dangerous.
OSWALD   I may not, madam.
    My lady charged my duty in this business.   20

Regan urges Oswald to give her Gonerill's letter, and claims that she should be Edmond's partner. She offers to reward anyone who kills Gloucester. Edgar deceives Gloucester into believing that they are climbing a slope.

---

1 More evil intent (in pairs)

Scene 4 contains only forty-two lines (32 spoken by Regan) but it is full of eddies and currents of intrigue, jealousy, betrayal and self-interest.

Take parts and read the scene through, then change parts for a second reading. Afterwards talk together about the ways in which both Regan and Oswald are trying to manipulate each other.

Now rehearse a presentation of the whole scene ready to be performed to others in your group. Consider in particular the following points:

- How the actors could play lines 21–4 where Regan appears to keep changing her mind.
- Whether or not Regan opens and reads the letter (lines 24–5).
- Whether 'note' in line 31 refers to a letter or means 'note this carefully'.
- What it is that Oswald 'may gather more' of (line 34).
- What Regan gives Oswald at line 35.

When you come to act out the scene make clear your decisions on each of the above issues and try to create as many eddies of intrigue, jealousy, betrayal and self-interest as you can.

2 'Look how we labour'

In lines 1–6 of Scene 5 Edgar tries to convince his father that they are climbing a hill. What advice would you give the actor playing Edgar? Bear in mind that his father's blindness means that Edgar does not have to prevent his real feelings from showing.

---

oeilliads significant glances
of her bosom in her confidence
call her wisdom to her to act with
  good sense

Preferment promotion
cuts him off kills him

REGAN Why should she write to Edmond? Might not you
        Transport her purposes by word? Belike –
        Some things – I know not what. I'll love thee much:
        Let me unseal the letter.
OSWALD   Madam, I had rather –
REGAN I know your lady does not love her husband.   25
        I am sure of that; and at her late being here
        She gave strange oeilliads and most speaking looks
        To noble Edmond. I know you are of her bosom.
OSWALD I, madam?
REGAN I speak in understanding. Y'are, I know't.   30
        Therefore I do advise you take this note:
        My lord is dead; Edmond and I have talked;
        And more convenient is he for my hand
        Than for your lady's. You may gather more.
        If you do find him, pray you give him this;   35
        And when your mistress hears thus much from you,
        I pray desire her call her wisdom to her.
        So, fare you well.
        If you do chance to hear of that blind traitor,
        Preferment falls on him that cuts him off.   40
OSWALD Would I could meet him, madam, I should show
        What party I do follow.
REGAN   Fare thee well.   *Exeunt*

Act 4 Scene 5
The countryside near Dover

Enter GLOUCESTER and EDGAR (dressed like a peasant)

GLOUCESTER When shall I come to th'top of that same hill?
EDGAR You do climb up it now. Look how we labour.
GLOUCESTER Methinks the ground is even.
EDGAR   Horrible steep.
        Hark, do you hear the sea?
GLOUCESTER   No, truly.
EDGAR Why, then your other senses grow imperfect   5
        By your eyes' anguish.

Edgar describes the alarming view which he claims to see. Gloucester asks to be set at the very edge of the cliff. Edgar says that he is misleading his father in order to save him from despair.

---

1 Creating an imaginary view (in pairs)

a Edgar has deceived his father into believing they have climbed the steep slope leading to the cliff edge at Dover. To convince him they are at the very edge, he describes the view from the clifftop. Practise speaking lines 11–24 as persuasively as possible.

b Edgar describes the noise of the waves in lines 20–1 ('The murmuring surge . . . chafes'). His words suggest the sound of the sea. Using words which echo their meaning in their sound is called 'onomatopoeia'. Try saying the lines aloud to express how the tide shifts pebbles at the sea's edge.

2 Why does Edgar lie?

Gloucester ironically suffers deception at the hands of both his sons. But of course where Edmond uses deception for evil purposes, Edgar believes his motives are benign.

When Edgar first began to deceive his blinded father he said, 'Bad is the trade that must play fool to sorrow' (Act 4 Scene 1, line 38), apparently regretting the unpleasant necessity of playing the fool to someone so vulnerable and distressed.

Now, in Act 4 Scene 5, Edgar tells an elaborate sequence of lies about what he can see and, in lines 33–4, states his motive for misleading his father, perhaps to reassure the audience as well as himself.

a How do you respond to Edgar's behaviour in this scene?

b Make a list of all the deceptions practised on Gloucester by both his sons.

---

phrase and matter style and content
choughs type of crow (pronounced 'chuffs')
samphire an edible plant
barque ship
cock small boat towed behind a larger one

For all beneath the moon for the whole world
Prosper increase (fairies were believed to increase hidden treasure)

GLOUCESTER   So may it be indeed.
　　　　Methinks thy voice is altered, and thou speak'st
　　　　In better phrase and matter than thou didst.
EDGAR　Y'are much deceived. In nothing am I changed
　　　　But in my garments.
GLOUCESTER   Methinks y'are better spoken.　　10
EDGAR　Come on, sir, here's the place. Stand still. How fearful
　　　　And dizzy 'tis to cast one's eyes so low.
　　　　The crows and choughs that wing the midway air
　　　　Show scarce so gross as beetles. Half-way down
　　　　Hangs one that gathers samphire, dreadful trade!　　15
　　　　Methinks he seems no bigger than his head.
　　　　The fishermen that walk upon the beach
　　　　Appear like mice, and yon tall anchoring barque
　　　　Diminished to her cock; her cock, a buoy
　　　　Almost too small for sight. The murmuring surge,　　20
　　　　That on th'unnumbered idle pebble chafes,
　　　　Cannot be heard so high. I'll look no more,
　　　　Lest my brain turn and the deficient sight
　　　　Topple down headlong.
GLOUCESTER   Set me where you stand.
EDGAR　Give me your hand. You are now within a foot　　25
　　　　Of th'extreme verge. For all beneath the moon
　　　　Would I not leap upright.
GLOUCESTER   Let go my hand.
　　　　Here, friend, 's another purse: in it, a jewel
　　　　Well worth a poor man's taking. Fairies and gods
　　　　Prosper it with thee. Go thou further off.　　30
　　　　Bid me farewell, and let me hear thee going.
EDGAR　Now fare ye well, good sir.
GLOUCESTER   With all my heart.
EDGAR　[Aside] Why I do trifle thus with his despair
　　　　Is done to cure it.

Gloucester tells the gods he intends to kill himself. He throws himself forward. Edgar pretends to be someone standing on the beach who saw him fall and land in safety. Gloucester is confused and distressed.

---

1 Defiance, patience or despair? (in pairs)

Gloucester is determined to kill himself. In Shakespeare's time Christians saw suicide as a terrible, unforgivable sin against God. Those who committed suicide were denied Christian burial. Gloucester tells the gods that, even if he continued to endure life ('bear it longer') and did not challenge the destiny the gods have decreed for him ('great opposeless wills'), his exhausted body would die like a burnt-out candle.

Practise speaking Gloucester's lines 34–40 in different ways. Choose a version that you think would be appropriate on stage; for example, despairingly (emphasising his helplessness), defiantly (emphasising his feeling of being in control), patiently (emphasising his humility).

2 Gloucester's 'leap'

Gloucester, believing that he is at the cliff's edge, throws himself forward, expecting to die. It can be a stunning moment of theatre, enhanced in many modern productions by a flat, bare stage, giving full weight to the suggestive power of Shakespeare's language to sustain the illusion (see colour section, p. x, top). Nineteenth-century productions used backdrops to create the illusion of being near the edge of a real cliff.

Describe how you would stage this. What effects would you seek?

3 Edgar – manipulator or rescuer?

Many people find it painful to watch this scene because Gloucester's suffering is so intense and because he is being so oddly manipulated by his son. Advise the actor playing Edgar how he could deliver each speech in lines 41–80 so as to minimise the audience's unease.

---

opposeless irresistible
snuff smouldering candle-end (old age)
conceit imagination
pass die
aught but gossamer anything but fine silk

shivered shattered
perpendicularly straight down
bourn boundary (Dover cliff)
shrill-gorged shrill-throated
beguile . . . his proud will cheat the fury of a dictator and disobey his wishes (by suicide)

GLOUCESTER [*Kneels*]   O you mighty gods!
    This world I do renounce, and in your sights   35
    Shake patiently my great affliction off.
    If I could bear it longer and not fall
    To quarrel with your great opposeless wills,
    My snuff and loathèd part of nature should
    Burn itself out. If Edgar live, O bless him.   40
    Now, fellow, fare thee well.
EDGAR   Gone, sir; farewell.
    [*Gloucester throws himself forward and falls*]
    [*Aside*] And yet I know not how conceit may rob
    The treasury of life, when life itself
    Yields to the theft. Had he been where he thought,
    By this had thought been past. – Alive or dead?   45
    Ho, you sir, friend! Hear you, sir? Speak!
    [*Aside*] Thus might he pass indeed. Yet he revives. –
    What are you, sir?
GLOUCESTER   Away, and let me die.
EDGAR Hadst thou been aught but gossamer, feathers, air,
    So many fathom down precipitating,   50
    Thou'dst shivered like an egg. But thou dost breathe,
    Hast heavy substance, bleed'st not, speak'st, art sound.
    Ten masts at each make not the altitude
    Which thou hast perpendicularly fell.
    Thy life's a miracle. Speak yet again.   55
GLOUCESTER But have I fall'n or no?
EDGAR From the dread summit of this chalky bourn.
    Look up a-height: the shrill-gorged lark so far
    Cannot be seen or heard; do but look up.
GLOUCESTER Alack, I have no eyes.   60
    Is wretchedness deprived that benefit
    To end itself by death? 'Twas yet some comfort
    When misery could beguile the tyrant's rage
    And frustrate his proud will.
EDGAR   Give me your arm.
    Up; so. How is't? Feel you your legs? You stand.   65
GLOUCESTER Too well, too well.

Gloucester determines to endure his suffering. Edgar urges him to feel free of guilt. Lear's disordered talk is of archers, mice and challenges. He acknowledges that flatterers misled him.

---

1 *Enter* Lear, [*mad*]

The Folio edition just has the stage direction 'Enter Lear'. It is the Quarto version that describes Lear as 'mad' when he enters at line 80. Later editors have added a reference to his being dressed 'fantastically' and many productions of the play have used the wild flowers and weeds mentioned by Cordelia in Scene 3 as a key element of his costume.

How would Lear appear in your version of the play? What visual impression would you seek to create? Present your ideas as a display for others to look at.

2 Sense in madness (in pairs)

It is not only Lear's costume and behaviour that signal his madness; he also speaks in a jumbled, volatile, distracted manner, his words seeming to gush and tumble out.

Yet it is possible to detect strands of sense and references to key elements of the king's past experience. For example, in lines 85–90, Lear talks of money being paid to enlisted troops ('There's your press-money'), orders an archer to stretch his bow to its full extent ('Draw me a clothier's yard'), imagines the arrow hitting the centre of the target ('i'th'clout, i'th'clout!') and imitates its whistling noise ('Hewgh!').

a Take turns to read Lear's three speeches (83–101). As one reads, the other listens closely for connections to the storm, to the issues of power, of flattery, of lies and deception and . . . After both readings, share and compare the ideas you have spotted.

b Why do you think Shakespeare chose to have Lear speak in prose at this point? (And why should Lear revert to verse at line 103?)

---

whelked twisted
make them . . . impossibilities gain reverence by performing miracles
The safer . . . master thus a sane mind would never allow its owner to dress like this

side-piercing heart-breaking
marjoram a herb (with healing properties)
no good divinity bad theology
ague-proof immune to fevers

EDGAR   This is above all strangeness.
         Upon the crown o'th'cliff what thing was that
         Which parted from you?
GLOUCESTER   A poor unfortunate beggar.
EDGAR As I stood here below, methought his eyes
         Were two full moons. He had a thousand noses,   70
         Horns whelked and waved like the enragèd sea.
         It was some fiend. Therefore, thou happy father,
         Think that the clearest gods, who make them honours
         Of men's impossibilities, have preserved thee.
GLOUCESTER I do remember now. Henceforth I'll bear   75
         Affliction till it do cry out itself
         'Enough, enough', and die. That thing you speak of,
         I took it for a man. Often 'twould say
         'The fiend, the fiend!' He led me to that place.
EDGAR Bear free and patient thoughts.

                     Enter LEAR, [*mad*]

                              But who comes here?   80
         The safer sense will ne'er accommodate
         His master thus.
LEAR No, they cannot touch me for crying. I am the king himself.
EDGAR O thou side-piercing sight!
LEAR Nature's above art in that respect. There's your press-   85
         money. That fellow handles his bow like a crow-keeper. Draw
         me a clothier's yard. Look, look, a mouse! Peace, peace, this
         piece of toasted cheese will do't. There's my gauntlet. I'll prove
         it on a giant. Bring up the brown bills. O well flown bird:
         i'th'clout, i'th'clout! Hewgh! Give the word.   90
EDGAR Sweet marjoram.
LEAR Pass.
GLOUCESTER I know that voice.
LEAR Ha! Gonerill with a white beard? They flattered me like a
         dog and told me I had the white hairs in my beard ere the black 95
         ones were there. To say 'ay' and 'no' to everything that I said
         'ay' and 'no' to was no good divinity. When the rain came to
         wet me once and the wind to make me chatter, when the
         thunder would not peace at my bidding, there I found 'em,
         there I smelt 'em out. Go to, they are not men o'their words.   100
         They told me I was everything; 'tis a lie, I am not ague-proof.

Gloucester recognises the king's voice. Lear embarks on a frenzied condemnation of women's sexuality. Gloucester asks whether Lear recognises him. The king seems to mock Gloucester's empty eye sockets.

1 The language of sexual disgust (in small groups)

Lear's language reflects the disturbance and distress of his mind. He shows an obsessive interest in sex, and an intense fear and loathing of women's sexual desires. He sees evidence of sexuality all around him: 'lecher' = copulate, 'luxury' = lust, 'fitchew' = a polecat (a slang term for a prostitute), 'soilèd' = oversexed, 'centaurs' = legendary creatures (half horse, half human). Lear seems fixated by the way in which the seeming purity of a woman can mask her dark desire and lust.

Try different ways of speaking lines 103–27 to bring out Lear's initial haughtiness followed by his deep sexual loathing. Afterwards talk together about each of the following:

- What does Lear's sexual disgust suggest about his character?
- How would Lear's daughters react if they heard his words?
- How might the listening Gloucester respond to what he hears?
- What challenges do you think this speech poses for an actor?

2 Gloucester – more humiliation?

Gloucester chooses to show Lear the courtesy due to a king by wanting to kiss his hand. His love and respect for the king also lead him to comment on Lear's demise in cataclysmic terms: 'This great world / Shall so wear out to naught.' Yet Lear responds by (unintentionally?) reminding Gloucester of his blindness, referring at least four times to eyes and seeing in lines 132–4.

Edgar has silently watched the excruciating exposure of his father to the king's gaze since line 84. Write his 'stream of consciousness' thoughts, culminating in the words of his Aside at lines 136–7.

---

cause offence
pell-mell promiscuously, riotously
face between . . . snow face predicts that she will be sexually frigid ('forks' = legs)
minces pretends to prefer
girdle waist

inherit possess
civet perfume
Shall so wear out to naught will similarly decay to nothing
squiny squint
challenge summons to a duel
take believe

GLOUCESTER The trick of that voice I do well remember.
      Is't not the king?
LEAR   Ay, every inch a king.
      When I do stare, see how the subject quakes.
      I pardon that man's life. What was thy cause?   105
      Adultery?
      Thou shalt not die. Die for adultery? No,
      The wren goes to't, and the small gilded fly
      Does lecher in my sight.
      Let copulation thrive: for Gloucester's bastard son   110
      Was kinder to his father than my daughters
      Got 'tween the lawful sheets.
      To't, luxury, pell-mell, for I lack soldiers.
      Behold yon simp'ring dame,
      Whose face between her forks presages snow,   115
      That minces virtue, and does shake the head
      To hear of pleasure's name.
      The fitchew nor the soilèd horse goes to't
      With a more riotous appetite.
      Down from the waist they're centaurs,   120
      Though women all above.
      But to the girdle do the gods inherit;
      Beneath is all the fiend's.
There's hell, there's darkness, there is the sulphurous pit,
burning, scalding, stench, consumption. Fie, fie, fie; pah, pah!   125
Give me an ounce of civet, good apothecary, sweeten my
imagination: there's money for thee.
GLOUCESTER O, let me kiss that hand!
LEAR Let me wipe it first; it smells of mortality.
GLOUCESTER O ruined piece of nature! This great world   130
      Shall so wear out to naught. Dost thou know me?
LEAR I remember thine eyes well enough. Dost thou squiny at me?
      No, do thy worst, blind Cupid, I'll not love.
      Read thou this challenge; mark but the penning of it.
GLOUCESTER Were all thy letters suns, I could not see.   135
EDGAR [*Aside*] I would not take this from report; it is,
      And my heart breaks at it.

Lear condemns the hypocritical and distorted justice exercised by those with power but without morality. He complains that the rich can escape punishment while the poor cannot. Lear recognises Gloucester.

1 Seeing without eyes (in pairs)

Lear seems to taunt Gloucester further with his blindness, ordering him to read and using the words 'eyes', 'see' and 'look' repeatedly in lines 138–48. In response to Lear's 'you see how this world goes', Gloucester replies 'I see it feelingly.' He both 'sees' the world by touch and, because of his suffering, understands its injustices more fully than before. He has learned by bitter experience.

Talk together about whether or not you believe that it is only through personal suffering that someone can really understand the unhappiness of others.

2 The great image of authority

Lear says that the image of a dog chasing off a beggar is symbolic of authority: anyone will be obeyed if they hold a position of power, irrespective of their personal worth or merit. How far do you agree with Lear's claim?

3 Double standards (in small groups)

Lear condemns hypocrisy and gives examples of hypocritical behaviour: a beadle whipping a prostitute while wishing he were one of her clients; a powerful money-lender having a minor cheat executed for lesser crimes than his own; and the fact that the sinful rich are protected from justice by their wealth, while the sinful poor are vulnerable.

Read lines 150–65 several times, changing the speaker at the end of each sentence. Experiment with different ways of speaking to reflect Lear's possible changing mood – for example anger, disbelief, resignation, bitterness. Then mark a photocopy of the speech with your thoughts about when and how Lear's mood changes. Display your version for others to look at.

case of eyes empty eye sockets	**pygmy's straw** tiny, weak weapon
rails upon criticises	**I'll able 'em** I'll support them
handy-dandy make a guess	**scurvy** vile, scheming
beadle parish officer	**matter and impertinency** sense and
usurer money-lender	nonsense
cozener cheat	**wawl** wail

LEAR Read.

GLOUCESTER What – with the case of eyes?

LEAR O ho, are you there with me? No eyes in your head, nor no   140
money in your purse? Your eyes are in a heavy case, your purse
in a light; yet you see how this world goes.

GLOUCESTER I see it feelingly.

LEAR What, art mad? A man may see how this world goes with no
eyes; look with thine ears. See how yon justice rails upon yon   145
simple thief. Hark in thine ear: change places, and handy-
dandy, which is the justice, which is the thief? Thou hast seen
a farmer's dog bark at a beggar?

GLOUCESTER Ay, sir.

LEAR And the creature run from the cur? There thou mightst   150
behold the great image of authority. A dog's obeyed in office.
    Thou rascal beadle, hold thy bloody hand.
    Why dost thou lash that whore? Strip thy own back.
    Thou hotly lusts to use her in that kind
    For which thou whip'st her. The usurer hangs the coz-
       ener.   155
    Through tattered clothes great vices do appear:
    Robes and furred gowns hide all. Plate sin with gold,
    And the strong lance of justice hurtless breaks;
    Arm it in rags, a pygmy's straw does pierce it.
    None does offend, none, I say none. I'll able 'em.   160
    Take that of me, my friend, who have the power
    To seal th'accuser's lips. Get thee glass eyes,
    And, like a scurvy politician, seem
    To see the things thou dost not. Now, now, now, now.
    Pull off my boots. Harder, harder! So.   165

EDGAR [Aside] O matter and impertinency mixed,
    Reason in madness.

LEAR If thou wilt weep my fortunes, take my eyes.
    I know thee well enough; thy name is Gloucester.
    Thou must be patient. We came crying hither.   170
    Thou know'st the first time that we smell the air
    We wawl and cry. I will preach to thee: mark.

GLOUCESTER Alack, alack the day.

Lear imagines revenge on his enemies. He greets the search party enigmatically, then runs away. Edgar learns that the French and British armies will soon meet in battle.

1 Stage of fools (in pairs)

Lear's description of the world as 'this great stage of fools' (line 175) is echoed in other plays by Shakespeare, for example *As You Like It* (Act 2 Scene 7, line 139) and *Macbeth* (Act 5 Scene 5, lines 17–27). But here the image connects specifically with tears shed at the moment of birth.

Discuss together different possible reasons why Lear uses the image of the 'stage of fools' at this point in the play.

2 Catching the king (in small groups)

Lear quickly emerges from his brief reflective mood in lines 174–5 to imagine taking bloody revenge on his enemies (lines 175–9). He appears confused and unsettled by the arrival of Cordelia's men and, in a manner that has echoes of a children's pursuit game, he manages to elude his Attendants (lines 193–4).

Suggest what might be motivating him to run away, then work out how his escape might be staged. Remember that he is old and frail, and that the Attendants are probably very fit soldiers.

3 'A sight most pitiful' (in pairs)

Cordelia's Gentleman comments on the king's sorry state and how low he has sunk (lines 195–6).

Take turns to experiment with different readings of the Gentleman's lines to find the most moving expression of his personal grief at Lear's decline.

---

delicate stratagem cunning plan
put't in proof test it
natural fool born idiot
seconds servants
man of salt man of tears
Sa, sa, sa, sa! a hunting cry
nature human nature

twain Gonerill and Regan
sure and vulgar certain and widely known
the main descry . . . hourly thought we expect to see the main body of the army at any time

LEAR When we are born, we cry that we are come
    To this great stage of fools. This' a good block.   175
    It were a delicate stratagem to shoe
    A troop of horse with felt. I'll put't in proof,
    And when I have stol'n upon these son-in-laws,
    Then kill, kill, kill, kill, kill, kill!

Enter a GENTLEMAN [*with Attendants*]

GENTLEMAN O here he is: lay hand upon him. Sir,   180
    Your most dear daughter –
LEAR No rescue? What, a prisoner? I am even
    The natural fool of fortune. Use me well.
    You shall have ransom. Let me have surgeons,
    I am cut to th'brains.
GENTLEMAN   You shall have anything.   185
LEAR No seconds? All myself?
    Why, this would make a man a man of salt,
    To use his eyes for garden water-pots.
    I will die bravely, like a smug bridegroom. What?
    I will be jovial. Come, come, I am a king.   190
    Masters, know you that?
GENTLEMAN You are a royal one, and we obey you.
LEAR Then there's life in't. Come, an you get it, you shall get it by
    running. Sa, sa, sa, sa!
                Exit [*running, Attendants following*]
GENTLEMAN A sight most pitiful in the meanest wretch,   195
    Past speaking of in a king. Thou hast a daughter
    Who redeems nature from the general curse
    Which twain have brought her to.
EDGAR   Hail, gentle sir.
GENTLEMAN Sir, speed you: what's your will?
EDGAR Do you hear aught, sir, of a battle toward?   200
GENTLEMAN Most sure and vulgar: everyone hears that,
    Which can distinguish sound.
EDGAR   But, by your favour,
    How near's the other army?
GENTLEMAN Near and on speedy foot: the main descry
    Stands on the hourly thought.
EDGAR   I thank you, sir. That's all.   205

Gloucester says that he is no longer suicidal. Edgar, expressing pity, offers to lead him to shelter. Oswald plans to kill Gloucester for the reward. Edgar, speaking as a peasant, defies Oswald. They fight.

---

1 'known and feeling sorrows'

Gloucester has suffered and learned much. In lines 212–14 Edgar describes himself (in words which could apply equally to his father) as someone who through his sorrows has learned the importance of pity. Think back over the play so far and recall the different 'sorrows' that have 'educated' Edgar and his father.

2 'father' (in pairs)

Edgar calls Gloucester 'father', as he did earlier at line 72. It could simply mean 'old man', but Edgar may intend it quite literally, wanting to be recognised.

Try out different ways of saying lines 210–11. Should the actor playing Gloucester make line 211 suggest a hazy recognition of his son?

3 Oswald, brave killer of blind old men? (in groups of four)

Read Oswald's lines 217–21 and 222–5 around the group, changing speaker at each punctuation mark. Which words could be emphasised to highlight Oswald's gloating, threatening, confident behaviour?

4 A voice in disguise

Edgar adopts a country accent to challenge Oswald. You may find his words easier to understand if you speak them aloud ('Chill' = I will, 'gait' = way, 'chud' = I should, 'zwaggered' = boasted, 'che vor'ye' = I tell you, 'costard' = head, 'ballow' = staff, 'foins' = sword strokes).

Some think that Edgar's rural speech is intended to mock Oswald's courtly, swaggering style. What is your view on why Edgar should change his accent yet again?

---

special cause particular mission
art . . . sorrows teaching of painfully experienced sorrows
Am pregnant to good pity have learned to pity

biding safe place
To boot, and boot may also greatly profit you
Briefly thyself remember prepare yourself for death

GENTLEMAN Though that the queen on special cause is here,
  Her army is moved on.
EDGAR   I thank you, sir.

          Exit [*Gentleman*]

GLOUCESTER You ever gentle gods, take my breath from me.
  Let not my worser spirit tempt me again
  To die before you please.
EDGAR   Well pray you, father.   210
GLOUCESTER Now, good sir, what are you?
EDGAR A most poor man, made tame to fortune's blows,
  Who by the art of known and feeling sorrows
  Am pregnant to good pity. Give me your hand;
  I'll lead you to some biding.
GLOUCESTER   Hearty thanks;   215
  The bounty and the benison of heaven
  To boot, and boot.

     Enter OSWALD

OSWALD   A proclaimed prize! most happy!
  That eyeless head of thine was first framed flesh
  To raise my fortunes. Thou old, unhappy traitor,
  Briefly thyself remember: the sword is out 220
  That must destroy thee.
GLOUCESTER   Now let thy friendly hand
  Put strength enough to't.
OSWALD   Wherefore, bold peasant,
  Dar'st thou support a published traitor? Hence,
  Lest that th'infection of his fortune take
  Like hold on thee. Let go his arm.   225
EDGAR Chill not let go, zir, without vurther 'casion.
OSWALD Let go slave, or thou di'st.
EDGAR Good gentleman, go your gait, and let poor volk pass. And
  chud ha' been zwaggered out of my life, 'twould not ha' been
  zo long as 'tis by a vortnight. Nay, come not near th'old man. 230
  Keep out, che vor'ye, or I s' try whether your costard or my
  ballow be the harder; chill be plain with you.
OSWALD Out, dunghill!

     [*They fight*]

EDGAR Chill pick your teeth, zir: come, no matter vor your foins.

Oswald, mortally wounded, asks Edgar to deliver his letters to Edmond. Edgar reads a letter from Gonerill urging Edmond to kill Albany and marry her. Edgar plans to take the letter to Albany.

1 'O untimely death' (in pairs)

Oswald believes that he will easily overcome an untrained peasant. Edgar has to fight armed only with a staff. Oswald is often shown on stage to be startled by the ferocity and skill with which Edgar fights. In one production Edgar felled Oswald and then repeatedly pounded Oswald's eyes with his staff, as if avenging his father's blinding.

Plan how to stage their fight to show Oswald's overconfidence and Edgar's attitude to violence. How should Oswald speak his final lines, 235–9: with nobility or bitterness, or in some other way?

2 'a serviceable villain'

Edgar describes Oswald as a 'serviceable villain' (someone who fawns, flatters, makes themselves useful). What is your final assessment of him?

Look back at the part Oswald plays in Act 1 Scenes 3 and 4, Act 2 Scene 2, Act 4 Scene 4 and this scene. Is he merely a 'serviceable villain' or might an actor see more to him than that?

3 'To know our enemies' minds' (in pairs)

Edgar has no knowledge of Edmond's relationship with Gonerill until he reads the letter. To help you understand how Edgar explores the meanings and tone of the letter, stand back to back. One reads the letter in a matter-of-fact way. The other then reads it in a way that emphasises the suggestions of a conspiracy and an intimate relationship.

What does this exercise suggest to you about the way Edgar should react to the letter (lines 259–66)?

---

deathsman   executioner
Leave   by your leave, pardon
gentle wax   seal on letter
reciprocal   jointly sworn
for your labour   as a reward for your efforts / sexual exertion
indistinguished   indefinable, puzzling, limitless

rake up   bury
post unsanctified   unholy messenger
ungracious paper   wicked letter
strike   blast
death-practised duke   intended assassination victim (i.e. Duke of Albany)

OSWALD Slave, thou hast slain me. Villain, take my purse.   235
    If ever thou wilt thrive, bury my body,
    And give the letters which thou find'st about me
    To Edmond, Earl of Gloucester: seek him out
    Upon the English party. O untimely death, death.

                                                    [He dies]

EDGAR I know thee well – a serviceable villain,   240
    As duteous to the vices of thy mistress
    As badness would desire.
GLOUCESTER   What, is he dead?
EDGAR Sit you down, father; rest you.
    Let's see these pockets. The letters that he speaks of
    May be my friends. He's dead. I am only sorry   245
    He had no other deathsman. Let us see.
    Leave, gentle wax; and manners, blame us not:
    To know our enemies' minds, we rip their hearts;
    Their papers is more lawful.

                  Reads the letter

'Let our reciprocal vows be remembered. You have many   250
opportunities to cut him off. If your will want not, time and
place will be fruitfully offered. There is nothing done, if he
return the conqueror; then am I the prisoner, and his bed my
gaol, from the loathed warmth whereof, deliver me, and supply
the place for your labour.   255
                Your (wife, so I would say)
                    affectionate servant,
                            Gonerill.'

    O indistinguished space of woman's will,
    A plot upon her virtuous husband's life –   260
    And the exchange my brother! Here in the sands
    Thee I'll rake up, the post unsanctified
    Of murderous lechers; and in the mature time
    With this ungracious paper strike the sight
    Of the death-practised duke. For him 'tis well   265
    That of thy death and business I can tell.

                [Exit, dragging out the body]

Gloucester wishes he were insane and could forget his griefs. Edgar plans to take him to safety. Cordelia thanks Kent for his loyalty. She prays that the sleeping Lear will wake to sanity.

---

1 Cordelia and Kent reunited

Scene 6 begins in marked contrast to the death-by-combat drama of the previous one. Kent and Cordelia have not met since Act 1 Scene 1, and now they meet again, albeit under very different circumstances.

How would you stage the opening to signal a strong contrast with Scene 5?

2 'Lear's servant' and the queen

Despite Cordelia's pleading ('Be better suited'), Kent refuses to remove his disguise ('weeds' = clothes) because it would interfere with his 'made intent'.

What do you think Kent is planning? Suggest why he chooses to remain in disguise.

3 Appealing to the gods (in pairs)

Cordelia compares Lear's state of mind to an untuned and discordant musical instrument. Her image is full of hope, since it suggests that recovery is possible, just as an ill-tuned instrument can be tuned back into harmony. She prays for the healing of the 'breach' in Lear's nature, which will bring about his recovery.

- Prayer in almost all religions is accompanied by ritualised movements, such as kneeling, pressing hands together or bowing. Devise a suitable ritual for Cordelia (and others on stage) to use when she speaks lines 14–17.
- One of you reads her prayer while the other performs the invented ritual. Would you recommend a similar kind of ritual to accompany the words in a stage production? Give reasons for your decision.

---

ingenious acute
wrong imaginations madness
every measure all ways of measuring (Kent's goodness)
modest truth simple accuracy
Nor more, nor clipped neither exaggerated nor understated

shortens my made intent interferes with my plans
boon request, favour
breach wound
Th'untuned . . . O wind up restore to harmony his discordant emotions

GLOUCESTER The king is mad. How stiff is my vile sense,
    That I stand up and have ingenious feeling
    Of my huge sorrows! Better I were distract,
    So should my thoughts be severed from my griefs,   270
        Drum afar off
    And woes by wrong imaginations lose
    The knowledge of themselves.

                    [*Enter* EDGAR]

EDGAR   Give me your hand.
    Far off methinks I hear the beaten drum.
    Come, father, I'll bestow you with a friend.

                                        Exeunt

Act 4   Scene 6
The French camp near Dover

Enter CORDELIA, KENT (disguised) and GENTLEMAN

CORDELIA O thou good Kent, how shall I live and work
    To match thy goodness? My life will be too short,
    And every measure fail me.
KENT To be acknowledged, madam, is o'erpaid.
    All my reports go with the modest truth,   5
    Nor more, nor clipped, but so.
CORDELIA   Be better suited:
    These weeds are memories of those worser hours.
    I prithee, put them off.
KENT   Pardon, dear madam.
    Yet to be known shortens my made intent.
    My boon I make it that you know me not   10
    Till time and I think meet.
CORDELIA Then be't so, my good lord. – How does the king?
GENTLEMAN Madam, sleeps still.
CORDELIA O you kind gods,
    Cure this great breach in his abusèd nature;   15
    Th'untuned and jarring senses O wind up
    Of this child-changèd father!

The sleeping Lear is carried on stage, dressed in fresh clothes. Cordelia speaks of him with pity and love. On waking, Lear thinks that he may be dead and that Cordelia is an angel.

---

1 Lear reclothed?

As in the previous scene, Lear's entrance on to the stage signals a crucial dramatic moment. In that scene he was 'mad'. Now, as he is reunited with Cordelia, he is carried in asleep, and in virtually all productions he has been reclothed, the 'weeds' of madness replaced by a different costume. See colour section, page x (bottom) for how one production dressed him.

Look back at Activity 1 on page 154 and remind yourself how Lear might have been costumed for Act 4 Scene 5. Then draw a sketch showing your ideas for Lear's reappearance here. How is he dressed and how is he carried in?

2 A wheel of fire (in pairs)

Lines 42–5 are the recovering Lear's first words after his long ordeal of mental suffering. He speaks as if he were dead and suffering torment, using imagery which recalls Christian ideas about heaven, hell and the afterlife.

Experiment with different ways of speaking the lines. Which of your interpretations do you prefer and why?

3 Music and additional lines

In the Quarto version of the play (see p. 240), music is played as Cordelia speaks to Lear, and she has four additional lines after line 32:

> To stand against the deep dread-bolted thunder?
> In the most terrible and nimble stroke
> Of quick cross lightning? to watch, poor perdu,
> With this thin helm?

Imagine that you are directing the play. Decide, with reasons, whether or not you would include music and these lines in your production ('perdu' = lost one, 'thin helm' = uncovered head).

I'th'sway of your own will as you think best	**challenge** demand
arrayed formally clothed	**fain** pleased
temperance self-control, sanity	**hovel thee** stay in a dirty hut
white flakes white hairs	**far wide** wide of the mark (still mad)

GENTLEMAN So please your majesty,
　　　That we may wake the king? He hath slept long.
CORDELIA Be governed by your knowledge, and proceed　　20
　　　I'th'sway of your own will. Is he arrayed?

　　　Enter LEAR [*asleep*] *in a chair carried by servants*

GENTLEMAN Ay, madam: in the heaviness of sleep
　　　We put fresh garments on him.
　　　Be by, good madam, when we do awake him;
　　　I doubt not of his temperance.　　25
CORDELIA O my dear father, restoration hang
　　　Thy medicine on my lips, and let this kiss
　　　Repair those violent harms that my two sisters
　　　Have in thy reverence made.
KENT　　　　　　　　　　　　　　Kind and dear princess!
CORDELIA Had you not been their father, these white flakes　　30
　　　Did challenge pity of them. Was this a face
　　　To be opposed against the warring winds?
　　　Mine enemy's dog,
　　　Though he had bit me, should have stood that night
　　　Against my fire. And wast thou fain, poor father,　　35
　　　To hovel thee with swine and rogues forlorn
　　　In short and musty straw? Alack, alack,
　　　'Tis wonder that thy life and wits at once
　　　Had not concluded all. He wakes. Speak to him.
GENTLEMAN Madam, do you; 'tis fittest.　　40
CORDELIA How does my royal lord? How fares your majesty?
LEAR You do me wrong to take me out o'th'grave.
　　　Thou art a soul in bliss, but I am bound
　　　Upon a wheel of fire, that mine own tears
　　　Do scald like molten lead.
CORDELIA　　　　　　　　　　　Sir, do you know me?　　45
LEAR You are a spirit, I know. Where did you die?
CORDELIA Still, still far wide.
GENTLEMAN He's scarce awake. Let him alone a while.
LEAR Where have I been? Where am I? Fair daylight?
　　　I am mightily abused. I should ev'n die with pity　　50
　　　To see another thus. I know not what to say.
　　　I will not swear these are my hands. Let's see:
　　　I feel this pin prick. Would I were assured
　　　Of my condition.

Cordelia asks her father for his blessing. He attempts to kneel before her. Although still confused, he is calm and recognises Cordelia, who expresses total forgiveness. As Lear leaves, he again asks Cordelia for forgiveness.

1 The moment of reconciliation

Finding that Cordelia's tears are real convinces Lear of her sincerity. Cordelia's repeated 'No cause' expresses the unconditional love which she has for her father, and which forgives all injuries.

- Lear's kneeling to Cordelia is in dramatic contrast with his kneeling to Regan in Act 2 Scene 4. Compare the circumstances and effects of his actions in both cases.
- When Cordelia offers Lear her support (line 80), some see in the gesture echoes of Lear with his Fool (Act 3) and Edgar with his father (Act 4). What similarities can you see in these three relationships?

benediction blessing
fond silly
mainly completely

abuse deceive
great rage frenzy
settling calming

CORDELIA   O look upon me, sir,
            And hold your hand in benediction o'er me.   55
            You must not kneel.
LEAR   Pray do not mock me:
            I am a very foolish, fond old man,
            Fourscore and upward,
            Not an hour more nor less; and to deal plainly,
            I fear I am not in my perfect mind.   60
            Methinks I should know you and know this man;
            Yet I am doubtful: for I am mainly ignorant
            What place this is, and all the skill I have
            Remembers not these garments, nor I know not
            Where I did lodge last night. Do not laugh at me,   65
            For, as I am a man, I think this lady
            To be my child Cordelia.
CORDELIA And so I am: I am.
LEAR Be your tears wet? Yes, faith. I pray, weep not.
            If you have poison for me, I will drink it.   70
            I know you do not love me; for your sisters
            Have, as I do remember, done me wrong.
            You have some cause; they have not.
CORDELIA No cause, no cause.
LEAR Am I in France?
KENT   In your own kingdom, sir.   75
LEAR Do not abuse me.
GENTLEMAN Be comforted, good madam. The great rage
            You see is killed in him. Desire him to go in.
            Trouble him no more till further settling.
CORDELIA Will't please your highness walk?   80
LEAR You must bear with me. Pray you now, forget
            And forgive. I am old and foolish.

                                                    Exeunt

Looking back at Act 4
Activities for groups or individuals

1 Setting the scene

Shakespeare did not specify the scene settings used at the head of each scene in this edition of the play. On the Globe stage there were few props and little or no scenery. The action flowed swiftly and continuously. Since Shakespeare's time, directors and editors have decided on the location for each scene. Remind yourself of the scene settings suggested throughout this edition of the play. Think about how appropriate each one seems to you. Where you disagree with the setting chosen, suggest an alternative, giving reasons for your choice.

2 Madness, sight and blindness

There are many moments in Act 4 (particularly in Scene 5) in which the themes of madness, sight and blindness are dramatically explored. Make a list of all examples and then write a short essay on the kinds of effects created.

3 Edmond

In Act 4 Edmond appears only in Scene 2, and speaks just one line, 'Yours in the ranks of death' (line 26). Imagine that Shakespeare thought of giving him a short soliloquy in which he could comment on his progress, on how he views his relationships with Regan and Gonerill, on his feelings about his father, and on his hopes for the future. Write seven or eight lines for Edmond to deliver as an Aside after his one line.

4 The road to Dover

By the end of the act, all the major characters are either travelling to Dover or are already there. Establish why each character has chosen to go there and what they hope to achieve. Speculate about what meetings will take place in Dover during Act 5.

5 The king and the duke

Act 4 has followed the fortunes of two 'old and foolish' men. There are many similarities between their experiences. Summarise what has happened to them during the act. Try to establish similarities and differences in their experience.

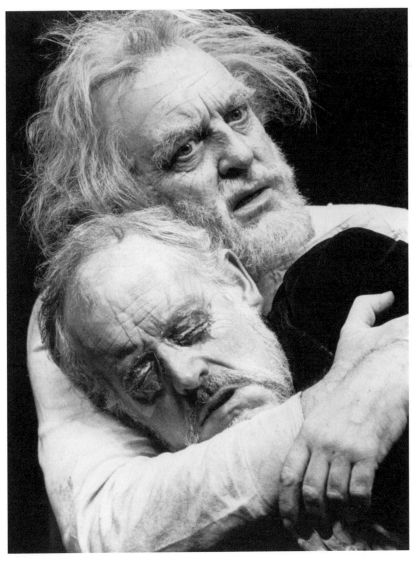

Lear and the blinded Gloucester. Find a line from Scene 5 as an appropriate caption for this moment from the Royal Shakespeare Company's 1976 production.

Edmond is unsure if Albany still intends to fight the French invaders. Regan jealously warns Edmond not to love Gonerill. Albany brings news that Lear and Cordelia have been joined by British rebels.

---

1 Regan's plans for Edmond (in pairs)

Regan, now a widow, is keen to marry Edmond and is anxious about his relationship with her sister. She questions him about his feelings for Gonerill and asks whether they are lovers.

Talk together about possible reasons that could be suggested in productions to explain why Regan is so interested in Edmond and so jealous of her sister. For example, could the actors show that she is desperate for a strong husband to lead her army or that she is in the grip of sexual obsession?

2 Mistrust between allies (in groups of four)

There seem to be tensions and unspoken issues in the conversation between Regan, Gonerill and Albany.

- Take parts and speak lines 15–26, with one group member taking the role of the silent Edmond.
- Read the lines again. This time each reader should pause at the end of every sentence so that Edmond can state what he thinks may lie behind the words that have been spoken.

3 What's the riddle?

After an initial refusal to attend the council of war, Gonerill changes her mind, and agrees to leave with Regan and Albany to discuss the battle plan. Her remark about the riddle (line 26) suggests that she knows the real reason for Regan's invitation. Decide what you think is running through Gonerill's mind at this moment.

---

course plans
constant pleasure firm decision
Our sister's . . . miscarried something's happened to Oswald
forfended forbidden
I never . . . her I won't have her as a rival
well bemet welcome

With others . . . out with rebels against the harshness of our rule
Why is this reasoned? why go into that now?
domestic . . . broils internal arguments
th'ancient . . . proceeding senior officers about our battle plan

Act 5   Scene 1
The British camp near Dover

Enter with drum and colours, EDMOND, REGAN, *Officers and Soldiers*

EDMOND [*To an Officer*] Know of the duke if his last purpose hold,
Or whether since he is advised by aught
To change the course. He's full of alteration
And self-reproving. Bring his constant pleasure.
                                        [*Exit Officer*]

REGAN Our sister's man is certainly miscarried.   5
EDMOND 'Tis to be doubted, madam.
REGAN   Now, sweet lord,
You know the goodness I intend upon you.
Tell me but truly, but then speak the truth,
Do you not love my sister?
EDMOND   In honoured love.
REGAN But have you never found my brother's way   10
To the forfended place?
EDMOND   No, by mine honour, madam.
REGAN I never shall endure her. Dear my lord,
Be not familiar with her.
EDMOND   Fear me not.
She and the duke her husband –

Enter with drum and colours, ALBANY, GONERILL, *Soldiers*

ALBANY Our very loving sister, well bemet.   15
Sir, this I heard: the king is come to his daughter,
With others whom the rigour of our state
Forced to cry out.
REGAN   Why is this reasoned?
GONERILL Combine together 'gainst the enemy;
For these domestic and particular broils   20
Are not the question here.
ALBANY Let's then determine with th'ancient of war
On our proceeding.
REGAN   Sister, you'll go with us?
GONERILL No.
REGAN 'Tis most convenient. Pray, go with us.   25
GONERILL [*Aside*] O ho, I know the riddle. – I will go.

Gonerill suspects Regan. Edgar gives Albany a letter: a warrior will verify it if Albany is victorious. Edmond reveals that he has sworn love to both sisters. He wishes to see Albany, Lear and Cordelia dead.

1 Brothers together

Edgar and Edmond are on stage together briefly at lines 27–8. Some directors ignore the stage direction at line 28 and keep Edmond on stage for Edgar's words with Albany. How might a director want Edgar to react to the sight of his brother?

2 'Hear me one word' (in pairs)

Albany is a high-ranking nobleman about to lead his army into battle, yet for some reason he pauses to listen to a poor peasant who asks to speak to him.

Taking parts as Edgar and Albany, first read through lines 27–39 with Edgar acting as a humble peasant grateful for Albany's attention. Then read through the lines again with Edgar acting in a courteous but self-assured way as though he were Albany's equal.

Decide which approach you feel is more appropriate, or suggest another way the lines could be performed.

3 Edmond's future plans (in groups of six)

Despite the pressures of the imminent battle, Edmond pauses to review his prospects (lines 44–58). In rehearsal actors sometimes use the following activity to bring out the full implications of his soliloquy.

Five of you, as Gonerill, Regan, Albany, Lear and Cordelia, stand in a circle. The sixth, as Edmond, walks around the space, speaking his lines to each of the characters as they are mentioned and adding gestures where they seem appropriate. Discuss whether the audience would find Edmond's words chilling in their ruthlessness or amusing in their exuberance.

---

avouchèd claimed
miscarry lose
machination all plots
diligent discovery careful reconnaissance
We will greet the time I can't wait to start

carry out my side achieve my aims, play my part
countenance power, support
taking off murder
state well-being
defend, not to debate act, not talk

Enter EDGAR *[dressed like a peasant]*

EDGAR If e'er your grace had speech with man so poor,
　　Hear me one word.
ALBANY *[To the others]*　　I'll overtake you.
　　　　　　　　　　　　　　　　　Exeunt both the armies
　　Speak.
EDGAR Before you fight the battle, ope this letter.
　　If you have victory, let the trumpet sound　　　　　30
　　For him that brought it. Wretched though I seem,
　　I can produce a champion that will prove
　　What is avouchèd there. If you miscarry,
　　Your business of the world hath so an end,
　　And machination ceases. Fortune love you.　　　　　35
ALBANY Stay till I have read the letter.
EDGAR　　　　　　　　　　　I was forbid it.
　　When time shall serve, let but the herald cry,
　　And I'll appear again.　　　　　　　　　　　*Exit*
ALBANY Why, fare thee well. I will o'erlook thy paper.

Enter EDMOND

EDMOND The enemy's in view; draw up your powers.　　40
　　Here is the guess of their true strength and forces
　　By diligent discovery; but your haste
　　Is now urged on you.
ALBANY　　　　　　　We will greet the time.　　*Exit*
EDMOND To both these sisters have I sworn my love,
　　Each jealous of the other as the stung　　　　　　45
　　Are of the adder. Which of them shall I take?
　　Both? one? or neither? Neither can be enjoyed
　　If both remain alive. To take the widow
　　Exasperates, makes mad her sister Gonerill,
　　And hardly shall I carry out my side,　　　　　　50
　　Her husband being alive. Now then, we'll use
　　His countenance for the battle, which being done,
　　Let her who would be rid of him devise
　　His speedy taking off. As for the mercy
　　Which he intends to Lear and to Cordelia,　　　　55
　　The battle done, and they within our power,
　　Shall never see his pardon; for my state
　　Stands on me to defend, not to debate.　　　　*Exit*

Edgar leaves Gloucester, but returns with the news that Albany's forces have won. Edgar comforts Gloucester. Edmond orders the imprisonment of Cordelia and Lear. Cordelia expresses compassion for Lear.

---

1 The battle at Dover (in pairs)

The battle is fought off stage ('*within*', line 4), but some productions choose to show glimpses of the fighting, or its aftermath. One production staged a non-realistic 'symbolic' battle as though imagined by the blind Gloucester. Others have shown the consequence of battle with lines of refugees or prisoners being mistreated by soldiers – one included the hanging of the Fool. Some productions show nothing of the battle, but suggest, through lighting changes and 'the shadow of this tree', the passage of some hours between lines 4 and 5.

Talk about the different effects you think each of the above methods of presenting the battle would have on an audience.

2 'Ripeness is all' (in pairs)

After the battle Edgar finds Gloucester wishing for death ('a man may rot'). Edgar tries to lift his father's spirits. Lines 9–11 seem to say that the time of death is chosen by the gods. We should suffer death as we suffer birth, as a natural part of life. Some people find Edgar's words a stoic acceptance of fate, others find in them a pessimistic resignation to what might, in fact, be changed. What do you think? Discuss your preferred interpretation.

3 The triumph of Edmond (in large groups)

The play's long final scene gathers all the main characters together in one place. Their various meetings and confrontations bring their stories to a conclusion. It begins with the entrance of the victorious Edmond and his royal prisoners.

Experiment with staging this entrance in different ways: you could aim to emphasise Edmond's delight in his success, Cordelia and Lear's vulnerability or some other aspect of the situation.

---

good host shelter
ta'en captured
good guard watch them carefully
their greater pleasures the wishes of our superiors
censure judge

meaning intention
incurred suffered
cast down laid low, humbled
Myself could . . . frown I could withstand bad luck if I were the only one in trouble

Act 5 Scene 2
The countryside near Dover

Alarum within. Enter with drum and colours, LEAR, CORDELIA,
and Soldiers, over the stage, and exeunt

Enter EDGAR, *dressed like a peasant, and* GLOUCESTER

EDGAR Here, father, take the shadow of this tree
    For your good host; pray that the right may thrive.
    If ever I return to you again
    I'll bring you comfort.
GLOUCESTER   Grace go with you, sir.

                                  Exit [Edgar]

      Alarum and retreat within. Enter EDGAR

EDGAR Away, old man! Give me thy hand; away!   5
    King Lear hath lost, he and his daughter ta'en.
    Give me thy hand. Come on.
GLOUCESTER No further, sir; a man may rot even here.
EDGAR What, in ill thoughts again? Men must endure
    Their going hence even as their coming hither: 10
    Ripeness is all. Come on.
GLOUCESTER   And that's true too.

                                   Exeunt

Act 5 Scene 3
The British camp near Dover

Enter in conquest with drum and colours EDMOND; LEAR *and*
CORDELIA, *as prisoners; Soldiers;* CAPTAIN

EDMOND Some officers take them away: good guard,
    Until their greater pleasures first be known
    That are to censure them.
CORDELIA   We are not the first
    Who with best meaning have incurred the worst.
    For thee, oppressèd king, I am cast down,   5
    Myself could else outfrown false fortune's frown.
    Shall we not see these daughters and these sisters?

Lear is joyful to be imprisoned forever with Cordelia. They will mock the petty quarrels of the court. Edmond gives Lear and Cordelia's death warrant to the Captain. He promises promotion and warns against soft-heartedness.

This is how a Russian film version staged Lear's and Cordelia's capture. Describe the mood and atmosphere it has created.

1 Lear's and Cordelia's future (in pairs)

Lear speaks only to Cordelia, ignoring everyone else. After their exit Edmond immediately arranges for their execution, promising the Captain promotion if he agrees to carry out the orders.

To bring out the shocking contrasts between the two parts of this episode, take on the roles of Edmond and Lear. Edmond reads lines 26–35, pausing at each full stop. At each pause the person taking the part of Lear speaks a few of Lear's words taken from his lines 8–25. Lear could use the same line each time (possibly line 9) or different phrases that seem appropriate.

---

gilded butterflies overdressed poseurs
take upon 's . . . things learn the hidden meanings of the universe
shall bring . . . foxes will need a flaming torch from the gods to divide us
goodyears plagues

fell skin
One step . . . thee I've already promoted you once
men . . . time is morality changes with circumstances
become a sword suit a soldier

LEAR No, no, no, no! Come, let's away to prison.
　　　　We two alone will sing like birds i'th'cage.
　　　　When thou dost ask me blessing, I'll kneel down　　　　　　　10
　　　　And ask of thee forgiveness: so we'll live,
　　　　And pray, and sing, and tell old tales, and laugh
　　　　At gilded butterflies, and hear poor rogues
　　　　Talk of court news, and we'll talk with them too –
　　　　Who loses and who wins; who's in, who's out –　　　　　　　15
　　　　And take upon 's the mystery of things,
　　　　As if we were God's spies; and we'll wear out
　　　　In a walled prison packs and sects of great ones
　　　　That ebb and flow by th'moon.
EDMOND　　　　　　　　　　　　　　Take them away.
LEAR Upon such sacrifices, my Cordelia,　　　　　　　　　　　　20
　　　　The gods themselves throw incense. Have I caught thee?
　　　　He that parts us shall bring a brand from heaven
　　　　And fire us hence like foxes. Wipe thine eyes.
　　　　The goodyears shall devour them, flesh and fell,
　　　　Ere they shall make us weep. We'll see 'em starved first.　　25
　　　　Come.
　　　　　　　　　　　　　　Exeunt Lear and Cordelia, guarded
EDMOND Come hither, captain. Hark.
　　　　Take thou this note. Go follow them to prison.
　　　　One step I have advanced thee; if thou dost
　　　　As this instructs thee, thou dost make thy way　　　　　　　30
　　　　To noble fortunes. Know thou this: that men
　　　　Are as the time is; to be tender-minded
　　　　Does not become a sword. Thy great employment
　　　　Will not bear question: either say thou'lt do't,
　　　　Or thrive by other means.
CAPTAIN　　　　　　　　　　　　I'll do't, my lord.　　　　　　　35
EDMOND About it, and write 'happy' when th'hast done.
　　　　Mark, I say, instantly, and carry it so
　　　　As I have set it down.
　　　　　　　　　　　　　　　　　　　　Exit Captain

Albany demands that Edmond hand over Lear and Cordelia. Edmond delays, provoking Albany to assert Edmond's social inferiority. Regan defends Edmond. Gonerill resents Regan's patronage of Edmond.

---

1 The alliance falls apart (in pairs)

The tone of this meeting is very different from the touching exchange between the captive Lear and Cordelia and from Edmond's authoritative commands to the Captain. Now the tensions between the victorious allies come to the surface: Edmond and Albany clash, Regan resents Albany's leadership – which she feels unable to challenge fully without support from a husband – and the two sisters compete for Edmond's favours.

Talk together about where in the scene a director should emphasise the outward show of formal courtesy breaking down. Which lines would you want the actors to use as insults?

2 Foresight, hindsight

Regan's comment, 'Jesters do oft prove prophets' (line 65), is a reminder of the Fool, who had, as early as Act 1 Scene 4, predicted the ill effects of Lear giving away his kingdom.

Gonerill and Regan can now see each other's scheming clearly. Gonerill's put-down of her sister, 'That eye that told you so' (line 66), is probably based on the proverb 'Love, being jealous, makes a good eye look asquint' (jealous people see things wrongly).

Once again the imagery of distorted perception, which runs through the play, is employed. It is hinted at in lines 49–50 ('turn . . . eyes': blind ourselves with our own weapons, make our conscripted soldiers rebel).

As you read to the end of the play, make a note of the various references to damaged sight and think about how the theme of moral blindness is important to the whole story.

---

strain   nature
Whose age . . . it   since Lear's old age provokes sympathy
common bosom   public sympathy, hearts of the people
I hold . . . brother   you're my subordinate, not my equal

we list   I choose
Bore . . . person   acted on my behalf
The which immediacy   and that connection
compeers   equals
Holla, holla!   a loud cry to attract attention

Flourish. Enter ALBANY, GONERILL, REGAN, [*Officers,*] *Soldiers*

ALBANY Sir, you have showed today your valiant strain,
And fortune led you well. You have the captives   40
Who were the opposites of this day's strife.
I do require them of you, so to use them
As we shall find their merits and our safety
May equally determine.
EDMOND   Sir, I thought it fit
To send the old and miserable king   45
To some retention and appointed guard,
Whose age had charms in it, whose title more,
To pluck the common bosom on his side
And turn our impressed lances in our eyes
Which do command them. With him I sent the queen: 50
My reason all the same, and they are ready
Tomorrow, or at further space, t'appear
Where you shall hold your session.
ALBANY   Sir, by your patience,
I hold you but a subject of this war,
Not as a brother.
REGAN   That's as we list to grace him.   55
Methinks our pleasure might have been demanded
Ere you had spoke so far. He led our powers,
Bore the commission of my place and person,
The which immediacy may well stand up
And call itself your brother.
GONERILL   Not so hot.   60
In his own grace he doth exalt himself
More than in your addition.
REGAN   In my rights,
By me invested, he compeers the best.
ALBANY That were the most if he should husband you.
REGAN Jesters do oft prove prophets.
GONERILL   Holla, holla!   65
That eye that told you so, looked but asquint.

Regan betrothes herself to Edmond. Albany forbids the marriage, accusing Edmond and Gonerill of treason and adultery. Albany challenges Edmond to a duel. He accepts. Regan falls ill, poisoned by Gonerill.

1 Regan claims Edmond (in pairs)

Edmond could not decide between the two sisters in Act 5 Scene 1, lines 44–54. Now Regan announces publicly that he is to be her husband and says that she surrenders everything to him, like a city at the end of a siege ('the walls is thine').

How could the actor playing Edmond show his response to this very public declaration? As Regan and Edmond, try different ways of speaking and reacting to lines 68–72.

2 Ready to kill (in groups of four)

Albany has read the letter Edgar took from Oswald and consequently arrests Edmond for treason, saying that he also knows of Gonerill's guilt. Because Edmond is now Earl of Gloucester, Albany allows him the aristocratic right to defend his honour in single combat and pledges to challenge him himself should no one else be prepared to do so.

Take parts as Albany, Edmond, Gonerill and Regan. As you read lines 84–95, decide what movements and gestures each character could make. Consider in particular how differently each of the four might react when the two gauntlets are thrown down.

3 Gonerill, the 'gilded serpent'?

What image does Albany's insulting description of his wife (line 78) conjure up in your mind? Look back through this scene and imagine how Gonerill might watch her sister showing the first effects of poisoning. Exactly how serpent-like should she be?

From a full-flowing stomach   with the full force of anger
patrimony   father's inheritance
let-alone   permission
Half-blooded   semi-noble, bastard
in thy attaint   also your dishonourable accomplice

subcontracted   already promised
banns   public intention to marry
make . . . bespoke   try your luck with me, as Gonerill is spoken for
An interlude!   what a farce!
heinous   evil
manifest   obvious

REGAN   Lady, I am not well, else I should answer
　　　　　From a full-flowing stomach. [*To Edmond*] General,
　　　　　Take thou my soldiers, prisoners, patrimony.
　　　　　Dispose of them, of me; the walls is thine. 70
　　　　　Witness the world that I create thee here
　　　　　My lord and master.
GONERILL 　　　　　　　　Mean you to enjoy him?
ALBANY   The let-alone lies not in your good will.
EDMOND   Nor in thine, lord.
ALBANY 　　　　　　　　Half-blooded fellow, yes.
REGAN   [*To Edmond*] Let the drum strike, and prove my title thine. 75
ALBANY   Stay yet, hear reason. Edmond, I arrest thee
　　　　　On capital treason, and in thy attaint
　　　　　This gilded serpent. For your claim, fair sister,
　　　　　I bar it in the interest of my wife.
　　　　　'Tis she is subcontracted to this lord, 80
　　　　　And I, her husband, contradict your banns.
　　　　　If you will marry, make your love to me,
　　　　　My lady is bespoke.
GONERILL 　　　　　　　　An interlude!
ALBANY   Thou art armed, Gloucester; let the trumpet sound.
　　　　　If none appear to prove upon thy person 85
　　　　　Thy heinous, manifest, and many treasons,
　　　　　There is my pledge!
　　　　　　　　　[*Throws down a glove*]
　　　　　　　　　　　　I'll make it on thy heart,
　　　　　Ere I taste bread, thou art in nothing less
　　　　　Than I have here proclaimed thee.
REGAN 　　　　　　　　　　Sick, O sick!
GONERILL   [*Aside*] If not, I'll ne'er trust medicine. 90
EDMOND   There's my exchange!
　　　　　　　　　[*Throws down a glove*]
　　　　　　　　　　　　What in the world he is
　　　　　That names me traitor, villain-like he lies.
　　　　　Call by the trumpet: he that dares, approach;
　　　　　On him, on you – who not? – I will maintain
　　　　　My truth and honour firmly.

Albany has dismissed Edmond's soldiers, so Edmond must fight alone. Regan, sick, is taken to Albany's tent. At the third trumpet call Edgar appears, disguised and armed. Refusing to give his name, he challenges Edmond.

1 Waiting for a challenger (in small groups)

Shakespeare makes the audience wait for the arrival of Edgar. The ritual language and ceremonial behaviour suggest that traditional rules of chivalry are now at work, governing the deadly encounter of two knights. Repeated trumpet calls build up a sense of tension and expectation in some ways very reminiscent of the opening scene of the play, where the formal protocols of court also governed behaviour.

It is only at the third trumpet call that Edgar finally appears. In some productions he is dressed in shining armour or in pure white. Other productions present him still dressed as a poor man, even though Edmond describes him as 'fair and warlike' at line 132. Edgar's face must presumably be covered as Edmond does not recognise him.

a Decide in your group how Edgar could be costumed and the effect your choices will have on the scene.

b Take parts and work out how to stage lines 100–40. Suggest how to heighten the drama in the delayed entrance of Edgar and how to deliver the formal, but often vicious, language which the characters speak before the duel. Present your version to the rest of the class.

2 'my name is lost' (in pairs)

a Edgar refuses to give his name, saying it has been devoured 'by treason's tooth'. Why do you feel he does not want Edmond to know whom he is fighting?

b Edmond is not obliged to face a challenge from a nameless, unknown combatant. Why do you think he agrees to fight (lines 134–5)?

---

thy single virtue   your one good quality (your bravery)
levied   recruited
Took their discharge   been dismissed
quality or degree   nobility and rank

lists   list of officers
manifold   prolific
adversary   opponent
cope   fight

ALBANY   A herald, ho!   95

Enter a HERALD

Trust to thy single virtue, for thy soldiers,
All levied in my name, have in my name
Took their discharge.
REGAN   My sickness grows upon me.
ALBANY She is not well. Convey her to my tent.
                              [*Exit Regan, led by an Officer*]
Come hither, herald. Let the trumpet sound,   100
And read out this.
                              A trumpet sounds
HERALD *Reads* 'If any man of quality or degree within the lists of
    the army will maintain upon Edmond, supposed Earl of
    Gloucester, that he is a manifold traitor, let him appear by the
    third sound of the trumpet. He is bold in his defence.'   105
                              First trumpet
Again.
                              Second trumpet
Again.
                              Third trumpet

Trumpet answers within. Enter EDGAR, *armed*

ALBANY Ask him his purposes, why he appears
Upon this call o'th'trumpet.
HERALD   What are you?
Your name, your quality, and why you answer   110
This present summons?
EDGAR   Know, my name is lost,
By treason's tooth bare-gnawn and canker-bit.
Yet am I noble as the adversary
I come to cope.
ALBANY   Which is that adversary?
EDGAR What's he that speaks for Edmond, Earl of Gloucester?   115
EDMOND Himself. What sayst thou to him?

Edgar proclaims Edmond's treachery. Edmond denies his guilt. Edmond is fatally wounded in the fight. Albany shows Gonerill's letter to Edmond. Gonerill attempts to seize it, claiming to be ruler and law-maker.

Identify each character, and suggest which line you think is being spoken at this precise moment.

EDGAR   Draw thy sword,
    That if my speech offend a noble heart
    Thy arm may do thee justice. Here is mine.
    Behold, it is the privilege of mine honour,
    My oath, and my profession. I protest,   120
    Maugre thy strength, place, youth, and eminence,
    Despite thy victor-sword and fire-new fortune,
    Thy valour and thy heart, thou art a traitor:
    False to thy gods, thy brother, and thy father,
    Conspirant 'gainst this high illustrious prince,   125
    And from th'extremest upward of thy head
    To the descent and dust below thy foot,
    A most toad-spotted traitor. Say thou no,
    This sword, this arm, and my best spirits are bent
    To prove upon thy heart, whereto I speak,   130
    Thou liest.
EDMOND   In wisdom I should ask thy name,
    But since thy outside looks so fair and warlike,
    And that thy tongue some say of breeding breathes,
    What safe and nicely I might well delay
    By rule of knighthood, I disdain and spurn.   135
    Back do I toss these treasons to thy head,
    With the hell-hated lie o'erwhelm thy heart,
    Which, for they yet glance by and scarcely bruise,
    This sword of mine shall give them instant way
    Where they shall rest for ever. Trumpets, speak!   140
        Alarums. [They] fight. [Edmond falls]
ALBANY Save him, save him.
GONERILL   This is practice, Gloucester;
    By th'law of war thou wast not bound to answer
    An unknown opposite. Thou art not vanquished,
    But cozened and beguiled.
ALBANY   Shut your mouth, dame,
    Or with this paper shall I stop it. – Hold, sir.   145
    Thou worse than any name, read thine own evil. –
    No tearing, lady. I perceive you know it.
GONERILL Say if I do; the laws are mine, not thine.
    Who can arraign me for't?   *Exit*
ALBANY   Most monstrous! O,
    Know'st thou this paper?

An Officer is sent to watch over Gonerill. The dying Edmond confesses his crimes. Edgar sheds his disguise and tells how, as Poor Tom, he helped Gloucester, only revealing his identity to his father afterwards.

---

1 'The wheel is come full circle' (in pairs)

Edmond acknowledges that he is fatally wounded: ''Tis past, and so am I' (line 154). He offers to forgive his killer if he is of noble blood. Edgar exchanges 'charity' before revealing his identity and affirming that the 'gods are just' in their punishment of both Edmond and Gloucester for their sins of pleasure. Edmond acknowledges the role of providence in his demise, returning him 'full circle' to the bottom of Fortune's wheel.

Take parts and speak lines 152–64. First, read the lines with Edgar standing formally while his wounded brother lies on the ground, then change the body language and have Edgar cradling and comforting his dying brother. Which interpretation works better, or do you feel the lines should be performed in some other way? Decide what gesture Edmond could use to accompany 'I am here' (line 164).

2 Edgar's story (in groups of four or five)

a Edgar recapitulates the 'brief tale' of his life as Poor Tom. As one person speaks lines 174–90, the others show a mimed version of Edgar's summary of his life since his betrayal by Edmond.

b Edgar describes how he saved Gloucester 'from despair', yet blames himself for not shedding his disguise sooner ('O fault!', line 183). Suggest why Edgar reproaches himself so bitterly, even though he comforted his father tenderly in his last hours, and why he only revealed his identity to his father at the point when he was about to fight Edmond.

c If you were the director, how would you instruct Edmond to behave during his brother's narrative, and why?

---

govern look after
thou / That hast . . . on you, who has better luck than
blood nobility
of our pleasant vices . . . us turn our pleasure-giving sins into pains

The dark . . . got his sordid fathering of you
That we the pain . . . once suffering is preferable to death
habit disguise
rings eye-sockets

EDMOND   Ask me not what I know.   150

ALBANY Go after her, she's desperate, govern her.

                                              [*Exit an Officer*]

EDMOND What you have charged me with, that have I done,
        And more, much more; the time will bring it out.
        'Tis past, and so am I. But what art thou
        That hast this fortune on me? If thou'rt noble,   155
        I do forgive thee.

EDGAR   Let's exchange charity.
        I am no less in blood than thou art, Edmond.
        If more, the more th'hast wronged me.
        My name is Edgar, and thy father's son.
        The gods are just, and of our pleasant vices   160
        Make instruments to plague us.
        The dark and vicious place where thee he got
        Cost him his eyes.

EDMOND   Th'hast spoken right; 'tis true.
        The wheel is come full circle; I am here.

ALBANY Methought thy very gait did prophesy   165
        A royal nobleness. I must embrace thee.
        Let sorrow split my heart if ever I
        Did hate thee or thy father.

EDGAR Worthy prince, I know't.

ALBANY Where have you hid yourself?   170
        How have you known the miseries of your father?

EDGAR By nursing them, my lord. List a brief tale,
        And when 'tis told, O that my heart would burst!
        The bloody proclamation to escape
        That followed me so near (O, our lives' sweetness,   175
        That we the pain of death would hourly die
        Rather than die at once!) taught me to shift
        Into a madman's rags, t'assume a semblance
        That very dogs disdained; and in this habit
        Met I my father with his bleeding rings,   180
        Their precious stones new-lost; became his guide,
        Led him, begged for him, saved him from despair,
        Never – O fault! – revealed myself unto him
        Until some half hour past, when I was armed.

Edgar reports that Gloucester died happily. News comes of Gonerill's suicide and Regan's poisoning. Kent arrives to bid farewell to Lear. Albany demands that Edmond reveal the whereabouts of Lear and Cordelia.

1 The dying brother (in pairs)

a Edmond says he is affected by Edgar's words but, although he claims it might move him to 'do good', he does nothing to revoke the death sentences on Lear and Cordelia. Suggest a gesture an actor could use to remind the audience of Edmond's earlier instructions to the Captain.

b Both Gonerill and Regan die off stage. Edmond greets the news with what could be a grim joke against his own agreement to marry both of them (lines 202–3). If you were playing Edmond, decide if you would want to make the audience smile at this point. Would humour add to, or detract from, the horror of this death-ridden scene?

2 'Produce the bodies' (in small groups)

Albany orders the bodies of the dead sisters to be carried on. He echoes Edgar's and Edmond's lines 160–4 in affirming the all-powerful 'judgement of the heavens'. Decide how you would stage the bringing-in of the bodies: casually, with great ceremony, or in some other manner? Also suggest how Albany should react to seeing his dead wife.

In some productions line 204 is omitted and the bodies are not brought on stage. What are the advantages and the disadvantages of this?

3 Kent's freedom

The loyal Kent appears '*as himself*' to bid farewell to Lear, perhaps for the last time. Although he fought on Lear's side, Kent has freedom of movement and does not seem to be a prisoner. Suggest how you could ensure that the audience realises that Kent has dropped his disguise as Caius and is now appearing as his true self.

---

of this good success for victory in the duel
our pilgrimage about our journey together
flawed weakened
smilingly and he died happily

perchance perhaps
contracted engaged
marry unite
compliment ... urges greeting that courtesy would normally demand

Not sure, though hoping of this good success,   185
I asked his blessing, and from first to last
Told him our pilgrimage; but his flawed heart –
Alack, too weak the conflict to support –
'Twixt two extremes of passion, joy and grief,
Burst smilingly.

EDMOND   This speech of yours hath moved me,   190
And shall perchance do good. But speak you on,
You look as you had something more to say.

ALBANY If there be more, more woeful, hold it in,
For I am almost ready to dissolve,
Hearing of this.   195

Enter a GENTLEMAN [*with a bloody knife*]

GENTLEMAN Help, help, O help!
EDGAR   What kind of help?
ALBANY   Speak, man.
EDGAR What means this bloody knife?
GENTLEMAN   'Tis hot, it smokes.
It came even from the heart of – O, she's dead.
ALBANY Who dead? Speak, man.
GENTLEMAN Your lady, sir, your lady; and her sister   200
By her is poisoned: she confesses it.
EDMOND I was contracted to them both; all three
Now marry in an instant.
EDGAR   Here comes Kent.

Enter KENT [*as himself*]

ALBANY Produce the bodies, be they alive or dead.
Gonerill's and Regan's bodies brought out
This judgement of the heavens, that makes us tremble,   205
Touches us not with pity. – O, is this he?
[*To Kent*] The time will not allow the compliment
Which very manners urges.
KENT   I am come
To bid my king and master aye good night.
Is he not here?
ALBANY   Great thing of us forgot!   210
Speak, Edmond; where's the king, and where's Cordelia?
Seest thou this object, Kent?

Edmond urges that someone be sent to cancel his death warrant on Lear and Cordelia. She was to be hanged to give the appearance of suicide. Lear enters, carrying the dead Cordelia and grieving for her.

'Howl, howl, howl, howl!' The entrance of Lear carrying the dead Cordelia is one of the most famous and heart-rending scenes in world drama. See also colour section, p. xi. Here, moments later, Lear searches Cordelia's face for signs of life. The sight prompts Kent to ask if the end of the world has come (line 237). In the seventeenth century, to satisfy audience demand for a happy ending, Nahum Tate rewrote Act 5 so that Cordelia survives (see p. 236). Was Shakespeare right, or is Tate's rewrite an improvement?

1 A supreme acting challenge (in pairs)

How do you feel an actor playing Lear should speak the four 'howls' (line 231) as he enters carrying his dead daughter? Take turns to play the king and try out different ways of saying the words. Then perhaps try speaking the even more challenging five 'nevers' at line 282.

---

writ death warrant
office task (of killing Lear and Cordelia)
commission orders

fordid killed
promised end end of the world, Judgement Day

KENT   Alack, why thus?

EDMOND Yet Edmond was beloved.
      The one the other poisoned for my sake,
      And after slew herself.   215

ALBANY Even so. – Cover their faces.

EDMOND I pant for life. Some good I mean to do,
      Despite of mine own nature. Quickly send –
      Be brief in it – to th'castle; for my writ
      Is on the life of Lear and on Cordelia.   220
      Nay, send in time.

ALBANY   Run, run, O run!

EDGAR To who, my lord? – Who has the office? Send
      Thy token of reprieve.

EDMOND Well thought on. Take my sword. The captain,
      Give it the captain.

EDGAR   Haste thee for thy life.   225

                                  [*Exit an Officer*]

EDMOND He hath commission from thy wife and me
      To hang Cordelia in the prison and
      To lay the blame upon her own despair,
      That she fordid herself.

ALBANY The gods defend her. Bear him hence a while.   230

                                  [*Edmond is borne off*]

Enter LEAR *with* CORDELIA *in his arms* [*and the* OFFICER *following*]

LEAR Howl, howl, howl, howl! O, you are men of stones.
      Had I your tongues and eyes, I'd use them so,
      That heaven's vault should crack. She's gone for ever.
      I know when one is dead and when one lives.
      She's dead as earth.
                [*He lays her down*]
                Lend me a looking-glass;   235
      If that her breath will mist or stain the stone,
      Why then she lives.

KENT   Is this the promised end?

EDGAR Or image of that horror?

ALBANY   Fall and cease.

Lear desperately seeks for signs that Cordelia lives. He boasts that he killed her murderer. Filled with grief, he is unmoved by the reunion with Kent and by the deaths of his other daughters. Edmond is reported dead.

Lear grieves for Cordelia. Choose one of Lear's lines as a caption.

redeem cure
falchion curved sword
crosses troubles
spoil disable
brag boast
That from . . . steps I've followed your decline from the very start

Nor no man else no one's welcome here, if not me
present us to bother, question, talk with
bootless futile

LEAR   This feather stirs, she lives: if it be so,
      It is a chance which does redeem all sorrows   240
      That ever I have felt.
KENT   O my good master!
LEAR   Prithee, away.
EDGAR   'Tis noble Kent, your friend.
LEAR   A plague upon you murderers, traitors all.
      I might have saved her; now she's gone for ever.
      Cordelia, Cordelia, stay a little. Ha?   245
      What is't thou sayst? – Her voice was ever soft,
      Gentle, and low, an excellent thing in woman. –
      I killed the slave that was a-hanging thee.
OFFICER   'Tis true, my lords, he did.
LEAR   Did I not, fellow?
      I have seen the day with my good biting falchion   250
      I would have made them skip. I am old now,
      And these same crosses spoil me. [*To Kent*] Who are you?
      Mine eyes are not o'th'best, I'll tell you straight.
KENT   If fortune brag of two she loved and hated,
      One of them we behold.   255
LEAR   This' a dull sight. Are you not Kent?
KENT   The same,
      Your servant Kent. Where is your servant Caius?
LEAR   He's a good fellow, I can tell you that.
      He'll strike, and quickly too. He's dead and rotten.
KENT   No, my good lord, I am the very man –   260
LEAR   I'll see that straight.
KENT   That from your first of difference and decay
      Have followed your sad steps.
LEAR   You're welcome hither.
KENT   Nor no man else. All's cheerless, dark, and deadly.
      Your eldest daughters have fordone themselves   265
      And desperately are dead.
LEAR   Ay, so I think.
ALBANY   He knows not what he says, and vain is it
      That we present us to him.

Enter a MESSENGER

EDGAR   Very bootless.
MESSENGER   Edmond is dead, my lord.

197

Albany returns authority to Lear. Lear again grieves for Cordelia, then dies. Albany asks Edgar and Kent to share power. Kent hints that he has not long to live. Edgar urges plain speaking, not dishonest formality.

1 Albany restores Lear's power (in groups of five or six)

Faced with these appalling events, Albany attempts to ensure that villains and victims are appropriately treated. In most productions his lines will be merely a background to the central tableau of Lear cradling his dead daughter.

Stage lines 269–78, taking a named part each. The person playing Albany speaks the lines. Decide on the appropriate speed for his words and how Edgar and Kent might respond. Decide whether something specific should occur to explain Albany's words 'O see, see!' or whether he should be overcome by the pity of it all.

2 Lear's last lines (in pairs)

a 'And my poor fool is hanged.' In Shakespeare's time 'fool' was often used as a term of affection. Do you think Lear is referring to Cordelia or to the Fool here?

b 'Look there, look there.' What does Lear see? Lear's dying words are often spoken as he searches Cordelia's face for signs of life. But in one production he seemed to glimpse something hopeful and beautiful in the distance. How do you feel Lear's final line should be performed?

3 Final words

In the Quarto version of the play, lines 297–300 are given to Albany (see p. 240). Decide, with reasons, who you think should have the last word: Edgar, Albany, or one of the other survivors?

4 'Exeunt with a dead march'

The way the final moments of a play are staged can have a powerful effect on the audience. What final image would they see in your production of the play?

---

trifle triviality
What comfort . . . applied everything will be done to help the nation and King Lear
boot, and such addition extra titles
wages reward

rack instrument of torture (used to stretch the victim's limbs)
usurped stole
Bear them carry the bodies
the gored state sustain care for this damaged nation

ALBANY   That's but a trifle here.
          You lords and noble friends, know our intent.   270
          What comfort to this great decay may come
          Shall be applied. For us, we will resign
          During the life of this old majesty
          To him our absolute power; [*To Edgar and Kent*] you, to
                your rights,
          With boot, and such addition as your honours   275
          Have more than merited. All friends shall taste
          The wages of their virtue, and all foes
          The cup of their deservings. O see, see!
LEAR   And my poor fool is hanged. No, no, no life?
          Why should a dog, a horse, a rat have life,   280
          And thou no breath at all? Thou'lt come no more,
          Never, never, never, never, never.
          Pray you, undo this button. Thank you, sir.
          Do you see this? Look on her! Look, her lips.
          Look there, look there.   *He dies*
EDGAR   He faints. My lord, my lord!   285
KENT   Break, heart, I prithee break.
EDGAR   Look up, my lord.
KENT   Vex not his ghost. O, let him pass. He hates him
          That would upon the rack of this tough world
          Stretch him out longer.
EDGAR   He is gone indeed.
KENT   The wonder is he hath endured so long.   290
          He but usurped his life.
ALBANY   Bear them from hence. Our present business
          Is general woe. Friends of my soul, you twain
          Rule in this realm and the gored state sustain.
KENT   I have a journey, sir, shortly to go: 295
          My master calls me; I must not say no.
EDGAR   The weight of this sad time we must obey,
          Speak what we feel, not what we ought to say.
          The oldest hath borne most; we that are young
          Shall never see so much, nor live so long.   300
                          Exeunt with a dead march

Looking back at the play
Activities for groups or individuals

1 Enjoying tragedy?

In spite of all its cruelty and bleakness, *King Lear* is one of Shakespeare's most popular plays and is frequently performed. Talk together about what audiences gain from seeing the play. Do you think it is possible to enjoy *King Lear*?

A practical problem faced when staging the play in a modern theatre is where to place the interval. Directors usually choose just before or just after Act 3 Scene 7, the scene in which Gloucester is blinded. Decide on the advantages and disadvantages of each choice.

2 Mourning Cordelia

This activity may help you to share the intensity of Lear's words at the death of Cordelia. You could try it in the hall or the drama studio, but it can be just as effective in a classroom, especially if it 'blacks out'. Everyone in the class can be involved.

- Identify all the phrases or sentences in Act 5 Scene 3, lines 230–69, that express grief or sympathy for Cordelia or Lear. Write them on slips of paper. Two of you play Cordelia and Lear. Distribute the slips to everyone except Cordelia. Each person memorises their phrase or sentence of mourning language.
- Make a tableau of Lear and the dead Cordelia surrounded by a circle of sympathetic onlookers.
- Make the tableau again. This time speak the memorised words in turn as a soundtrack to the picture. Use stage lights or candles and, at low volume, play appropriate music to add atmosphere.
- Try introducing movement. For example, each mourner, in turn, could step into the circle, then move close to Lear and Cordelia, adding gesture to emphasise their words, before returning to the circle of mourning.

3 Costumes and appearance

Clothes are important in a play where two characters are in disguise for much of the time, and the central character rebels against the deceptive sense of status that they provide by trying to strip naked during the storm: 'Off, off, you lendings! Come, unbutton here.' (Act 3 Scene 4, line 97).

Look at the various styles of costume used in the production photos and consider what approach to costume design you would wish to take. Consider in particular how Edgar should be dressed as he assumes various disguises and how Lear's different costumes might help an audience visualise his state of mind.

4 The wheel of fortune

This activity could take place in a classroom, but a larger space is preferable. Draw, or mark out with ribbon/string, a circle to represent the wheel of fortune, indicating in some way the top and bottom. Each of you takes the role of one of the principal characters in the play.

Decide where each character is on the wheel at various points in the play: for example, just before the love test in Act 1 Scene 1; at the end of the same scene; during the terrible storm; just before the battle.

Remember Edgar's words 'Who is't can say "I am at the worst"?' from Act 4 Scene 1, and decide where in the play you think each character is at the lowest point in their personal journey.

5 Time scale

Draw a time line plotting the sequence of events in the play. Decide how much time could have passed between the start and end of the play and how much time has passed between the various acts. You could extend this to create 'back-stories' for the main characters that help to explain their behaviour in the play itself.

6 The most interesting question

What is the question you would most like to ask of each of the following: Lear, Cordelia, Edmond, Edgar, the Fool? Write a separate question for each. Pool all your questions in the class. Decide which are the most interesting, and use them to hot-seat members of the class in role as the characters.

7 Modern relevance

Make a list of all the things you would say in a debate about *King Lear*'s relevance to today's world.

Shakespeare finds his story

No one can be certain why, in about 1605, Shakespeare chose to write a play with a story-line similar to *Cinderella*: a fairy-tale about a foolish father, a pair of ugly sisters and one loving, but mistreated daughter. The following four possibilities may help explain his interest in the ancient legend of King Leir and his three daughters.

1 The gossip of the day: a topical play?

Lurid real-life stories of greed and suffering among the moneyed classes were sensational and popular sources of gossip in the early seventeenth century. Sir William Allen, for example, a former lord mayor of the city, in old age made the disastrous mistake of splitting his estate between his three daughters and arranging to live with them in turn. Once they had his money, the old man was treated with cruelty and disrespect. Unlike Lear's daughters, all three of Sir William's daughters mistreated him.

Sir Brian Annesley, however, did have one child who cared. She was Cordell, the youngest of his three daughters. In 1603 Sir Brian's eldest daughter tried to have him certified as infirm of mind and memory and 'altogether unfit to govern himself or his estate'. Cordell challenged her sister in court, protesting that it was unjust to her elderly father 'at his last gasp to be registered a lunatic'.

2 The hazards of transferring power: a political play?

Inheritance in Elizabethan and Jacobean England was determined by male primogeniture (i.e. the first-born son inherits). Lack of sons was very dangerous. At the start of the seventeenth century, as the childless Queen Elizabeth's life drew to a close, many feared a disputed succession and possible civil war.

The folly of deliberately dividing up a kingdom would have been obvious to Shakespeare's audience. They would have certainly understood Kent's outrage at Lear's carving up of Britain. English history had been traditionally seen as a steady movement towards the security, strength and cohesion of a single realm. The contrast between the recent peaceful succession of King James in 1603, which had united the crowns of England and Scotland, and Lear's unwise division of his kingdom would have been all too clear to Shakespeare's audiences.

3 Legendary stories: a history play?

Geoffrey of Monmouth wrote about King Lear and his three daughters in his *History of England*, over 400 years before Shakespeare's day. It was clearly a mixture of myth and legend, but many people in the seventeenth century regarded it as historical fact. In 1577 Raphael Holinshed retold the legend in his *Chronicles of England, Scotlande and Irelande*. This is a summary of Holinshed's account of the King Lear story:

> Leir, the ageing king of Britain has three daughters, Gonorilla, Regan and Cordeilla, of whom his favourite is the youngest, Cordeilla. In order to help him to decide on the succession, he asks which of his daughters loves him best. Gonorilla and Regan speak extravagantly of the love they bear their father, but Cordeilla says that she loves him only according to his worth. Leir is furious and arranges for the two older daughters to marry the Dukes of Cornwall and Albany, between whom the kingdom will be divided after his death. The dukes are immediately given half of this inheritance. Cordeilla is to receive nothing, but the Prince of Gallia, who rules a part of France, chooses to marry her despite the fact that she has no dowry.
>
> Cornwall and Albany resent having to wait for power. They rise against Leir, forcing him to give up all his power. Leir's oldest daughters, with whom he has no choice but to live alternately, treat him unkindly and reduce the number of his servants.
>
> Leir flees the kingdom, and travels to Gallia. Before he appears at court, Cordeilla gives her father money so he can arrive with clothes and servants befitting a king. Cordeilla and her husband make him welcome.
>
> The Prince of Gallia raises an army to restore Leir to his throne. Cordeilla accompanies her father when he returns to his kingdom, and is named as his heir. The army of the Dukes of Cornwall and Albany is defeated, and the two Dukes die in battle. Leir regains his throne and reigns for two years before he dies. Cordeilla succeeds him, but her reign is cut short by a rebellion led by her sisters' sons. She is imprisoned, despairs and commits suicide. Her nephews then make war against each other, and England is only restored to peace after one of them is killed and the other is able to rule uncontested.

Some of the alterations and additions that Shakespeare made to Holinshed's story include: adding the characters of the Fool, Kent and Oswald; inventing Lear's madness and the storm; inserting the entire sub-plot of Gloucester and his sons; having Cordelia die before her father and the play finish with the deaths of Lear's entire family; ending with the rightful king restored.

◆ Choose one of the alterations or additions listed above. Write a paragraph discussing what the play gains from that 'change'.

4 Shakespeare's reading: a literary play?

Shakespeare may have read or seen *The True Chronicle History of King Leir*, a play first performed in the 1590s but not published until 1605. In this dramatised version of the story, no characters die and Leir is restored to his realm at the end. It contains stage directions of 'thunder and lightning', which may have been Shakespeare's inspiration for the storm in Act 3.

Shakespeare certainly read Samuel Harsnett's *A Declaration of Egregious Popish Impostures* (1603). Much of the strange language used by Edgar when pretending to be the mad Poor Tom, especially the lists of demons' names (see p. 114), is taken from this anti-Catholic pamphlet. It claimed to expose the evils of false exorcism (driving out devils from mad people), and quoted speeches supposedly made by people who pretended to be possessed by demons. By giving such evil language to Edgar, a 'good' character, Shakespeare increases the dramatic intensity of the play.

Shakespeare's most significant addition to the old legend is the story of Gloucester and his sons. This sub-plot mirrors the main plot of Lear and his daughters and is based on an episode in *Arcadia* (1590), a prose romance story by Sir Philip Sidney. Although in *Arcadia* the main character is a king rather than an earl and the illegitimate son is directly responsible for blinding his own father after seizing his throne, the virtuous son (as in *King Lear*) is betrayed by his brother, loses his father's favour, and is driven into exile. The virtuous son then returns to protect his father but, while he guides his blinded father, he refuses to help him commit suicide. The blind king eventually crowns his virtuous son and dies happy.

Shakespeare's Gloucester sub-plot has many similarities with the main plot of *King Lear*. Both are about powerful men and their relationships with their grown-up children. Both involve the father's unjust rejection of a faithful child who continues to love and protect the father. Both show the fathers mistreated by the children whom they favour.

◆ Write a short essay in response to the following statement: 'In *King Lear* the sub-plot deepens the atmosphere of horror. The tragic effect of the play is heightened as the sufferings of the two families unfold.'

Family relationships

At the beginning of the play, Lear and Gloucester both appear to believe that they head successful and happy families. Their illusions do not last long. By the end of the first scene Lear has torn his family apart. In the opening lines of the second scene Edmond reveals the plot against his brother that will destroy Gloucester's family.

Shakespeare's sharp dramatic focus is on fathers and their children. Neither family has a mother. The fracturing of bonds between fathers and children is mirrored in the play by the terrible storm in nature, and by the breakdown of society itself. Gloucester, troubled by the discovery of his son Edgar's supposed treachery, expresses that mirror-image: 'Love cools, friendship falls off, brothers divide. In cities, mutinies; in countries, discord; in palaces, treason; and the bond cracked 'twixt son and father'. In *King Lear* a family problem is a sign of much wider national and cosmic discord.

The family can be viewed as an economic unit which allows one generation to build on the success of the previous one through the inheritance of property and power. In *King Lear* the riches of a kingdom and an earldom await the heirs of Lear and Gloucester. The issue of inheritance generates great resentment in some children on reaching adulthood. They must await the death of a parent before being able to acquire the family wealth. The letter which Edmond pretends has been written by Edgar makes that resentment clear: 'This policy and reverence of age makes the world bitter to the best of our times, keeps our fortunes from us till our oldness cannot relish them.'

Gonerill and Regan, as well as Edmond, detest such 'aged tyranny', and want to take over the power, wealth and status of their father. Parents sometimes try to control children by manipulating their expectations of inheritance. Lear makes the dangerous mistake of dividing his kingdom between his two ambitious daughters. Gonerill and Regan receive their inheritance and have nothing more to gain by tolerating their father's caprices. Gloucester, however, does not choose to abdicate his role, so his ruthless son Edmond must scheme and plot to replace Edgar as heir, and then seek an opportunity to depose his father.

A family's tragic journey

The royal family, together in the play's opening scene.

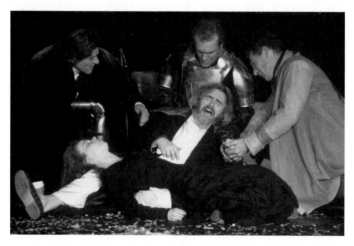

Lear and Cordelia reunited in death at the play's end. The bodies of Gonerill and Regan lie nearby, but out of sight.

The play begins and ends with the complete royal family on display before the audience. In contrast to the strong visual image of Lear's family, established by their appearance together in the opening scene, the three members of Gloucester's family never appear together on stage.

The family: a source of love and care

Families satisfy the profound human need for a sense of belonging and for the security of love. Although it may seem obvious that the families of Lear and Gloucester are unsuccessful, they are not totally unloving. Despite the fact that they are both badly treated, Edgar and Cordelia remain selflessly devoted to their fathers.

At the beginning of the play Lear seems unable to understand and value family love. He demands that his daughters make public statements about how much they love him. His absurd and insensitive command produces glib and overblown statements from Gonerill and Regan. Lear expects Cordelia to outdo her sisters in flattery, and is angered and humiliated by her refusal to participate. He condemns her for what he believes are harsh words, disregarding all his love for her up to that point. She says that she loves him 'According to my bond', as a daughter ought to love a father. Lear finds this universal statement of family obligation 'untender'. He wants an elaborate and fawning expression of love. Failing to get it, he violently rejects the only one of his children who has real affection for him.

After rejecting Cordelia, Lear announces that he will divide his time between Regan and Gonerill. It does not occur to him that such an action makes him vulnerable. Only respect and love will protect him once he has given up his power. Both Cordelia and Kent suspect the flattery of Gonerill and Regan, and may fear that they do not love or respect Lear enough for him to be safe with them.

A major function of the family is to provide security for its members as they pass through childhood, sickness and old age. Indeed, it is sometimes claimed that one reason why people have children is in order to provide care for themselves in old age. Lear, over 80 years old, certainly expects to be cared for by his daughters after he has given up power. He had hoped to live with Cordelia:

> I loved her most, and thought to set my rest
> On her kind nursery.

Lear later shows a calculating attitude to love when he rates Regan's and Gonerill's affection according to the number of his servants they are willing to support. Whoever accepts the larger number must love him the most:

> Thy fifty yet doth double five and twenty,
> And thou art twice her love.

a Are Gonerill and Regan completely evil? Look back at their conversation at the end of Act 1 Scene 1 where they discuss Lear's 'rash' behaviour in the love trial. Suggest any ways in which their actions and attitudes might be reasonably defended as they prepare to look after their ageing father.

b Find examples of Cordelia's unconditional love in Acts 4 and 5, and describe in detail how profoundly it impacts on her father's thoughts and behaviour.

Lear's descent into madness and his growing awareness of the needs of others help him to a true understanding of the love which Cordelia has for him. Lear is healed by Cordelia's unconditional love, and finds in it a model for the selfless love of father and daughter. It gives him happiness at the prospect of their imprisonment together, and it cruelly intensifies his agony of grief at her death.

Women in the family

Women often had powerful roles within their families during the sixteenth and seventeenth centuries. However, the power they had outside the family was limited by the rules of inheritance, ingrained traditions, and the prejudiced attitudes of the state, the law and the Church. Nonetheless, powerful women were not unknown. King James's mother was Mary Stuart, Queen of Scotland. His immediate predecessor on the English throne was Queen Elizabeth I.

Women in positions of authority caused much consternation in the sixteenth century. In 1558, the year of Elizabeth's accession, John Knox, a Scottish Protestant reformer, issued a pamphlet attacking women rulers. Entitled *First Blast of the Trumpet against the Monstrous Regiment of Women*, it argued that giving women, who are 'weak, frail, impatient, feeble and foolish creatures', any sort of authority was the 'subversion of good order, of all equity and justice'.

By the time *King Lear* was written, attitudes to women in power had been modified by Elizabeth I's success as monarch, but women still had low status in society. In the play, although Lear's daughters are his heirs, the power and authority of the crown is transferred to their husbands. The daughters are not made queens regnant, monarchs in their own right. Regan and Gonerill are strong and influential figures, but have to wield that influence through their husbands. Consequently, Gonerill has to goad Albany into action when he has doubts about how to react to the political crisis. She knows it would be difficult, if not impossible, for her to act alone.

Gonerill and Regan both want Edmond, not just as a lover but as a consort. Their reasons may be entirely personal, or may be connected with their appraisal of his skills as a commander and ruler. Although all three princesses play authoritative roles in the preparations for battle, it is Albany and Edmond who lead the British army. Cordelia acts as commander-in-chief of the invading French army, but has been invested with that authority by her husband (Act 4 Scene 3, lines 25–6).

Lear's wife, the mother of his daughters and the queen of Britain, is dead before the play begins. In the Gloucester family, too, both the mothers are absent from the play. Edmond's mother is mentioned only when he or his father refer lewdly to his conception. There are no references to Edgar's mother.

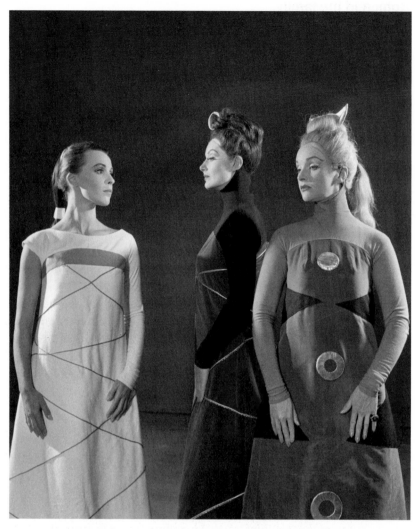

Cordelia, Gonerill and Regan. What family likenesses and differences can you see in this portrayal of the three sisters? Think about how far the picture matches your own image of the sisters, and suggest how you would like to see them portrayed on stage (actors, costumes, movements, style of speech, and so on).

Sons and brothers

The sub-plot of Gloucester and his two sons very obviously increases the dramatic effect of the main plot of Lear and his daughters. The good and evil qualities of the king's daughters are reflected in Edgar's struggles to protect his father, and Edmond's schemes to harm him. The play's exploration of family life offers every new production a challenge in how to portray the brothers.

Brothers can be remarkably similar or very different in appearance and character. There are obvious and stark contrasts between the two Gloucester half-brothers. For example, Edgar plays a number of roles: a gullible dupe who believes his brother's false story; a madman, as Poor Tom; a choric commentator on suffering ('ripeness is all'); a defender of right as he slays both Edmond and Oswald. In contrast, Edmond seems to be unremittingly devious, seeking whatever will serve his own interests. Only in the closing minutes of the play, near to death, is he prompted to do good, and unsuccessfully tries to prevent the deaths of Lear and Cordelia.

'My name is Edgar, and thy father's son.' Edgar reveals his identity to his dying brother. The wheel has come full circle, and Edmond pays the price for his wrong-doing.

Different views of 'Nature'

The words 'Nature', 'natural' and 'unnatural' occur over forty times in the play. Almost every character appeals in some way to 'nature': to justify their actions or to help them, or to explain why things are as they are. Lear begins the 'love test' by inviting his daughters to compete for the largest share of his kingdom by combining their natural affection for their father with exaggerated statements of their love ('Where nature doth with merit challenge'). But within minutes he rejects Cordelia as 'a wretch whom nature is ashamed / Almost t'acknowledge hers'. Later, he will call Gonerill and Regan 'unnatural hags'.

Why is 'nature' so important in the play? One major reason is that it is a powerful means of controlling people. Like all tyrants, Lear knows that if he can make everyone believe that it is 'natural' for him to rule and for his every wish to be obeyed, then he has power over them. They will think that what is 'natural' is right, and that it must not be challenged. If daughters think that it is natural to obey all their father's commands, or if people believe that society is naturally hierarchical, with a king at the top, then they are unlikely to challenge that 'natural' state of affairs.

For much of the play Lear believes that everything he does is natural. Any person who frustrates his desires is unnatural, because it is natural that everyone should obey him without question. His view of his family is the same as his view of England: rigidly hierarchical with himself as father-king at the top, entitled to immediate and unstinting obedience. Nature herself is a goddess to whom he can appeal for revenge on his unnatural daughter Gonerill ('Hear, Nature, hear').

One way of understanding the play is to see it as the slow and agonising transformation of Lear's view of the natural order of things. Through his suffering, Lear's original view of nature is painfully stripped away.

Two views of nature

A traditional way of understanding the play has been to see it as depicting two different views of nature, malign or benign (bad or good). Characters are grouped according to their view of nature. That view defines their opinion of society, of what men and women are like, and of how they should behave. Although this two-fold view of nature is a simple stereotype, it can be a valuable first step in developing your thinking about the significance of 'nature' in the play.

Nature as malign   The view of nature as spitefully malevolent links the ruthless individualism of Edmond, Gonerill and Regan. Nature is seen as a malign force which acts as a powerful motivator. It drives and feeds ruthless and selfish impulses. Humans behave like violent predatory animals, preying on the naive, innocent and vulnerable. They lack conscience and moral sensitivity, and are concerned only with their own advancement and profit. Like Lear, Edmond thinks of nature as a deity ('Thou, Nature, art my goddess'), but sees her favouring the merciless, self-motivated individual. This 'natural' (illegitimate) son of Gloucester is coldly calculating and cunning. He mocks Gloucester's superstitions, and is scornful of any notion that his nature was determined by the stars.

Gonerill and Regan flatter Lear shamelessly to gain a share of their father's wealth, but then renounce all family bonds and duties. Hard-heartedly, they cruelly exile Lear into the storm.

Nature as benign   Gloucester, Kent, Edgar and Cordelia are shaped by a benign vision of nature as a kind-hearted and benevolent force which strives for order, stability and harmony. Gloucester sees the world as orderly and hierarchical, valuing trust, loyalty and family bonds. His response to Edgar's apparent villainy is to proclaim him an 'unnatural, detested, brutish villain'. Kent's loyalty to his master, Lear, expresses itself in his unwavering and unquestioning sympathy and concern for the king throughout the play. Cordelia's nature, like Kent's, is truthful and honest. Her constancy and devotion to Lear act as healing, cleansing forces. Edgar cloaks his true nature in the disguise of a mad beggar, but redeems, heals and restores his father, to whom he remains faithful.

a To help you make up your mind about the appropriateness of the two views of nature given above, work through the list of characters on page 1. Consider each character in turn, and think about to what extent their view of nature is malign or benign.

b Organise a class debate on the following claim: '*King Lear* shows that nothing to do with human society is "natural". Everything is shaped by men and women (mostly men!), and could be otherwise. Nature itself is completely indifferent to human beings.'

Justice

At the end of *King Lear* Albany confronts the bloody reality of the death and suffering caused by Lear's division of his kingdom and declares that both 'friends' and 'foes' will get what they deserve (Act 5 Scene 3, lines 276–8). But do they? It is true that Edmond has been killed by the brother he wronged, and the wicked Gonerill and Regan are dead. But the innocent Cordelia has died cruelly, hanged in prison, and Gloucester's blinding and mental suffering are hardly fit punishment for the 'crime' of fathering the bastard Edmond. Does Lear, for all his flaws of character or judgement, deserve the agonies of madness he has undergone ('I am bound / Upon a wheel of fire'), or the twisted irony of being reconciled with Cordelia only to have her ruthlessly snatched away from him?

◆ Poetic justice means that people get what they deserve, but it seems hard to find it in *King Lear*. Discuss Albany's statement (above) in the light of all that has happened by the end of the play.

Divine justice

A belief in the power of divine justice runs through the play. Lear strengthens his early displays of authority and paternal cursing by appealing to pagan deities. He swears by 'the sacred radiance of the sun', 'The mysteries of Hecate and the night', 'Apollo' and 'Jupiter'. Regan appeals to the 'blessed gods' when Lear turns his anger on her. Lear himself begs for help from the 'heavens': 'If you do love old men . . . send down and take my part', and acknowledges the authority of 'high-judging Jove'.

Attitudes towards the gods see-saw in the play. Sometimes characters see them as 'kind' and 'mighty', at other times arbitrary, indifferent and cruel. Albany finds them just: 'you are above / You justicers'. Gloucester thinks them spitefully unjust: 'As flies to wanton boys are we to th'gods; / They kill us for their sport', then revises his opinion: 'You ever gentle gods'. To Cordelia the gods are benevolent: 'O you kind gods'. With his brother dying and his sightless father dead, Edgar acknowledges a divine justice that watches over and judges all human actions: 'The gods are just, and of our pleasant vices / Make instruments to plague us.'

Human justice

There are five 'trials' in the play in which one human being judges another:

1 Lear's 'love trial' of his three daughters (Act 1 Scene 1). Lear, as judge and jury, metes out the 'justice' he thinks is appropriate.

2 Cornwall's 'trial' of Kent, whose bluntness earns him instant punishment in the stocks (Act 2 Scene 2).

3 Cornwall and Regan's 'trial' of Gloucester (Act 3 Scene 7) at which the old man is not allowed any representation or defence.

4 Lear's 'mock trial' of Gonerill and Regan (only in the Quarto edition – see p. 240), showing how Lear's 'madness' craves justice against his ungrateful daughters.

5 The trial by battle (Act 5 Scene 3). Edgar challenges Edmond to trial by combat on the charge of treason.

Throughout the play men or women pass judgement on their fellows, always appealing to some higher power or authority. Lear exiles Kent for daring to criticise him; Gloucester impulsively condemns Edgar; Gonerill and Regan, having assumed their father's power, 'judge' Lear and pronounce punishment; Edmond sentences Lear and Cordelia to imprisonment and issues their death warrant.

The play clearly shows that, when humans exercise justice, there is no guarantee that it will be fair, proper or right. Possession of power is more important than fairness. Gonerill sees herself as the queen, unchallengeable, controlling the law and yet beyond it: 'the laws are mine, not thine. / Who can arraign me for't?' In his madness Lear damningly criticises the hypocrisy of the parish officer who lusts after the prostitute even as he is punishing her and how even 'A dog's obeyed in office.' He displays piercing insight into the fallibility of judges, and into the way powerful, rich people can avoid punishment for their crimes: 'Plate sin with gold, / And the strong lance of justice hurtless breaks'.

But there are incidents in the play that suggest that some kind of natural justice *is* at work: a loyal servant protests about Gloucester's horrific treatment and mortally wounds Cornwall, another helps his blinded master make his way to Dover, and Oswald is killed by Edgar when he attempts to murder the old man.

Madness

In Shakespeare's time attitudes and responses to madness were much harsher and less sympathetic than they are today. Nowadays, doctors rarely use such words as 'mad' or 'lunatic', preferring alternative descriptions such as 'mentally ill' or 'disturbed'. But Elizabethan and Jacobean audiences had no such scruples, and in *King Lear* (and other plays) Shakespeare's language reflects the beliefs of the time. The 'mad' were thought to be possessed by devils and therefore had to be confined and whipped to expel the demonic spirits. Held in secure hospitals like Bethlehem ('Bedlam'), the insane provided a grotesque form of entertainment for curious, well-to-do onlookers. Much of Edgar's language, as Poor Tom, is taken from a 1603 pamphlet describing how devils were 'cast out of lunatics' (see p. 204).

Throughout his career, Shakespeare explored various forms of madness in his plays. He seems to have been particularly interested in madness as an agent of beneficial change. The suffering of mental disturbance could transform characters' views of themselves and others. In the comedies, the 'madness' of love becomes an altered state of consciousness which produces sharper insight. The tragedies offer a more sombre perspective on the effects of madness, but its outcome is also clearer perception. For example, Hamlet (whether his madness be real or feigned) finds calm and understanding after his journey of mental suffering.

Madness in this play is most evident in the portrayal of Lear himself: his mind tormented and unsettled by his experience. But *King Lear* is not simply a psychological depiction of the insanity of an individual. Human madness is reflected in disturbance at two other levels, the natural and the social. The onset of the terrible storm in Act 3 suggests that tempests in nature mirror those in an individual's mind. Lear's abdication of his power and the division of his kingdom would have been seen as acts of political madness by Shakespeare's contemporaries. By tearing up his country, Lear sets off a chain of social frenzy that results in cruelty, blindness, madness and death.

King Lear portrays different types of mental derangement. Lear's madness is that of a selfish, autocratic old man whose will is thwarted. His moral blindness, misjudgements and lack of understanding of himself and others inevitably lead to breakdown: 'O fool, I shall go mad.' As Poor Tom, Edgar puts on the madness of a Bedlam beggar. The Fool's 'madness' is professional, eccentric, witty, exposing weakness and folly: 'May not an ass know when the cart draws the horse?'

Cornwall and Regan become possessed by the madness of evil in their obsession with Gloucester's punishment and torture: 'Hang him instantly'. Gloucester, near to death, thinks it better to be 'distract' and lose his sorrow in 'wrong imaginations' as if, perhaps, madness were a blessing which would release him from his terrible sufferings.

Lear's journey through madness to self-knowledge

Act 1   Lear's tendency to mental instability is established. He subjects his daughters to a bizarre love trial, banishes his loyal adviser Kent and disowns Cordelia. He reacts with violent curses to Gonerill's challenge to his wilful behaviour.

Act 2   Lear's sanity is undermined by his obsession with 'filial ingratitude', the 'unnatural' behaviour of Gonerill and Regan. Infuriated by Kent's punishment in the stocks, Regan's refusal to speak to him and Gonerill's alliance with her sister, Lear rants impotently about revenge. Fearing the onset of madness, he storms out of Gloucester's castle.

Act 3   Lear rages at the storm, calling for universal destruction. His moods swing violently from raging in the storm to quieter sympathy for those less fortunate than himself: 'Poor naked wretches'. Lear's 'mad' companions, the Fool and Poor Tom, deepen the sense of his decline into insanity. He rips off his clothes ('Off, off you lendings!'), and hallucinates about devilish spirits.

Act 4   A stage direction in Scene 5 indicates '*Enter* LEAR, [*mad*]'. Talking with the blinded Gloucester, Lear's language combines sexual loathing with hallucinations about hell and damnation: 'Let copulation thrive … there is the sulphurous pit, burning, scalding, stench, consumption'. Lear's disordered thoughts range over mortality, justice and authority, and erupt in savage emotion: 'And when I have stol'n upon these son-in-laws / Then kill, kill, kill, kill, kill, kill!' At last, reunited with Cordelia, Lear's mental torment ceases.

Act 5   The cruel murder of Cordelia threatens Lear's wits once more: 'Howl, howl, howl, howl!' He dies, his final words suggesting that he is deluding himself with the thought that she lives.

◆ Use the outline above to help you collect quotations from each act to trace the course of Lear's mental state. Choose a style of presentation for your quotations that seems to you powerful and effective, for example an essay, a set of drawings, a short play or set of tableaux.

Politics

King Lear is firmly rooted in the political and social conditions of Shakespeare's times. The play reflects the political issues which were heatedly debated in Elizabethan and Jacobean England: the divine right of kings, the unity of the kingdom, the changing social order which triggered a growth of conflicting factions and a threatening underclass. From this standpoint *King Lear* may be seen as a play about the struggle for power, property and inheritance in early seventeenth-century England.

The play opens with Lear portrayed as an absolute monarch who demands unquestioning obedience. In Shakespeare's time monarchs regarded themselves as ruling on God's behalf. When it attempted to go against her wishes, Queen Elizabeth I reminded Parliament that she was their anointed queen and God's representative on earth. Her successor, King James, took this belief in the divine right of kings even further. He asserted that it was blasphemous and unlawful to question any action taken by a king. In 1610 he declared to Parliament: 'The state of monarchy is the supremest thing upon the earth; for kings are not only God's lieutenants upon earth, and sit upon God's throne, but even by God himself they are called gods'.

However, such absolute rulers also acknowledged a God-given obligation. It was their sacred duty to keep their kingdom intact. Elizabeth emphasised that she had to answer to God for her government of the realm. She and James shared the conviction that it would be a sin against their divinely given authority to abdicate, or to divide their country. It was an ideology embraced by most of their subjects. So the audience in 1605 probably shared Kent's horror at Lear's decision to throw off the responsibility of kingship and divide his kingdom. They probably also admired Kent's good sense in refusing to share power at the end of the play. To Shakespeare's contemporaries *King Lear* was a play about how *not* to rule a country.

The England of Elizabeth and James was a society in transition. The feudal world of medieval times, with its strong allegiances and rigid hierarchy, had virtually collapsed. A newly prosperous gentry and commercial class challenged the power of the king and of an aristocracy divided among itself. Political factions abounded, strongly hinted at in the dangerous rivalry existing between Albany and Cornwall, and gossiped about by Kent and Gloucester as the play opens.

Newly acquired property gave power to a new kind of individual. Powerful men emerged who felt no obligation to the old feudal loyalties. They were men on the make, filled with the spirit of radical individualism, driven by self-interest. Edmond, Gloucester's unscrupulous, illegitimate son, refuses to 'Stand in the plague of custom'. In rejecting tradition he seeks to thrive by his own cunning, mocking the superstitious beliefs of his father, an upholder of the old feudal loyalty to the king. There is no place for an outdated system of chivalry in Edmond's moral scheme. At a different social level, the corrupt Oswald is another example of the 'new man'. His self-serving character is ridiculed by Kent in Act 2 Scene 2 ('Such smiling rogues as these'). Power-seeking, quarrelling aristocrats and the emerging thrusting individualists of Tudor and Jacobean England find their counterparts in Shakespeare's play.

Shakespeare also gives expression to a dispossessed underclass who did not share in the affluence of the times. The enclosure of common fields provoked protest and revolt. What the wealthy classes saw as necessary to more efficient farming, the poor saw as landgrabbing. In the twenty years before the play was written, there were a number of food riots. Shortly after its first performance, serious riots against enclosures took place in the Midlands, including Warwickshire, Shakespeare's home county. Bedlam beggars, the disguise adopted by Edgar, were familiar and deeply worrying figures who roamed 'from low farms, / Poor pelting villages, sheep-cotes, and mills', pleading for charity.

In *King Lear* Shakespeare gives expression to crucial political and social issues of his times. Some of these issues remain relevant today. In the twenty-first century the future of the British monarchy and of the union of the countries of the United Kingdom have again become subjects of political debate.

a Conduct your own research into the political and social conditions of Shakespeare's time. Focus particularly on Elizabethan and Jacobean attitudes to kingship and the emergence of a new middle class.

b Suggest ways of staging the play to help bring out its relevance to political and social issues in today's society.

Characters

King Lear

Lear is a tragic hero very much in the mould of classical Greek tragedy: a powerful but fatally flawed ruler who, through *hubris* (excessive pride or arrogance), destroys both himself and those around him.

At the start of the play Lear has clearly been accustomed to exercising absolute power for many years, but the old man's weaknesses quickly become apparent. His artificial 'love test' ('Which of you shall we say doth love us most . . .?') shows that he craves flattery rather than truth, inexplicably valuing Gonerill's and Regan's fawning declaration of false love above the integrity of his youngest daughter's sincere expression of filial devotion and duty. Lear's angry disinheriting of Cordelia, and banishment of the loyal Kent, affirm the picture of a despotic monarch, unused to opposition. By the end of the first scene, Regan's comment about her father's sanity ('he hath ever but slenderly known himself') becomes increasingly pertinent.

Once Lear has given away his kingdom, the play proceeds to chart his painful journey from pride and arrogance to self-knowledge and redemption. He rages at challenges to his wilful behaviour, finds his tenuous hold on sanity threatened by his daughters' 'filial ingratitude' and begins to question his identity ('Who is it that can tell me who I am?'). In the storm scenes his mood oscillates between violent raging against the elements and quieter reflection on the state of his kingdom and the plight of the 'Poor naked wretches'. But he has yet to become fully self-aware: 'I am a man / More sinned against than sinning.'

Ironically, the further Lear descends into madness, the sharper becomes his awareness of the world's evils, his scathing attack on the hypocrisy of judges and the vulnerability of the poor revealing just how much he has learned through his suffering. Briefly he emerges from his tortured madness to find some kind of peace and reconciliation with Cordelia, his youngest daughter, even contemplating the joy of their imprisonment together. But their moment of happiness is all too short.

Lear may be a flawed man, infuriatingly self-obsessed, morally blind, unjust and unfair, who acquires self-knowledge and sympathy for others only through suffering, but he is also a great man. Kent's faithful service bears testament to the qualities of loyalty and devotion that Lear, the king and the man, could inspire in others.

A Shakespearian actor's most challenging role?

Two images of King Lear from the 2001 production of the play at Shakespeare's Globe in London. Which scenes do you think these images came from? Give your reasons. Read and discuss the character notes on the opposite page. Then write a brief essay outlining the major challenges you think an actor would face when playing King Lear.

Gonerill, Regan and Cordelia

Gonerill, Lear's eldest daughter, speaks first in the 'love test', instantly displaying how devious and deceitful she is. Her words, slick, oily and probably rehearsed ('Sir, I love you more than word can wield the matter'), are clearly designed to appeal to her father's vanity. She knows Lear's weaknesses all too well – his volatile moods, poor judgement and lack of self-knowledge – and carries her ability for cold, objective assessment into her later dealings with him. Systematically she schemes with Regan to erode the last vestiges of the old king's power, to reduce the number of his followers and to make him homeless. She has nothing but contempt for her 'Milk-livered' husband, openly plotting adultery with Edmond ('To thee a woman's services are due') and poisoning her sister to keep him for herself. When Edmond is mortally wounded, she stabs herself through the heart. Is this an act of courage or merely perverse self-destruction?

Lear's second daughter, Regan, initially seems less spiteful and more restrained than her elder sister but, as the play unfolds, her sadistic disposition comes to the fore. It is Regan who proposes that Kent's punishment in the stocks be extended ('Till night, my lord, and all night too'), who wants to deny Lear even one follower ('What need one?') and who orders the castle gates to be locked against him as the storm rages outside. Most savagely of all, she participates fully in torturing Gloucester, urging Cornwall to take out both of the old man's eyes lest 'One side will mock another'. Like Gonerill, she is ambitious and keen to seek sexual pleasure, competing unashamedly with her for Edmond's favours. She is also confident and assertive, wilful and defiant. When she is poisoned by her sister, she meets what many see as a symbolically just demise.

Cordelia, Lear's youngest daughter, interestingly speaks in only four scenes, yet her presence permeates much of the play. Her early exchanges with Lear show unnerving honesty in the face of so much that is false and contrived, her Asides to the audience accentuating the integrity of what she says and feels. Although often played as more obviously feminine and gentle than her sisters, she is certainly not weak and vulnerable. It takes courage to stand up to her father, her candid assessments of her sisters' behaviour smack of insight and perception ('I know you what you are') and she abhors deception and pretence ('Who covers faults, at last with shame derides').

When Cordelia returns to England, productions often stress her regal qualities, or emphasise the fact that she is commander of an

invading army. However, her language resonates with words of healing and therapy, leading some to interpret her in a particularly Christian way. In displaying unconditional love and forgiveness for her
father, she is a symbol of hope and goodness. That her life should be
so pointlessly extinguished is perhaps the cruellest act of all in this
bleakest of plays.

(a)   (b)

(c)

(a) Regan licking blood from Gloucester's blinding (Act 3 Scene 7);
(b) Cordelia returning to the play as queen of France (Act 4 Scene 3);
(c) Gonerill facing Lear's anger (Act 2 Scene 4).

◆ How closely do these interpretations match your own ideas for
  these roles? Write advice for each actor about how to play these
  three difficult scenes.

Gloucester, Edgar and Edmond

Gloucester is Lear's loyal and long-serving counsellor. Like his master he is an elderly father who misjudges his children and who achieves self-knowledge and reconciliation with his virtuous child only after suffering extremes of pain and distress.

His flippant joking about his illegitimate son Edmond and the ease with which the latter exploits his gullible and superstitious nature do not create a good first impression. But that should not belie his essential seriousness and sobriety as he muses on the troubling breakdown in society following Lear's abdication. Although he feels deeply divided loyalty between the new and the old regimes, he consistently sympathises with Lear and seeks to offer him solace when he is cast out into the storm. For this 'treachery' his eyes are plucked out. Yet ironically this barbaric blinding, like Lear's madness, leads to new insight and understanding. He admits his earlier follies ('I stumbled when I saw'), but has still to learn the priceless virtue of patience. In deep despair he attempts to leap off the cliff at Dover, but is saved, and perhaps spiritually healed, by the disguised Edgar, who makes him realise that 'Men must endure / Their going hence even as their coming hither: / Ripeness is all.'

Edgar is Gloucester's legitimate and virtuous son. Like his father, he is easily duped by Edmond's scheming. Unfairly accused of plotting his father's murder, he is forced to disguise himself as the mad beggar Poor Tom to avoid capture. In this role and as various peasant figures, he then helps both Lear and Gloucester attain self-knowledge and understanding and also, as a kind of 'chorus' device, comments directly to the audience on the intensity of other characters' suffering. In the later stages of the play he becomes an overt force for good, killing Oswald who had been sent to murder Gloucester and then mortally wounding Edmond in trial by combat. When finally he tells his father who he really is, Gloucester's heart ''Twixt two extremes of passion, joy and grief, / Burst smilingly.' Neither Albany nor Kent has the heart to take over governance of England, so it is left to the young Edgar to try to pick up the pieces.

Edmond, Gloucester's bastard son, is generally perceived to be a more dynamic and charismatic character than his brother. He too speaks in Asides directly to the audience but his soliloquies are more powerful and engaging than Edgar's. Often portrayed as physically robust and attractive, he exudes raw energy and desire. He is unabashed in his selfishness and he ruthlessly seeks to better himself, using whatever means possible: 'All with me's meet that I can fashion fit'. He discredits Edgar, betrays his father to gain favour with Cornwall and exploits Gonerill's and Regan's sexual interest to strengthen his position further. There seems no pity or remorse in him: betraying his father 'must draw me / That which my father loses: no less than all.' Yet, close to death, he is strangely capable of one final gesture of decency in attempting to repeal Cordelia's death warrant: 'Some good I mean to do, / Despite of mine own nature.'

Identify the two scenes from which these images of Edgar might come. Then write a paragraph about what the different directors might have had in mind about the way they wished their Edgar to be portrayed.

Describe the impression you think this Edmond made on his audience at Shakespeare's Globe. In what ways does he match your idea of how the character should be played?

The Fool

Fools were popular well before Elizabethan times. In the Middle Ages jesters were very common as household servants to the rich. They often wore the traditional costume of the coxcomb (jester's cap) with bells, and a motley (multicoloured) coat. Their role was to entertain with witty words and songs, and to make critical comment on contemporary behaviour. An 'allowed fool', such as Feste in *Twelfth Night*, was able to say what he thought without fear of punishment.

Lear's Fool is 'all-licensed', and so can speak frankly and critically about anything and anyone, especially his master, the king. He acts as a kind of dramatic chorus, an ironic commentator on the action he observes. Although he is threatened with whipping for impertinence, the Fool constantly reminds Lear of his folly. Lear is relentlessly used as the butt of the Fool's barbed comments: 'this fellow has banished two on's daughters and did the third a blessing against his will'; 'thou hast pared thy wit o'both sides and left nothing i'th'middle'; 'I am a fool, thou art nothing'.

The Fool moves easily between different styles of humour: stand-up comedy ('Thou hadst little wit in thy bald crown when thou gav'st thy golden one away'); song ('Fools had ne'er less grace in a year'); rhyme or proverb ('Fathers that wear rags / Do make their children blind'); and sexual innuendo ('She that's a maid now').

The Fool's language seems to be a mixture of sense and nonsense. Attempting to analyse its exact meaning may destroy both its potential humour and its dramatic power. Some of the Fool's words may be puzzling, but all carry significance for Lear's plight. For example, 'So out went the candle, and we were left darkling', spoken as Gonerill begins to undermine Lear's sanity, is eerily prophetic of the blindness and confusion that will follow. The Fool appears in only six scenes. From his very first appearance, his special relationship with Lear is evident. It allows him to escape punishment for his stinging criticisms, and sees him following Lear selflessly into the storm, almost as if he were Lear's *alter ego*, his second, more sane self.

The Fool disappears from the play in Act 3 Scene 6. When Lear says 'And my poor fool is hanged' just before he dies, he may be speaking of the dead Cordelia ('fool' could be a term of endearment). But his sorrowing words create echoes of the Fool (who had 'much pined away' for Cordelia). One production highlighted the relationship between Cordelia and the Fool by beginning the play with an ominous tableau of them with their heads linked by a hangman's noose.

Every production faces the challenge of how the Fool should be portrayed. In one production he was played as a red-nosed comedian. In another a woman played the role. How would you portray the Fool if you were directing the play?

Kent

Kent is an important presence in *King Lear* for, although he does not speak a huge number of lines, he is on stage for almost half the play. Presented as Lear's loyal and devoted servant, he epitomises

227

the kind of unconditional love that the old king could inspire. He is also the voice of unflagging honesty and plain speaking, challenging Lear in the love trial to 'check / This hideous rashness' and to 'See better'. In disguise as Caius he remains constant in his dedication to his master, following him through misfortune, storm and subsequent madness. He is never afraid to speak bluntly, disdaining pomposity and hypocrisy and defending truth. He also acts as a bridge with Cordelia, reminding the audience that she still keeps a watchful eye on her father. His selflessness acts in marked contrast to the selfishness of others. Perhaps his ultimate act of loyalty to Lear is when he hints that he will follow his master into death: 'I have a journey, sir, shortly to go: / My master calls me; I must not say no.'

Match these two images of Kent to lines from either Act 1 Scene 4 or Act 2 Scene 2. Which actor better conveys the key qualities of Kent as you see them? Justify your views.

The language of *King Lear*

Imagery

King Lear abounds in imagery (sometimes called 'figures' or 'figurative language'): vivid words and phrases that conjure up emotionally charged pictures in the imagination (e.g. 'I am bound / Upon a wheel of fire, that mine own tears / Do scald like molten lead.') and help to create the atmosphere of the play. Shakespeare seems to have thought in images, and the whole play richly demonstrates his unflagging and varied use of verbal illustration.

Shakespeare's imagery uses metaphor, simile or personification. All are comparisons which in effect substitute one thing (the image) for another (the thing described).

Simile   Compares one thing to another using 'like' or 'as': 'We two alone will sing like birds i'th'cage'; 'My life I never held but as a pawn'.

Metaphor   Also a comparison, suggesting that two dissimilar things are actually the same: 'Come not between the dragon and his wrath'; 'How sharper than a serpent's tooth it is / To have a thankless child'.

Personification   Turns all kinds of things into persons, giving them human feelings or attributes: 'Thou, Nature, art my goddess'; 'Ingratitude! Thou marble-hearted fiend'.

♦ Identify a dozen striking and powerful images in the play. Draw them in a bold, visual way that highlights the comparisons at the heart of each one.

Antithesis

Antithesis is the opposition of words or phrases against each other, as when Lear accuses Cordelia, 'so young, and so untender?' and when she replies: 'So young, my lord, and true.' This setting of word against word ('young' against 'untender' and then 'young' against 'true') is one of Shakespeare's favourite language devices. He uses it extensively in all of his plays. Why? Because antithesis powerfully expresses conflict through its use of opposites, and conflict is the essence of all drama.

In *King Lear* conflict occurs in many forms: father against daughter, son against father, brother against brother, sister against sister, wife against husband. The kingdom itself is divided, and is invaded by the foreign army of France. Thematically, sight works against blindness, nature against the 'unnatural', man against animal, rich against poor, truth against deception.

Shakespeare's dramatic style is characterised by his concern for comparison and contrast, opposition and juxtaposition: he sets character against character, scene against scene, word against word, phrase against phrase. For example, when Kent is banished in the first scene, he expresses the moral and social confusion stemming from Lear's impulsive decision in a series of antitheses. 'Freedom' pivots against 'banishment'; 'hence' against 'here'; Cordelia is praised whilst her sisters are scorned. And Kent's speech culminates with his avowal to 'shape his old course in a country new.'

◆ Collect more examples of antithesis. Use them in an essay exploring how antithesis creates a sense of conflict in *King Lear*.

The language of *King Lear* is full of variety. What follows is a brief description of some key language features and image clusters that Shakespeare uses to provide insight into crucial concerns of the play.

1 Lear and the language of power

Shakespeare initially gives Lear an imperative style of speaking, which matches the old king's conviction at the play's outset that, like all tyrants, his every wish should be obeyed. His first words are an abrupt order to Gloucester: 'Attend the lords of France and Burgundy'. Throughout the opening scene his language bristles with the commands, imperious statements and questions of a king confident of his unshakeable authority: 'What can you say to draw / A third more opulent than your sisters? Speak.' Even in his madness Lear strives to dictate to the elements, instructing the storm, 'Blow, winds, and crack your cheeks!'

But when Lear is reconciled with Cordelia in Act 4, although he expresses himself in similarly direct language – 'Pray do not mock me', 'Do not laugh at me' – the tone is softer and more intimate. Even at the end of the play Lear still gives orders, but now they are radically changed into the style of polite request, 'Pray you, undo this button. Thank you, sir.' His final words, 'Look there, look there', are an impassioned plea for confirmation that Cordelia still lives.

So, while Lear may speak the language of power, there is great variation in his speech. For example, his dialogues with the Fool are quite different from those with Gonerill and Regan. As the play progresses he learns through his suffering that a king's role is not simply to command. When he is reunited with Cordelia, his language has changed completely.

Either in pairs, take parts and speak the following dialogues aloud:

- Lear and Cordelia, Act 1 Scene 1, lines 77–114 (from 'Now our joy' to 'Good my liege')
- Lear and Cordelia, Act 5 Scene 3, lines 3–26
- all that Lear says in Act 5 Scene 3, lines 231–85.

When you have spoken the lines, talk together about how you think Lear's language changes in these three scenes.

Or choose two or three major characters and trace the way in which Lear speaks to them throughout the play, noting any changes in his manner of addressing them.

2 Sight and blindness

When Lear banishes Kent with 'Out of my sight!', Kent's reply, beginning 'See better, Lear', highlights Lear's moral blindness, his lack of self-knowledge and understanding. The king is clearly unable to see through the falseness of Gonerill's claim to love him 'Dearer than eyesight'. In contrast, there is a terrible literalness in Gonerill's 'Pluck out his eyes', and in Cornwall's brutal execution of that order, 'Upon these eyes of thine I'll set my foot.' The many images of sight and blindness which pervade the play sharply underscore and emphasise the dramatic effect of Gonerill's and Cornwall's horrifying words.

Gloucester talks ironically of not needing 'spectacles' to read Edgar's traitorous letter. The villainous Edmond can clearly 'see the business'. Lear speaks of 'Old fond eyes' which threaten to shed tears, and the physical pain and suffering experienced by Gloucester as a result of his blinding bring him insight into his past errors, 'I stumbled when I saw'. His new-found compassionate awareness of the nature of the world is vividly expressed: 'I see it feelingly'.

◆ Collect four or five references to sight, eyes or blindness from each act. Work out a powerful way of presenting your collection to illustrate the importance of sight and blindness in *King Lear*. For example, you could write an essay, make a large diagram or wall display, or rehearse and present a short play.

3 Animal imagery

King Lear resonates with the imagery of animals. Lear likens his daughters' cruelty to that of predatory birds and beasts. He calls Gonerill a 'Detested kite' whose ingratitude is 'sharper than a serpent's tooth'. Her face is 'wolvish', her tongue 'serpent-like'. In his madness he sees Gonerill and Regan as 'pelican daughters', cruelly feeding on his flesh and blood. Disguised as 'Poor Tom', Edgar describes himself as 'hog in sloth, fox in stealth, wolf in greediness, dog in madness, lion in prey'. Gloucester's outburst 'As flies to wanton boys are we to the gods / They kill us for their sport' reduces humans to insignificant insects. Lear in his madness sees man without his fine clothes as little more than a 'poor, bare, forked animal' and howls like an animal himself over the dead Cordelia:

> Why should a dog, a horse, a rat have life,
> And thou no breath at all?

◆ Collect as many animal references as you can. Work out a way of presenting your collection that you find satisfying.

4 Disease and pain

The political and moral disruptions that result from Lear's division of his kingdom are echoed in recurring images of pain and disease, of bodies racked and tortured. Most obviously, Lear's madness and Gloucester's blinding illustrate the theme of mental and physical suffering.

The language of the play is studded with references to sickness and ailments. Kent identifies Lear's banishing of Cordelia as a 'foul disease'. Lear views the Fool's criticisms as a 'pestilent gall' (an infected irritant). On both his ungrateful daughters he wishes 'all the plagues that in the pendulous air hang'. To Lear, Gonerill is 'a disease that's in my flesh', 'a boil / A plague-sore, or embossed carbuncle'. In his madness, Lear's ravings trigger his disgust at the thought of sexually transmitted diseases, 'There's hell, there's darkness, there is the sulphurous pit, burning, scalding, stench, consumption'.

But although disease imagery runs through the play, it is partly counterbalanced by the language of healing. Cordelia, grieving for her father's madness, urges that:

> All you unpublished virtues of the earth,
> Spring with my tears; be aidant and remediate
> In the good man's distress.

Reunited with Lear in Act 4, Cordelia seeks to return him to health, 'restoration hang / Thy medicine on my lips'.

♦ Identify six to eight examples of images of disease and pain. Consider each example in turn, and suggest how far you think it could apply to: the state of Lear's England; Lear's mental, moral or physical state.

5 Christian or pre-Christian?

There is much argument about whether *King Lear* is a Christian play. Those who regard it as Christian see Lear redeemed by the 'crucifixion' of his suffering. They identify Cordelia as a symbol of Christian redemption, almost Christ-like. She is a healer of suffering, a purger of ills and sins. Her reconciliation with her father helps to restore his wits. Her language affirms such Christian qualities as tolerance and understanding: 'blest', 'virtues', 'aidant', 'remediate', 'love', 'goodness', 'cure', 'restoration', 'repair', 'pity', 'benediction'. When she returns at the head of an army to aid Lear, her words echo those of Jesus, 'O dear father / It is thy business that I go about' (Act 4 Scene 3, lines 23–4).

However, there is much evidence in *King Lear* of a pre-Christian world. Characters do not appeal to a Christian god, but to the sun, Hecate, Apollo and Jupiter. Lear proclaims his faith in 'high-judging Jove'. Gloucester's world is beset by superstitious beliefs in the 'late eclipses in the sun and moon'. Edmond puts his faith in Nature as his goddess. Gloucester, Albany, Cordelia and Kent constantly appeal to the gods as they try to make sense of the apparently arbitrary nature of fortune and justice which they dispense, 'That shows you are above / You justicers'.

♦ Work in two groups. One group collects non-Christian references in the play. The other group identifies possible allusions to a Christian world. Organise a discussion on what a production of *King Lear* gains and loses from being set in a pre-Christian environment.

6 Nothing

The word 'nothing' resounds throughout the play. Cordelia uses it first, saying 'Nothing, my lord' in answer to Lear's love test. She has nothing to say, no flattering words to embellish the dutiful love she feels for her father. Lear's response adds a new meaning, 'Nothing will come of nothing'. If she does not declare her love, she will inherit nothing. The word will shift its meaning constantly in the mouth of each character: no words, no wealth, no meaning, no brains, no identity.

Gloucester will reward Edmond ('it shall lose thee nothing') for his false loyalty. Kent criticises the Fool's joking advice, 'This is nothing, fool'. Lear's criticism of the Fool is returned with a sharp twist of meaning, 'thou hast pared thy wit o'both sides and left nothing i'th'middle'. The Fool gives the word yet another interpretation, loss of identity: 'I am a fool, thou art nothing.' It is a meaning that is echoed as Edgar discards his true personality, 'Edgar I nothing am'.

Gonerill and Regan chillingly remind Lear that his former power will be reduced to nothing, 'What need you five and twenty? ten? or five? ... What need one?' The consequences of Lear's rash act are devastatingly brought home to him, although 'nothing' remains unspoken. Many of the characters will be left with nothing at the play's end. In the most literal sense, they will be brought to nothing, losing life itself.

◆ Write a paragraph giving your response to this claim: 'The essence of the play can be summarised in Lear's five words, "Nothing will come of nothing"'.

7 Plain speaking

King Lear strikingly explores the differences between speaking sincerely and insincerely. Some characters' private thoughts quite clearly do not match their public voices. Cordelia recognises that her sisters speak untruthfully in Lear's love test, but she refuses to speak dishonestly: 'I want that glib and oily art, / To speak and purpose not'. Yet elsewhere, Gonerill and Regan's language is plain and direct, even though the duplicitous nature of their scheming pervades the play.

Kent is banished for his plain speaking, 'his offence, honesty' and returns as a character still committed to speaking candidly and bluntly. Edmond in contrast uses lies to prey on a 'credulous father' and his 'foolish honesty' and later uses his cunning to 'stuff his [Cornwall's] suspicions more fully'. The virtuous Edgar, disguised as Poor Tom, lies to his blinded father, but his motivation is benign and with almost the final words of the play he urges plain speaking, 'Speak what we feel, not what we ought to say.'

◆ Consider each character in turn, and assess to what extent they have spoken honestly throughout the play. Suggest reasons why the characters choose to hide their true thoughts.

8 Blank verse or prose?

How did Shakespeare decide whether his characters should speak in blank verse or prose? His theatre audiences generally expected to hear plays in verse, but it was conventional for prose to be used by low-status characters for comedy, to express madness, and in letters. It is a popular belief today that Shakespeare's high-status characters speak verse because it is particularly appropriate to the noble, 'serious' thoughts of aristocrats, and his lower-status characters use prose to reflect the everyday or comic thoughts of 'ordinary' people.

Is this belief true of *King Lear*? Shakespeare never followed any convention slavishly, and there are plenty of exceptions in the play to these verse/prose conventions. Consider, for example, Gloucester and Edmond's conversation in Act 1 Scene 2, Lear's dialogues with the Fool, and Lear's conversations with Poor Tom and the blinded Gloucester.

◆ The undoubtedly high-status King Lear uses prose and verse. Compare his blank verse speech 'Poor naked wretches' (Act 3 Scene 4, lines 28–36) with his prose speech 'Thou wert better in a grave' (lines 91–7). Both speeches are 'serious', so why do you think Shakespeare chose such different forms of expression?

King Lear in performance

King Lear was probably performed many times during Shakespeare's lifetime. The first record of a performance is 'before the King's majesty at Whitehall' on 26 December 1606. What would King James have made of a Christmas entertainment showing the spectacle of a mad king who divided and gave away his kingdom? He probably enjoyed it, partly because it confirmed his view that a divided kingdom was the utmost political folly, and partly because 26 December was traditionally a day on which human foolishness and the virtue of enduring hardship with patience were celebrated.

How King James 'watched' *King Lear* would have been greatly affected by the factors that influenced Shakespeare as he wrote it (see pp. 218–19), namely the prevailing political and cultural assumptions. Since those first performances, all subsequent productions have mirrored in some way the interests and anxieties, preoccupations, beliefs and values of their times. There is no one 'right way' to perform or interpret *King Lear*. Each performance reflects the current political, religious, literary or aesthetic ideologies.

After the English Civil War and the execution of King Charles I, audiences had little stomach for the harshness of Shakespeare's play. In 1681 the dramatist Nahum Tate rewrote *King Lear* with a happy ending, and produced a version that lasted on stage for over 150 years. Tate cut the Fool, invented a trusted woman friend for Cordelia (whom he married off to Edgar), and ensured that Lear, Kent and Gloucester survived into the happy retirement of old age, leaving Cordelia and Edgar to rule the kingdom.

Not until the nineteenth century did Shakespeare's original script of the play enjoy real stage success over Tate's happy-ending version. But even then the influence of political considerations on drama and theatre can be clearly seen. During the mental derangement of King George III, performances of *King Lear* were suspended because the play came too close to reality for comfort.

Nineteenth-century productions were increasingly concerned with spectacle. Large casts, lavish costumes and monumental sets were used in an attempt to give historical accuracy to the play. The problem was that historical accuracy is not a concept that lends itself happily to *King Lear*. Quite simply, no one knows where or when Shakespeare intended it to be set (and it is possible that he had no specific time or place in mind except 'long-ago England'). Famous productions set the play in Saxon times, among the ancient druids or at Stonehenge.

The twentieth century saw attempts to return to what Shakespeare originally wrote (given the problem of Quarto/Folio versions, see p. 240), and to face squarely the bleakness and horror of Shakespeare's vision. Although the tradition of extravagant productions lingered on, most no longer attempted to create an impression of realism. In a century that gave full expression to the terrors of mechanised warfare and human cruelty, *King Lear* became one of the most frequently performed of all Shakespeare's plays, and many people argue that it is Shakespeare's greatest play. Virtually all modern productions attempt to bring out the play's contemporary significance and relevance.

One of the most celebrated versions was Peter Brook's at Stratford in 1962, which emphasised the bleakness of existence and its pain and suffering. For example, there was no help from servants for Gloucester after his blinding (see p. 132, Activity 2), and Edmond's line 'Some good I mean to do' (Act 5 Scene 3, line 217) was cut. Paul Scofield's austere Lear seemed designed to resist audience sympathy and the hostile universe seemed indifferent to human suffering.

Antony Sher's dazzling performance as a red-nosed Fool in 1982 (see p. 227) received great critical acclaim, but he perhaps unfortunately upstaged some of the other characters, especially the traditionally dynamic and energetic villain, Edmond.

In 1997 the Young Vic theatre cast a female in the role of Lear (see colour section, p. xii, top) as if the king were so old that he was virtually beyond gender. In a wheelchair, with bald, shrunken head, he was presented as an inhabitant of a nursing home in a set that was full of steel scaffolding and huge wooden doors. In the same year the Old Vic production was marked by a clever staging of the storm scene in which a jagged slash opened up at the back of the stage through which Lear and the Fool stumbled, as if from another world.

The RSC production in 1999 (see colour section, p. vi, top) was directed by the renowned Japanese director Yukio Ninagawa, and its oriental soundscape and Japanese-costumed Fool suggested the universality of the play's themes.

◆ Use the illustrations throughout this edition to help you work out how you would stage *King Lear*. Consider costumes, historical period, set, and so on.

This 1936 production opened with great ceremony to the blast of trumpets. It began at line 29 of Scene 1.

This 1981 Hungarian production set the play on the site of an abandoned factory and railway. The loudspeakers and the stark set emphasise the director's intention to present the play as a political parable about authority in Eastern Europe in the 1980s.

A still from the 1962 film directed by Peter Brook. What additional opportunities might a film of *King Lear* provide for a director?

Shakespeare's plays are popular with audiences he could never have imagined. This photograph is a still from the Japanese film *Ran*, which sets *King Lear* in the traditional culture of Japan.

Quarto and Folio editions

Two different versions of the *King Lear* script exist: a Quarto version printed in 1608 and the famous First Folio version printed in 1623. What follows are selected lines from the Quarto version that do not appear in the Folio, the version used in this edition.

The mock trial of Gonerill (following line 14 in Act 3 Scene 6)

Lear conducts a trial to 'arraign' (bring before a court) Gonerill and Regan. He instructs Edgar to take the part of a judge in robes, the Fool to be his partner ('yoke-fellow'), and Kent to join them as a member of the 'commission' (panel of judges). A 'joint-stool', a low stool made by a carpenter, stands in for Gonerill.

EDGAR The foul fiend bites my back.

FOOL He's mad that trusts in the tameness of a wolf, a horse's health, a boy's
    love, or a whore's oath.

LEAR It shall be done; I will arraign them straight.
       [*To Edgar*] Come, sit thou here, most learnèd justicer.
       [*To the Fool*] Thou, sapient sir, sit here. – No, you she-foxes –

EDGAR Look where he stands and glares! Want'st thou eyes at trial, madam?
       [*Sings*] Come o'er the bourn, Bessy, to me.

FOOL [*Sings*]   Her boat hath a leak
              And she must not speak
              Why she dares not come over to thee.

EDGAR The foul fiend haunts poor Tom in the voice of a nightingale. Hoppe-
    dance cries in Tom's belly for two white herring. Croak not, black angel!
    I have no food for thee.

KENT How do you, Sir? Stand you not so amazed.
       Will you lie down and rest upon the cushions?

LEAR I'll see their trial first. – Bring in their evidence.
       [*To Edgar*] Thou robed man of justice, take thy place.
       [*To the Fool*] And thou, his yoke-fellow of equity,
       Bench by his side. [*To Kent*] You are o'th'commission;
       Sit you too.

EDGAR Let us deal justly.
       Sleepest or wakest thou, jolly shepherd?
       Thy sheep be in the corn;
    And for one blast of thy minikin mouth
       Thy sheep shall take no harm.
    Purr, the cat, is grey.

LEAR Arraign her first; 'tis Gonerill. I here take my oath before this
    honourable assembly, she kicked the poor king her father.

FOOL Come hither, mistress. Is your name Gonerill?
LEAR She cannot deny it.
FOOL Cry you mercy, I took you for a joint-stool.
LEAR And here's another whose warped looks proclaim
        What store her heart is made on. – Stop her there!
        Arms, arms, sword, fire! Corruption in the place!
        False justicer, why hast thou let her 'scape?

The lessons of suffering (following the last line in Act 3 Scene 6)

The Quarto includes a soliloquy for Edgar after Lear has been carried off to Dover. Edgar acknowledges that the king's suffering is far greater than his own. He plans to watch events and to reveal ('bewray') his true identity when the charges against him have been disproved.

EDGAR When we our betters see bearing our woes,
        We scarcely think our miseries our foes.
        Who alone suffers, suffers most i'th'mind,
        Leaving free things and happy shows behind.
        But then the mind much sufferance doth o'erskip,
        When grief hath mates, and bearing, fellowship.
        How light and portable my pain seems now,
        When that which makes me bend makes the king bow.
        He childed as I fathered. Tom, away!
        Mark the high noises, and thyself bewray
        When false opinion, whose wrong thoughts defile thee,
        In thy just reproof repeals and reconciles thee.
        What will hap more tonight, safe 'scape the king!
        Lurk, lurk!

Husband and wife hostility

Albany claims the sisters' cruel treatment of Lear will make them like 'monsters of the deep'. Gonerill replies by contemptuously mocking his manhood. Extract (i) appears in Act 4 Scene 2, after line 33 ('Blows in your face'), and extract (ii) after line 38 ('So horrid as in woman').

(i) ALBANY   I fear your disposition:
        That nature which condemns its origin
        Cannot be bordered certain in itself.
        She that herself will sliver and disbranch
        From her material sap, perforce must wither

              And come to deadly use.

GONERILL   No more, the text is foolish.

ALBANY Wisdom and goodness to the vile seem vile;
         Filths savour but themselves. What have you done?
         Tigers, not daughters, what have you performed?
         A father, and a gracious aged man,
         Whose reverence even the head-lugged bear would lick,
         Most barbarous, most degenerate, have you madded.
         Could my good brother suffer you to do it?
         A man, a prince, by him so benefited?
         If that the heavens do not stir their visible spirits
         Send quickly down to tame these vile offences,
         It will come.
         Humanity must perforce prey on itself
         Like monsters of the deep.

(ii) ALBANY Thou changed and self-covered thing, for shame
         Be-monster not thy feature. Were't my fitness
         To let these hands obey my blood,
         They are apt enough to dislocate and tear
         Thy flesh and bones. Howe'er thou art a fiend,
         A woman's shape doth shield thee.

GONERILL Marry, your manhood! Mew!

An additional scene

The Quarto includes a complete scene after Act 4 Scene 2, in which Kent and a Gentleman discuss the French invasion of Britain. The Gentleman describes Cordelia's compassionate reaction to news of her father's plight, and how Lear's sense of shame makes him unwilling to see her.

KENT Why the King of France is so suddenly gone back, know you no reason?

GENTLEMAN Something he left imperfect in the state which since his coming forth is thought of, which imports to the kingdom so much fear and danger that his personal return was most required and necessary.

KENT Who hath he left behind him general?

GENTLEMAN The Marshal of France, Monsieur La Far.

KENT Did your letters pierce the queen to any demonstration of grief?

GENTLEMAN Ay, sir. She took them, read them in my presence,
         And now and then an ample tear trilled down
         Her delicate cheek. It seemed she was a queen
         Over her passion, who most rebel-like
         Sought to be king o'er her.

KENT   O, then it moved her?

GENTLEMAN Not to a rage. Patience and sorrow strove
    Who should express her goodliest. You have seen
    Sunshine and rain at once; her smiles and tears
    Were like a better way; those happy smilets
    That played on her ripe lip seemed not to know
    What guests were in her eyes; which parted thence
    As pearls from diamonds dropped. In brief.
    Sorrow would be a rarity most beloved
    If all could so become it.

KENT Made she no verbal question?

GENTLEMAN Faith, once or twice she heaved the name of father
    Pantingly forth, as if it pressed her heart;
    Cried 'Sisters, sisters! Shame of ladies! Sisters!
    Kent! Father! Sisters! What, i'th'storm? i'th'night?
    Let pity not be believed!' There she shook
    The holy water from her heavenly eyes,
    And clamour moistened. Then away she started
    To deal with grief alone.

KENT   It is the stars,
    The stars above us, govern our conditions,
    Else one self mate and make could not beget
    Such different issues. You spoke not with her since?

GENTLEMAN No.

KENT Was this before the king returned?

GENTLEMAN   No, since.

KENT Well, sir, the poor distressèd Lear's i'th'town,
    Who sometime in his better tune remembers
    What we are come about and by no means
    Will yield to see his daughter.

GENTLEMAN   Why, good sir?

KENT A sovereign shame so elbows him: his own unkindness
    That stripped her from his benediction, turned her
    To foreign casualties, gave her dear rights
    To his dog-hearted daughters – these things sting
    His mind so venomously that burning shame
    Detains him from Cordelia.

GENTLEMAN Alack, poor gentleman!

KENT Of Albany's and Cornwall's powers you heard not?

GENTLEMAN 'Tis so. They are afoot.

KENT Well, sir, I'll bring you to our master, Lear,
    And leave you to attend him. Some dear cause
    Will in concealment wrap me up awhile.
    When I am known aright, you shall not grieve
    Lending me this acquaintance. I pray you, go
    Along with me.

William Shakespeare
1564–1616

1564 Born Stratford-upon-Avon, eldest son of John and Mary Shakespeare.

1582 Marries Anne Hathaway of Shottery, near Stratford.

1583 Daughter, Susanna, born.

1585 Twins, son and daughter, Hamnet and Judith, born.

1592 First mention of Shakespeare in London. Robert Greene, another playwright, describes Shakespeare as 'an upstart crow beautified with our feathers . . .'. Greene seems to have been jealous of Shakespeare. He mocks Shakespeare's name, calling him 'the only Shake-scene in a country' (presumably because Shakespeare was writing successful plays).

1595 A shareholder in 'The Lord Chamberlain's Men', an acting company that became extremely popular.

1596 Son Hamnet dies, aged eleven.
Father, John, granted arms (acknowledged as a gentleman).

1597 Buys New Place, the grandest house in Stratford.

1598 Acts in Ben Jonson's *Every Man in His Humour*.

1599 Globe Theatre opens on Bankside. Performances in the open air.

1601 Father, John, dies.

1603 James I grants Shakespeare's company a royal patent: 'The Lord Chamberlain's Men' become 'The King's Men' and play about twelve performances each year at court.

1607 Daughter, Susanna, marries Dr John Hall.

1608 Mother, Mary, dies.

1609 'The King's Men' begin performing indoors at Blackfriars Theatre.

1610 Probably returns from London to live in Stratford.

1616 Daughter, Judith, marries Thomas Quiney.
Dies. Buried in Holy Trinity Church, Stratford-upon-Avon.

The plays and poems
(no one knows exactly when he wrote each play)

1589–1595 *The Two Gentlemen of Verona, The Taming of the Shrew, First, Second and Third Parts of King Henry VI, Titus Andronicus, King Richard III, The Comedy of Errors, Love's Labour's Lost, A Midsummer Night's Dream, Romeo and Juliet, King Richard II* (and the long poems *Venus and Adonis* and *The Rape of Lucrece*).

1596–1599 *King John, The Merchant of Venice, First and Second Parts of King Henry IV, The Merry Wives of Windsor, Much Ado About Nothing, King Henry V, Julius Caesar* (and probably the *Sonnets*).

1600–1605 *As You Like It, Hamlet, Twelfth Night, Troilus and Cressida, Measure for Measure, Othello, All's Well That Ends Well, Timon of Athens, King Lear*.

1606–1611 *Macbeth, Antony and Cleopatra, Pericles, Coriolanus, The Winter's Tale, Cymbeline, The Tempest*.

1613 *King Henry VIII, The Two Noble Kinsmen* (both probably with John Fletcher).

1623 Shakespeare's plays published as a collection (now called the First Folio).